FDR'S DEADLY SECRET

FDR'S
DEADLY SECRET

STEVEN LOMAZOW, MD, AND ERIC FETTMANN

PUBLICAFFAIRS
New York

Published in the United States by PublicAffairs™,
a member of the Perseus Books Group.

Book Design by Brent Wilcox

Library of Congress Cataloging-in-Publication Data
Lomazow, Steven, 1948–
FDR's deadly secret / Steven Lomazow and Eric Fettmann.
p. cm.
Includes bibliographical references and index.
ISBN 978-1-58648-744-7 (alk. paper)
1. Roosevelt, Franklin D. (Franklin Delano), 1882–1945—Health.
2. Presidents—United States—Biography. 3. Presidents—Disability—United States. 4. Brain—Tumors—Patients—United States—Biography.
5. United States—Politics and government—1933–1945. I. Fettmann, Eric.
II. Title.
E807.L68 2009
973.917092—dc22
[B]

2009030873

First Edition

10 9 8 7 6 5 4 3

For Isabelle Faye Lomazow and Grace Maya Lomazow,
whose lives are just beginning,
and to the memory of
Sadie Feldman Fettmann (1920–1971)
and Morton Fettmann (1921–1978),
who grew up in the FDR years

CONTENTS

PREFACE

This story begins in 1979, with the publication of Dr. Harry Goldsmith's landmark paper, "Unanswered Mysteries in the Death of Franklin D. Roosevelt," by the medical journal *Surgery, Gynecology & Obstetrics*, the first peer-reviewed examination that challenged the traditional account of FDR's final illness. This paper by a well-respected surgeon, which garnered national attention, raised the possibility that a pigmented lesion over the thirty-second president's left eye—quite visible, but rarely commented on during his lifetime—may have been malignant.

If true, this would suggest the need for a whole new evaluation of Roosevelt's final years and the precise nature of the ill health that progressively overtook him. And it raises questions, long debated by historians, as to whether FDR was fully capable of functioning as chief executive and commander in chief during the global conflict of World War II.

In reaction to Goldsmith's article, Roosevelt's lone surviving primary physician, Howard Bruenn, emphatically denied that FDR ever had cancer, effectively quashing further speculation and investigation. But the 1991 death of Margaret "Daisy" Suckley, Roosevelt's cousin and frequent companion, led to a surprising discovery: Daisy had kept a secret diary that documented her relationship with FDR, along with many of his previously unknown letters to her. And, to the surprise of Roosevelt biographers, who had dismissed her as a historical footnote, it turns out that FDR had confided things to Daisy he didn't dare divulge to anyone else (save, perhaps, his onetime mistress, Lucy Mercer Rutherfurd), knowing she would protect his secrets.

Like Goldsmith's paper, the startling revelations in Daisy's diary, published in 1995, often directly contradicted many of the claims made years earlier by FDR's physicians, including what historians long had accepted as the definitive account of Franklin Roosevelt's medical history.

Working with these disclosures, and expanding on them with intensive research, we have produced what essentially is a medical biography of Franklin D. Roosevelt. It presents a strong circumstantial case, backed by surviving medical records and analysis, that Roosevelt did indeed have cancer—melanoma, to be exact, originating in the pigmented lesion above his eye—that eventually spread to his brain and his abdomen. In other words, the cerebral hemorrhage that struck him down less than a month before V-E Day was not a "bolt out of the blue," as his doctors contended, but the inevitable result of a deadly illness, compounded by catastrophic heart problems.

We did not intend this to be a political book, although it is impossible to avoid politics entirely when considering the effect that cancer had on Roosevelt's performance as president. Others can read into this information what they will: Some will see confirmation that FDR was indeed the "sick man of Yalta," incapable of negotiating skillfully with the determined Soviet dictator, Joseph Stalin. Others will see a determined champion, tirelessly guiding America through the global conflagration while contending with the ravages of the diseases that threatened his own life.

In fact, even as soldiers were fighting the enemy on the battlefields of Europe, Africa, and Asia, a parallel struggle was under way in the White House to preserve the president himself against the considerable medical challenges—polio, heart disease, and cancer—that surrounded him. Roosevelt himself was at the center of this battle—not as a disengaged and uninterested spectator, as historians have long believed, but as a chief executive who ultimately determined the course of his own medical struggle, just as he did in the fight against the Axis powers.

With the help of his doctors, Roosevelt was determined not only to stay alive for the time needed to accomplish his goals, but also to convince the nation—and the world at large—that he was always functioning at full capacity. Yet he knew that his was a desperate race against time. In this respect, Franklin Roosevelt took one of the greatest gambles in world history—and won.

An Orator Stumbles

CHAPTER 1

Over the course of his unprecedented twelve years as president of the United States, Franklin Delano Roosevelt had—whether standing before Congress, addressing a huge political rally, or simply sitting before a microphone while delivering one of his intimate Fireside Chats—enthralled his listeners with self-assured oratory that was simple, yet stirring. But on March 1, 1945, as FDR prepared to tell Congress and a national radio audience about his recent summit at the Crimean city of Yalta with British Prime Minister Winston Churchill and Soviet leader Joseph Stalin, at which they had planned nothing less than the political shape of the postwar world, something about his delivery was very different—and radically wrong.

For one thing, the president was sitting down, something he'd never before done while delivering a major address before Congress. And he'd been wheeled into the chamber, where previously the chief executive had "walked," heavy steel braces tightly supporting his withered legs, while tightly grasping an aide's arm. Indeed, in his opening remarks, FDR surprisingly would refer publicly, for the first and only time as president, to the paralysis that had crippled him more than two decades earlier. "I hope that you will pardon me for the unusual posture of sitting down during the presentation of what I want to say," Roosevelt told his astonished listeners. "But I know that you will realize that it makes it a lot easier for me in not having to carry around ten pounds of steel around the bottom of my legs." This in itself was startling: After all, Roosevelt had waged a determined—and successful—quarter-century-long campaign to keep the American people from fully understanding that he was physically unable to stand without his braces, or to walk unaided.

In his first appearance before Congress in twenty-six months, the president was a weary and exhausted man, both physically and emotionally drained. Just the day before, in a downpour of rain and sleet, he had attended the burial of Gen. Edwin "Pa" Watson, his trusted military aide and one of his closest friends and advisers. Watson's unexpected death of a stroke aboard the USS *Quincy* while returning from Yalta had been a crushing blow to the president, who, in an unusual display of emotion, spent the rest of the transatlantic voyage in an obvious state of depression. Physically, Roosevelt was a shell of the powerful and commanding figure he'd once presented: Over the past year, he'd lost at least forty pounds. He looked gaunt and emaciated, and dark shadows circled his eyes. Even some of FDR's closest aides, like his confidential secretary, William Hassett, were speculating privately that the president was "slipping away."[1]

But in front of Congress, Roosevelt had a more immediate and perilous problem. As he began to read from a loose-leaf binder containing thirty-one double-spaced typewritten sheets, the president came to a horrifying realization: *He could not fully see all of the words on the page.*

For at least six weeks, and possibly longer, FDR had been aware that he had a problem. Progressively, he had lost his ability to read—specifically, he could no longer see the words in the left side of his field of vision; they had either become incomplete or simply were no longer visible at all. To compensate, he'd developed a technique, first noticeable a few weeks earlier when he sat for newsreel cameras reading short excerpts from his upcoming State of the Union message, which he did not deliver live to Congress, as was traditional. Roosevelt used his hands as a stylus to mark his place, even crossing them over each other to keep track of his position on the page;[2] it was a procedure he'd never before employed while speaking publicly.

But the speech he was delivering this day was one he'd determined could not simply be sent to Congress in written form. The nation needed to hear him speak. In many ways, this was the most critical speech Roosevelt had ever given; one that, likely knowing his days were numbered, he meant to cement his postwar legacy. For beyond simply reporting on the events at Yalta, the president had a burning desire to convince both Congress and the American people of the need for a postwar global peacekeeping organization. As Margaret "Daisy" Suckley, the adoring distant cousin who, it was later revealed, had been Roosevelt's intimate confidante, confided to her diary: "FDR's one really great wish is to get this international organization for peace started. Nothing else counts, next to that."[3*]

Roosevelt's mentor, Woodrow Wilson, had envisioned a similar framework for global peacekeeping after World War I, but Congress, after a bitter and rancorous partisan debate, rejected his dream of U.S. participation in the League of Nations. Roosevelt knew all too well what that political defeat had done to Wilson, destroying him both politically and physically. And, as he'd been heard muttering during a screening of the 1944 film *Wilson*, as he watched the enfeebled leader being portrayed by Alexander Knox: "By God, that will never happen to me."[4]

But, with Congress and the country hanging on his words, Roosevelt could not deliver the clarion call to postwar solidarity that he'd envisioned. The greatest political orator of the twentieth century—the man who twelve years earlier had inspired a nation in the throes of a great depression by declaring that "the only thing we have to fear is fear itself"—failed to enthrall his listeners. Time after time he stumbled over the text, making mistakes that sometimes were simple and at other times were substantial. Over and over, he appeared to lose his place and tried to compensate by ad-libbing, buying time in order to find the right spot on the page or simply to rest from the intense mental gymnastics it must have taken to keep restructuring into intelligible form sentences whose words he could not fully see. *Time* magazine calculated that he'd departed from his text forty-nine times, adding a total of seven hundred words.[5]

---

*In fact, Roosevelt apparently confided to Daisy on several occasions that he planned to resign the presidency in order to head the United Nations once it had been set up.

"I was dismayed at the halting, ineffective manner of delivery," noted his aghast speechwriter, Judge Samuel Rosenman, who had worked with Roosevelt through seven drafts of the address. "Some of his extemporaneous remarks were wholly irrelevant and some of them almost bordered on the ridiculous."[6] Grace Tully, FDR's personal secretary, added: "Sam and I were sick [over it]; he wasn't himself at all."[7] Even his White House physician, Admiral Ross McIntire—who until his death contended that Roosevelt had never been in ill health before the attack that killed him—later wrote that "now and then he passed his hand over his eyes as if to clear his sight."[8] And Howard Bruenn, the Navy cardiologist who had assumed day-to-day responsibility as the president's attending physician, wrote a quarter-century later that "his speech at times was hesitant and . . . he occasionally appeared to be at a loss for words. When queried about this later, he laughingly reported that while giving the speech he had spoken from memory and 'off the record' and that he then had slight difficulty in finding the proper place when returning to read the printed word of his address."[9]

Senator Bourke B. Hickenlooper, an Iowa Republican, sitting only a few feet from Roosevelt on March 1, noticed something unusual as the president spoke to Congress: "Watch his hands," he told a colleague. FDR's right hand, Hickenlooper said, didn't seem to be working, and he was having trouble turning the pages of his loose-leaf binder with his left hand.[10] In fact, as he'd done in January for the newsreel cameras, Roosevelt's right hand was busy marking his place in the text.

Newspaper reporters, both friendly and unfriendly, commented widely on the president's unusually weak performance. The *New York Times* headlined its front-page report, "President Put Many Interpolations in Text," and wrote that FDR had taken "his carefully prepared congressional speech for a buggy ride."[11] The paper also noted that while stenographers from the *Congressional Record* had taken down Roosevelt's words, "they did not transcribe their notes immediately, because their instructions from the White House were to use the prepared text."[12] (Press Secretary Jonathan Daniels said it was nearly impossible later on to construct a comprehensible official text from the actual transcript.)[13] The *Times*'s Capitol Hill correspondent, Allen Drury,* wrote in his private

*Drury later wrote the Pulitzer Prize–winning political novel *Advise and Consent.*

journal that "it was a long, rambling, rather lifeless affair, delivered in a rambling and rather lifeless fashion.[14] Drury added that FDR's own vice president, Harry Truman, when asked afterward for his reaction to the speech, called it "one of the greatest ever given," then "burst into hearty laughter in which we all joined."[15] The notoriously anti-Roosevelt *Chicago Tribune* was far less circumspect: "FDR Rambles in Talk," the paper's lead headline read. Its story, by longtime Roosevelt bête noire Walter Trohan, noted that the speech's "delivery was sometimes marked by hesitancy as the president obviously lost his place several times after diverging from the typewritten text placed before him."[16]

Some of the mistakes Roosevelt made were in individual words, reading "conclusions" instead of "decisions," or "arrangements" instead of "agreements." Sometimes FDR's vision problem led him to repeat words in awkward construction: For example, his original notation of the period between the Teheran and Yalta summits "without conferences of civilian representatives" of the three major powers became "without conferences of representatives of civilian representatives." And many of the ad libs, which ranged from a few words to entire paragraphs, were rambling and often disjointed, as if Roosevelt had embarked upon a rhetorical path from which he could not always easily find his way back.*

Today, listening to recordings of FDR's speech and watching the short film excerpts that survive feels like an intrusion into a moment of private weakness because the speaker, a man of magnificent intellect and rhetorical skills, an unmatched orator who had flawlessly delivered hundreds of speeches and enthralled audiences, is so audibly struggling to read the words on the page in front of him. Yet FDR was by no means mentally impaired. On the contrary: His superb mental acuity demonstrated a remarkable ability to cover his visual deficit.

What exactly was Roosevelt's problem? The answer can be found in a close examination of the actual reading text from which the president delivered his speech, for it reveals that the mistakes FDR made were by no means random. The overwhelming majority stemmed from his visual

---

*A complete audio recording of the speech, as well as a copy of Roosevelt's actual reading text, annotated by the authors to indicate his many mistakes and ad-libs, can be found at this book's companion Web site, www.fdrsdeadlysecret.com.

President Roosevelt, seated—for the first and only time—in the well of the House of Representatives, reports to Congress and the nation on the summit at Yalta. FDR's listeners, including his top aides, were horrified by his rambling, tentative, and confused delivery. (Bettmann/CORBIS)

inability to find the left margin of each page or to see the left side of the individual words—forcing him to reconstruct sentences on the fly.

However, the problem was not with the president's eyes but with his brain. He was suffering from a neurological condition called left hemianopia, characteristic of a specific focal dysfunction in the right posterior portion of the brain. The errors Roosevelt made present the strongest evidence that a large pigmented lesion over his left eyebrow, which had grown and darkened over a period of nearly two decades, was not a harmless sunspot, but rather a deadly melanoma, or skin cancer. And that—just as the medical literature of the day predicted—in the four to five years since it had become malignant, the cancer had now metastasized to his brain, causing the growing tumor that would take Roosevelt's life a mere six weeks later. Even with all the advances in today's state of medical knowledge, the presence of symptomatic brain metastases from melanoma, from which FDR was suffering, is the inevitable harbinger of an inexorable and rapid demise.

Although hemianopia is most commonly seen in strokes, it can also be a consequence of a host of neurological diseases, including tumors involving the areas of the brain that affect vision.*

Roosevelt died two and a half hours after suffering a sudden catastrophic brain hemorrhage at Warm Springs, Georgia, on April 12, 1945. The notes taken by Bruenn, one of two doctors at FDR's bedside as his life ebbed, document physical findings that a neurologist easily would recognize as emanating from the posterior aspect of the right cerebral hemisphere—precisely the area of the brain that would produce the left-sided visual deficit Roosevelt exhibited for three months prior to his death. Coupled with the knowledge that melanoma is notorious for its rate of brain metastases, and that hemorrhages from them are the second most common cause of death among melanoma victims, the implications are obvious.

More evidence of Roosevelt's hemianopia comes from an incident that occurred on January 14, 1945, while the president was at his Hyde Park residence. Daisy Suckley records that FDR phoned her at her nearby home, Wilderstein, "at 5 minutes to 2—He had mistaken the time on his clock & had just come down for his lunch."[17] An inability to clearly see the left side of his clock might easily have led the president to mistake 2 p.m. for noon. Having a patient draw a clock face is a routine part of present-day neurological examinations to assess the integrity of the right cerebral hemisphere.

Yet even if Roosevelt's doctors had known about hemianopia, there was precious little they could have done about it. While the medical literature of FDR's day asserted that melanoma invariably was fatal and that it fairly consistently metastasized to the brain and the abdomen, as

---

*This was demonstrated dramatically in the case of the veteran political columnist Robert Novak, who in 2008 was diagnosed with a malignant brain tumor after he unknowingly struck a pedestrian while driving in Washington, D.C. As Novak later wrote:

> I had no idea I had hit anyone until they flagged me down. . . . [That] was soon confirmed by the diagnosis of my brain cancer, in which I have lost not only peripheral vision but nearly all my left vision, probably permanently. Several people have asked me whether the person I hit was crossing in front of me on my left. I answer, "I never saw him." (Robert Novak, "My Brain Tumor," September 7, 2008). He died in August 2009, barely a year after first being diagnosed.

did Roosevelt's, it's not at all clear that his doctors fully understood the nature of this neurological problem, though they certainly knew that the president's lesion was malignant and had metastasized. All Roosevelt and his doctors knew on March 1, 1945, was that he could not easily read the pages in front of him. And those listening to the distressed president were aware only that, as Sam Rosenman put it, "the great fighting eloquence and oratory that distinguished him in his [re-election] campaign only four months before were lacking."[18*]

When the frail, coughing sixty-three-year-old president was wheeled out of the House chamber at the end of his speech, many of those in the audience instinctively felt that they were seeing Franklin Delano Roosevelt for the last time.

They were right.

* * *

It is unlikely we will ever know with absolute certainty what killed the thirty-second president of the United States. No autopsy was performed (though none of those present could ever agree why), and, save for a few lab slips that turned up in 1957, the whereabouts of Roosevelt's medical file, maintained by Ross McIntire, has been unknown since his death.

For the first quarter-century, the official line on FDR's passing was the one given by his doctors on April 12, 1945, at the Little White House in Warm Springs, where he died: An otherwise healthy Roosevelt

---

*Just how rapidly Roosevelt's metastatic brain disease had progressed can be seen from this account by the Pulitzer Prize–winning playwright Robert Sherwood, one of FDR's speechwriters: In the middle of a campaign speech at Philadelphia's Shibe Park the previous October, Postmaster General Frank C. Walker told him, FDR could be seen shuffling through the pages of his text.

Now and then, Roosevelt would glance down at one of those earlier pages but proceeded with the delivery of the text that he was not even looking at. After the speech, Walker asked Roosevelt what he had been doing, and the president explained that there was some point he had made early in the speech that had gone over so well he thought he would like to make it again.

Added Sherwood: "This was another demonstration of Roosevelt's amazing assurance and command of the situation when delivering a speech." (Jonathan Daniels, *White House Witness*, p. 255)

had been brought down by a sudden and unforeseeable massive cerebral hemorrhage—"a bolt out of the blue," they called it—with arteriosclerosis as a contributing cause.[19] The president's gaunt appearance and his shocking weight loss and startling performance in his recent speech to Congress were not signs of ill health, they maintained, but sheer physical exhaustion, brought on by overwork and the strain of being a wartime chief executive. Americans accepted this explanation, though there had long been whispers in Washington circles that all was not right with the president's health.

Those whispers were vindicated in 1970, when Bruenn—a cardiologist who, virtually unknown to the outside world, had been at Roosevelt's side daily since April 1944—wrote a paper in a medical journal disclosing that the president had indeed been terribly ill, physically compromised during the last year of his life by severe cardiac illness and uncontrollable high blood pressure. Bruenn's paper was widely hailed at the time as a revelation and the irrefutable last word on Franklin Roosevelt's final illness.

That Roosevelt had critical heart problems—Bruenn's diagnosis of acute cardiac failure in March 1944—is undeniable. Dr. Wayne C. Levy, a cardiologist at the University of Washington who in 2006 developed a comprehensive model for predicting the short-term survival rates for patients with heart failure, has analyzed FDR's data and suggested that his estimated mortality at the time of Bruenn's diagnosis was 23 percent at one year and 78 percent at five years. This, he said, "is about the average mortality of a ninety-year-old male in the current era."[20]

But Bruenn's paper was not the final word on FDR's illness. It contains numerous discrepancies and significant omissions that have been contradicted by other available evidence. His insistence that the president was wholly unconcerned about the state of his health is utterly refuted by the 1995 publication of Daisy Suckley's diary. The diary, previously unknown and discovered only after her death in 1991, makes undeniably clear that Roosevelt was all too aware of the specific details of his fatally compromised health.

The present book goes even further—presenting a strong case that, far from being a submissive patient who just sat back and followed his doctors' orders, Roosevelt was in control of his own medical situation;

indeed, that whatever actions McIntire ultimately undertook came only at the president's specific direction. Roosevelt knew his condition as well, perhaps better, than many of the doctors who treated him. He gambled that he was, despite all the medical evidence, fit for the highest office at the most critical time: as America joined, fought, and won the Second World War, and then negotiated the shape of the postwar world.

Additionally, this book presents an alternate account of Roosevelt's final illness that not only explains the circumstances of the president's death better than any of his doctors offered at the time, but also raises anew the question of his competence in the last years of his life. Cancer of the brain has very different consequences than the heart condition that Roosevelt's doctors finally, and reluctantly, acknowledged. They said he was fatigued; we assert that the president was diagnosed with a highly malignant skin cancer, melanoma, which later metastasized to his abdomen and to his brain, producing a hemorrhage that was the most probable immediate cause of his death. And that he may also have suffered from prostate cancer, whose treatment ultimately was compromised by a multitude of serious health problems. Cancer, over many years, was Roosevelt's deadly secret.

Rumors that Roosevelt had prostate cancer circulated widely even while he was still alive. And the specific notion that a lesion over his eye was malignant first was raised as early as 1948; in particular, the groundbreaking work by Dr. Harry S. Goldsmith, who has spent forty years investigating FDR's health and whose 1979 paper in a leading medical journal provided the inspiration for this work, moved this theory forward. But none of the earlier researchers could offer anything more than the visual appearance of Roosevelt's lesion; this work provides a more solid basis for the scenario, based on medical evidence of the effect of the melanoma.

We cannot be incontrovertibly certain in our diagnosis, of course—absent an autopsy or objective confirmation from Roosevelt's still-missing contemporary medical records. Both McIntire and Bruenn repeatedly denied that the president ever had cancer. Moreover, his severe cardiovascular problems were sufficient to kill him, and likely would have done so before the end of his fourth term. And the many documented spells of unconsciousness, most consistent with seizures, that Roosevelt exhibited in the final year of his life, and that have gone largely undiscussed by most historians, most probably are attributable to the effects of his malignant hypertension.

But a very strong, albeit circumstantial case—based on surviving records, independent medical evidence, and reliable eyewitness reports of his condition—supports the notion that Roosevelt died of cancer. Moreover, there are the numerous reports, long after his death, quoting other doctors involved in his case—some of whose connections previously were known, such as Frank Lahey, and others not, such as William Calhoun Stirling—that Roosevelt did indeed have widespread malignancy.

If true, this presents a profound historical revelation. Conventional wisdom has it that Roosevelt took ill in early 1944, ran for a fourth term knowing he was ill, and then suffered a rapid physical breakdown only in the last few weeks before his death, retaining his mental powers to the end. But if the melanoma scenario is correct, it means that Roosevelt, while still in his *second* term, knew he was almost certainly doomed to die of cancer within five years. And that, even with this knowledge, he and his doctors covered it up—even as they are known to have kept from the public an honest understanding of the president's disability from polio—and forged ahead, believing in his tremendous force of will, combined with a firm conviction that his continued presence in the Oval Office was necessary to bring the country into and through the growing war against Germany and Japan.

This work also explodes another long-standing myth about FDR: that Ross McIntire, with limited medical skills, botched the president's medical care and that the knowingly false statements he made, both during Roosevelt's lifetime and afterward, were intended to disguise his own incompetence. A large body of evidence shows that Roosevelt's care—with the exception of a nearly fatal oversight in 1941—was on a level consistent with what would be expected for the president of the United States. Indeed, McIntire not only fully availed himself of the vast resources and expertise available from Navy medicine, then, as now, on the cutting edge of medical care, but when necessary did not hesitate to call in the finest and most skilled consultants available. And Bruenn's role, contrary to long-standing belief, went far beyond that of a superbly competent physician who passively treated a seriously ill president: He eventually became the caretaker of FDR's deadly secret, which he vigorously protected until his own death in 1995.

That McIntire and Bruenn acted in the best interests of their patient and commander in chief, arguably the most powerful and charismatic figure of the twentieth century, is undeniable. Whether by publicly misleading the country about the state of his health they also acted in the best interests of the American people is much more debatable.

Ultimately, though, did Roosevelt's concealment of his deadly secret make a difference on the course of events? Ironically, neither member of the Republican ticket that opposed FDR in 1940 for his third term (after he'd been diagnosed with melanoma), Wendell Willkie and Charles L. McNary, survived to the end of what would have been their term in office,* meaning that the United States, during the heart of the Second World War, would have been led by an unelected president—whomever Willkie might have chosen as secretary of state. And had FDR not run in 1940, the two leading candidates to succeed him were Vice President John Nance Garner, a seventy-two-year-old conservative who had broken with Roosevelt and the New Deal, and Postmaster General James A. Farley, whose electoral prospects, as a Catholic, would have been difficult. Like Willkie, neither of these candidates had any foreign-affairs experience. Nor, for that matter, did Thomas E. Dewey—who, had he defeated Roosevelt in 1944, would have become president in the midst of the war, with responsibility for negotiating the course of postwar Europe and Asia with Joseph Stalin and Winston Churchill.

At the same time, though, it is inexplicable that FDR, knowing his grim prognosis, made no effort to ensure that, should the worst occur, he would be succeeded by a strong and capable vice president. His running-mate selections in both races were determined entirely by domestic political considerations. Fortunately, in Harry Truman, he had a vice president who was up to the job, though that was not widely realized at the time. Truman, though, was not his first choice for the job, or even his second or third. Henry Wallace, who did become vice president during the third term, was dangerously naive about Stalin and the Soviet Union;

---

*McNary died in February 1944 at age seventy, after surgery on a brain tumor. Willkie died seven months later from a heart attack; he was only fifty-two.

had he become president during the war, it is inconceivable that the conflict and the postwar world would have taken the same course.

Franklin Roosevelt, with the help of his doctors, chose to roll the dice with history, believing that he was the best man for the times. He might have been right when he made the decision to run for a third term, even perhaps when he decided to campaign for a fourth. But he could not beat the medical odds for long. That his risky gamble succeeded for as long as it did hardly excuses the overwhelming danger of the choice he made—raising profoundly disturbing implications for future presidents.

Wilson's Example

CHAPTER 2

Once the initial shock of Franklin Delano Roosevelt's death had sunk in, popular sentiment held that an overworked president, taxed beyond reason by the demands of his office, had fallen victim to the strain of fighting first the Great Depression and then the greatest war in world history. Most people around the world doubtless shared the assessment of Senator Robert Taft, the Ohio Republican and conservative leader who declared that FDR had "literally worked himself to death in the service of the American people."[1]

But, at sixty-three, Roosevelt was hardly an old man and, unbeknownst to the American people, for the previous sixteen months his actual working hours had been severely limited to as little as four a day, with long periods of rest in between—hardly the schedule one might expect for a president presiding over the greatest conflagration in human history and whose personal physician insisted he was in superb physical condition. Moreover, fully half his time was spent away from Washington and the White House—at grueling international conferences and on the campaign trail, to be sure, but often for long periods of recuperation at Hyde Park, Warm Springs, the presidential retreat of

Shangri-La (later renamed Camp David), and Bernard Baruch's Hobcaw Barony in South Carolina.

Roosevelt had spent decades fighting off illnesses that ravaged his body—according to one medical chronicler, "a lifetime series of sieges of the common cold, sinusitis, pharyngitis, tonsillitis, laryngitis, tracheitis, bronchitis, influenza and pneumonia."[2] And, with the most serious health crisis of his pre-presidential years—the polio that permanently crippled him in the prime of life—he spent almost as much effort shielding the public from comprehending the true effects of his disability as he did in fighting the illness itself.

During his younger years, FDR faced an unusually high number of potentially life-threatening and debilitating ailments. In 1889, at the age of seven, he was diagnosed with typhoid fever while on a transatlantic cruise to England with his parents and received the special care and attention that was expected by a family of his wealth and social standing: The ship's captain gave young Franklin a private room on deck, then wired ahead for his own physician cousin and a nurse to meet the boat in port. For several weeks, Franklin lived in the doctor's home, receiving round-the-clock care—including bread and milk spiked with port—and close attention until he was well enough to travel.[3]

FDR had been born on January 30, 1882, the only child of the well-to-do squire of Hyde Park, James Roosevelt, and his second wife, Sara Delano. (Franklin had a half-brother, James, known as Rosy, who was thirty years his senior and who died in 1927.) His was a difficult birth: His mother spent over twenty-four hours in painful labor that nearly killed both of them, and the doctor had to administer chloroform to save her life.[4]

Franklin's childhood was both pampered and sheltered. He was homeschooled until the age of fourteen, and—save for six weeks spent in a German school in 1892—virtually the only people his own age with whom he came into contact were his cousins and the children of neighboring estates in New York's Dutchess County. He did, however, meet some of the notables of the day, including President Grover Cleveland, whom he visited at the White House with his father and who famously told the five-year-old Franklin: "My little man, I am making a strange wish for you. It is that you may never be president of the United States."

FDR's cloistered early childhood and isolation from his youthful peers shielded him from exposure to most of the common childhood diseases of the day. Once he began at the exclusive Groton Preparatory School in 1896, however, he fell victim to one ailment after another—beginning with the chronic sinus problems that would plague him throughout his life (and possibly attributable to the chloroform that was administered at his birth).[5] According to his biographer, Geoffrey C. Ward, he "seems to have been susceptible to every Groton germ."[6] Over the four years of his teenage schooling, he suffered bouts of measles, mumps, and hives, as well as frequent colds and athletic injuries, much to the distress of his overly protective mother. In 1898, following America's declaration of war against Spain, Franklin and two classmates made plans to run away and join the Navy—until they all came down with scarlet fever. (So FDR always claimed, anyway; Ward believes the story was heavily embellished, reflecting the young Roosevelt's wish, rather than what he actually did.) The illness, however, was no embellishment; FDR's parents, then traveling in Europe, quickly returned home when they were cabled that Franklin had developed inflamed kidneys, which may have had an effect on some of his later illnesses.[7]

Following a lackluster academic career at Harvard and Columbia Law School, Roosevelt married his cousin Eleanor in 1905 and passed the New York bar exam—despite a severe attack of sinusitis on the day of the test. While marking time at a Wall Street law firm, he plotted a political career, telling friends and colleagues he would follow the same path as his distant cousin, President Theodore Roosevelt, who was now his uncle by marriage: winning a seat in the New York state legislature; appointment as assistant secretary of the Navy; followed by election as governor of New York. From there, according to the later recollections of Grenville Clark, a law clerk, he would win the presidency.[8] And, in fact, this was the very route his political career would chart—albeit with one or two detours.

In 1910, he was offered the Democratic nomination for a safe seat in the state assembly, only to be forced out of the race when the incumbent changed his mind about retiring. Instead, he turned to the state Senate seat representing the Hyde Park area, even though the district was strongly Republican and his opponent had last been reelected by a 2-to-1 margin. But FDR had picked the right year to undertake his challenge: A national split in the GOP had a strong impact on New York, and Roosevelt, a natural campaigner, rode a nationwide Democratic wave to victory.

Though only a freshman legislator, Roosevelt rose to prominence on the strength of his nationally famous name and his role as the leader of an insurgent faction of Democrats that rebelled against the Tammany Hall machine over the selection of a United States senator. But his reelection campaign in 1912 was unexpectedly threatened when FDR once again was struck down, this time by a severe attack of typhoid fever while returning from a summer vacation at the family home on Campobello Island in New Brunswick, Canada. The illness left him bedridden at his family's Manhattan apartment and physically unable to campaign; it looked like Roosevelt's political career would be over almost before it had even begun.

Yet even at the darkest moments of his life, good fortune always seemed to smile on Franklin Roosevelt—and this time was no exception. He enlisted the services of a political genius named Louis McHenry Howe, the Albany correspondent of the *New York Herald* (and political ghostwriter for hire on the side), who had already taken a considerable shine to FDR as a political prospect. Indeed, while interviewing FDR for the *Herald* that same year, Howe had concluded that "nothing but an accident could keep him from becoming president." Over the next quarter-century, Howe would enjoy a relationship with his patron unlike any other in the Roosevelt inner circle. As *Time* magazine noted after his death in 1936: "Admirers [FDR] had by the millions, acquaintances by the thousands, advisers by the hundreds, friends by the score, but of intimates such as Louis Howe he had only one."[9]*

While FDR remained in bed for the remaining six weeks of the election, Howe personally canvassed the countryside for votes and waged a one-man campaign operation—with Roosevelt usually the last to find

*Like many of those who surrounded Roosevelt, Howe battled lifelong infirmities. Barely five feet tall, his face disfigured by a childhood accident, he cheerfully admitted that he resembled "a medieval gnome," adding: "Children take one look at me on the street and they run." He suffered from chronic bronchitis as well as cardiac and gastrointestinal ailments. His perpetual shortage of cash served as the catalyst for his joining forces with FDR in 1912, when he asked for Roosevelt's help in lining up a position with Woodrow Wilson's presidential campaign. The ailing candidate told his wife instead to hire Howe for his own race.

out precisely what his surrogate was up to. Spending the then-unheard-of sum of $3,000, Howe took out full-page newspaper ads, dispatched more than 11,000 personal letters to voters over FDR's signature, and, in the words of biographer Jean Edward Smith, personally "promis[ed] in Franklin's name whatever would win votes." And it worked: Without a single day's campaigning of his own, Roosevelt was reelected by an increased margin.[10] From that moment on, Howe dedicated himself to attaining the goal he'd set in a letter he sent Roosevelt during the campaign, addressed to "Beloved and Revered Future President."[11]

No sooner had Roosevelt been reelected, however, than he made plans to desert Albany for Washington. After declining President-elect Wilson's offers of a position as either deputy secretary of the Treasury or collector of the Port of New York, he finally got the job he'd been after at the Navy Department under incoming Secretary Josephus Daniels, a North Carolina newspaper publisher who was wholly ignorant of naval affairs. Louis Howe went along as his special assistant—his real job was to expand FDR's public visibility and political contacts.

As assistant secretary, Roosevelt—despite his personal loyalty to the president—was at odds with the Wilson administration's reluctance to become entangled in the European war that broke out in 1914; he even secretly fed information to his cousin Theodore and Wilson's other hawkish Republican interventionist critics as he worked to drastically expand the Navy's manpower.[12] Though convinced that Daniels was not up to the task of preparing for what he believed was America's inevitable entry into the conflict, he prepared to leave the Navy Department, campaigning for a U.S. Senate seat from New York in the fall of 1914, only to lose the Democratic primary to a Tammany-based candidate.*

During this time, health problems continued to follow Franklin: In July 1915, a burst appendix forced him to spend five weeks convalescing at Campobello, while a peritonsillar abscess in August 1917 led to four

---

*When the U.S. finally entered the world war in April 1917, FDR's first thought was to once again follow in the footsteps of his cousin Theodore, who became a national hero through his command of the Rough Riders during the Spanish-American War, and resign his post to join the Army. Theodore Roosevelt not only agreed, he actually demanded emphatically that Franklin enlist. But both President Wilson and Secretary Daniels ordered FDR to remain at his post.

days' hospitalization. During a tour of the front in France shortly before the war's end, he came down with a heavy attack of flu; on the return trip to New York, he collapsed with double pneumonia, spent most of the voyage in a semiconscious state, and had to be carried ashore by stretcher, followed by four weeks' recovery in bed.[13] Within days of returning to work, however, he fell victim once again to influenza.

Roosevelt also witnessed firsthand, as he would again later on, the devastating effects of serious illness on a president, privately expressing his fear that Wilson was on the verge of suffering "a breakdown" following the death of his wife from cancer in 1914.

It was at the Navy Department that Roosevelt first met and befriended another man who would play a key role in his life: Rear Admiral Cary T. Grayson, President Wilson's personal physician. Grayson, who had earlier tended to the health of presidents Theodore Roosevelt and William Howard Taft, was more than just Wilson's doctor; the *New York Times* described him as the president's "closest confidant and friend"[14]—a role very much akin to that of FDR's own presidential physician, Ross McIntire. And, as with McIntire later on, Grayson's personal devotion and loyalty to the president led him to conspire to keep the true state of the chief executive's precarious health from the American public.

In Grayson's case, however, that cover-up extended far beyond simply lying about how sick the president really was. On April 3, 1919, in the midst of his fierce battle with Senate isolationists over America's participation in the new League of Nations, Wilson broke down under the strain. Grayson diagnosed an attack of influenza, which was then raging in a worldwide pandemic, though Wilson had actually suffered a stroke that left him neurologically impaired. Weeks of increasingly bizarre behavior followed, culminating in a near-fatal cerebral embolism on September 26 and an even more severe stroke a week later that left Wilson completely paralyzed on one side and suffering the same vision loss that would, more than a quarter-century later, provide the medical smoking-gun clue to FDR's own final illness.[15]*

---

*According to medical historians Kenneth Crispell and Carlos Gomez, Wilson also suffered from a prostate condition that necessitated surgery. But a top urologist who was called in declined to operate, fearing the weakened president would not survive the surgery. Coincidentally, FDR would face a similar circumstance.

Dr. Cary Grayson, who, along with First Lady Edith Wilson, engineered the cover-up of Woodrow Wilson's debilitating stroke and later found for FDR a White House physician who "knows how to keep his mouth shut." (Franklin D. Roosevelt Library)

Grayson, fearing that the impaired Wilson would be forced to resign or temporarily step aside in favor of his lightly regarded vice president, Thomas R. Marshall (he flatly told Secretary of State Robert Lansing that he would never certify that the president was hopelessly disabled), Grayson conspired with Wilson's second wife, Edith (whom he'd first introduced to the president), to deceive the cabinet, Congress, and the American people about the perilous state of his health. Wilson was largely kept hidden from public view, including visitors from Capitol Hill and even the president's own aides. While admitting to the cabinet that Wilson had suffered "a nervous breakdown . . . and a depleted nervous system," Grayson warned the secretaries against "bothering" the president during what he assured them was a steady path to recovery.

Meanwhile, unbeknownst to everyone, the First Lady, with Grayson's connivance, functioned as a surrogate president, essentially seizing the reins of government and making key political and policy decisions, in the name of protecting "my husband and his health." Amazingly, at one point Wilson himself told Grayson that the country would be better off if he left office—only to be dissuaded by his doctor, who assured him that he was still politically in touch and insisted that even an impaired Woodrow Wilson was better than a healthy Thomas Marshall. And so Wilson, his physical health broken, his mind and judgment weakened, lingered on for the remainder of his second term, holding the title of president but never fully performing the functions of his office.

There is no evidence that FDR was privy to the full extent of Wilson's dark secret, but he did witness the president's disability firsthand during the final year of his second term. Years later, Roosevelt recalled his visit to the White House: "As we came in sight of the portico, we saw the president in a wheelchair, his left shoulder covered with a shawl which concealed his left arm, which was paralyzed. . . . Wilson looked up and in a very low, weak voice said, 'Thank you for coming.' . . . His utter weakness was startling."[16] The sight of the fragile and vulnerable president, whose fight to bring the United States into a postwar organization designed to ensure global peace had ended in a crushing personal defeat at the hands of his political foes, left an indelible mark on Franklin Roosevelt, as will later be seen.

By then, he and Grayson had formed a strong personal bond that lasted until the latter's death a quarter-century later. So close was their relationship that Roosevelt would enlist Grayson, then retired from the Navy, to chair and organize his first two presidential inaugurations, in 1933 and 1937. More important, when FDR needed to select his own White House physician, he would turn to Grayson for a recommendation.

All that was in the future, though, as the Wilson administration, and Roosevelt's role in the sub-cabinet, drew to a close. In the summer of 1920, the political spotlight unexpectedly shone on FDR and turned him into a national figure: The Democrats, sunk low in the polls, nominated him for vice president on the ticket headed by Governor James Cox of Ohio. It made little sense politically—Roosevelt was just thirty-eight years old, the third-youngest major-party nominee in history, with little political experience. But he had a magical last name, and that's what his party was counting on. Not that it really mattered; the Cox-Roosevelt ticket went down to a crushing defeat against the Republican team of Warren G. Harding and Calvin Coolidge. But the campaign provided FDR with important national political experience: He barnstormed the country by railroad, speaking an average of seven times a day and building a network of important contacts.

Despite the landslide loss, Roosevelt had to be feeling supremely confident as 1921 dawned. Not yet forty, his name already was nationally known, he had a record as a legislator and a wartime administrator, and he had shown considerable skill on the campaign trail. On the personal front, however, things were far less rosy. In 1918, while unpacking his luggage as her husband lay bedridden with double pneumonia, Eleanor had discovered a packet of love letters essentially confirming that, as long rumored in Washington circles, Franklin had been having an affair with her social secretary, Lucy Mercer. Her first response had been to offer Franklin "his freedom," but, under intense pressure from both Louis Howe and FDR's mother, who argued vehemently that divorce would end his political career, Eleanor agreed to preserve the marriage (although, by all accounts, their physical relationship ended), provided Franklin vowed never to see Lucy again.[17] He did promise—but it was a promise he would not keep.

Politicians' personal lives being considered off-limits to journalists at the time, not a word of this appeared in the press. As a result, Roosevelt weathered the personal crisis and his political standing was undamaged. He was universally acknowledged as a rising star and his prospects seemed limitless. Then fate intervened and threatened to shatter all of his dreams and ambitions in a single, literally crippling, blow.

Triumph Over Mortal Matter

CHAPTER 3

August 10, 1921—the last day that Franklin Delano Roosevelt would ever walk unassisted—was much like any other summer day at Campobello. It was filled with nonstop recreation for FDR and his five young children, particularly sailing aboard his new sloop, the *Vireo*. It was only the fourth day of what Roosevelt was expecting to be his first real vacation since joining the Navy Department more than eight years earlier.

A couple of weeks before journeying north, FDR had joined a delegation to a Boy Scout camp for underprivileged children near Bear Mountain, some forty miles from Hyde Park. He spent the day roughhousing with the youngsters, who, having grown up in the crowded city slums, had developed natural immunity to those serious diseases to which Roosevelt remained susceptible—diseases like the much-dreaded, and very prevalent, poliomyelitis. Polio was a disease with which FDR was not entirely unfamiliar: In 1916, during a particularly virulent outbreak along the East Coast, with mortality rates reaching as high as 25 percent, he insisted that his family remain at Campobello while he returned to Washington, refusing to allow them to leave until after the epidemic had abated—and, even then, arranging for Navy Secretary Daniels's private yacht to bring them home, rather than subject them to the perceived risks of public transportation.[1]

Franklin Roosevelt's personal confrontation with the disease that would prove to be the defining event of his life began with a family sail on the *Vireo*. Along the way, they noticed a forest fire on a nearby island and spent several hours battling the blaze. They then jogged two miles for a swim in a lagoon, followed by a longer plunge in the Bay of Fundy and another lengthy run home. The day before, FDR had accidentally fallen into Fundy's icy waters while baiting some fishing hooks. "I'd never felt anything as cold as that water!" he wrote a decade later, adding that "the water was so cold it seemed paralyzing."

By the time the family returned home at 4 p.m., Roosevelt was feeling unusually tired—too tired even to change out of his wet bathing suit. After an hour or so of reading the mail, he began to feel chills and went to bed, wrapped in heavy blankets, without eating dinner. The next morning, he was unsteady on his feet, his back was wracked with pain, and he had a raging fever. The family's elderly local physician, Edward Bennett, diagnosed the problem as "a severe cold," but by the following day, Roosevelt had lost the use of his legs and was having problems urinating. Moreover, his skin had become so painfully sensitive that he could not even bear the pressure of his bedclothes.[2]

After frantic telephoning, Louis Howe managed to locate the venerable Philadelphia surgeon William W. Keen, a former president of the American Medical Association, who was vacationing in Maine. The eighty-four-year-old Keen was world-famous; four years earlier, in an article for the *Saturday Evening Post*, he'd disclosed how he and a fellow surgeon in 1893 had secretly performed a series of operations on President Grover Cleveland to remove a cancerous growth from the roof of his mouth. His diagnosis of Roosevelt: "A clot of blood from a sudden congestion" that had "settled in the lower spinal cord, temporarily removing the power to move, though not to feel"; Keen prescribed heavy massage of his legs and predicted a quick recovery. A few days later, though, he wrote Eleanor to change his diagnosis; now, he said, the problem was a "lesion of the spinal cord" with a much worse long-term prognosis. Along with his letter, Keen enclosed a bill for the then-staggering sum of $600—the equivalent of $7,000 in 2009.

For the next ten days. Eleanor and Howe spent countless hours vigorously kneading the muscles in FDR's legs—to no avail. By this time, Roosevelt was completely paralyzed from his chest downward and was slipping in and out of delirium; as Eleanor later put it in a draft of her autobiography, he was "out of his head." (FDR excised the description from her manuscript.) When Franklin's uncle, Frederic Delano, showed Eleanor's letters detailing her husband's symptoms to several doctors, one—Samuel Levine, an internist at the Peter Bent Brigham Hospital (and later a famous cardiologist)—did not hesitate before offering a diagnosis of poliomyelitis.[3] According to his unpublished manuscript on the case, a spinal tap was performed in the hopes of relieving cerebrospinal pressure and lessening any further paralysis. Although Levine urged that the procedure take place at once, it was not performed for four days.[4]

By this time, the family had enlisted the aid of Dr. Robert W. Lovett of Boston, considered the leading expert on infantile paralysis. It didn't take long for him to concur with Levine and to order an immediate halt to the painful massage, which in fact had both hastened and worsened Roosevelt's condition.* Still, Lovett provided some optimism: "The case was not of the severest type," he told Eleanor, and "some of the important muscles might be on the edge where they could be influenced either way—towards recovery or turn into completely paralyzed muscles."[5] But FDR's condition failed to improve, and he became increasingly anxious and disturbed, to the point where he proposed to Lovett that massage therapy be resumed. To this, the doctor replied: "There is nothing that can be added to the treatment."[6]

---

*In a 2003 paper in the *Journal of Medical Biography*, Dr. Armond Goldman of the University of Texas presented a case that Roosevelt's illness was not polio but probably related to Guillain-Barré Syndrome, a disorder in which the body's immune system attacks part of the peripheral nervous system and causes paralysis. Guillain-Barré had first been described in 1916, though it likely was known to Lovett, the world's foremost expert on polio. The results of the spinal tap, which were available to FDR's doctor at the time, would have been a key diagnostic factor in differentiating between the two conditions. And a 1958 paper by Dr. Noah Fabricant, who made a close study of Roosevelt's early illnesses, raised a possible connection between the attack of polio and FDR's having undergone a tonsillectomy twenty-one months earlier: "If poliomyelitis strikes shortly after a tonsillectomy is performed, there is increased likelihood that the disease will come on in a very severe form."

The first public word of Roosevelt's illness appeared on the front page of an Augusta newspaper, the *Daily Kennebec Journal*, on August 27. Under the headline "Franklin Roosevelt Improving After Threat of Pneumonia," the short Associated Press dispatch, datelined Eastport and based on information selectively supplied by Louis Howe, reported that Roosevelt "has been seriously ill at his summer home at Campobello, but is now improving," adding that he "took a heavy cold and was threatened with pneumonia, but was slightly improved and progressing favorably."[7] There wasn't even the slightest hint of either polio or Roosevelt's continuing paralysis—for, even at this point, as the anguished family grew more and more panicked, Howe's overwhelming concern was to preserve Roosevelt's political future. "I'm not going to mention the word 'paralysis' unless I have to," he said. "If it's printed, we're sunk. Franklin's career is *kaput*, it's finished."[8]

With this in mind, he arranged to bring FDR back to New York, where he could be treated by specialists without the public's realizing the extent of his incapacity. Frederic Delano, a successful railroad operator, provided a private railway car for the trip from Maine; Howe arranged for Roosevelt to be strapped to a stretcher and loaded onto a boat for the short but painful trip to the railway siding. Meanwhile, he diverted well-wishers and reporters to the opposite end of the port. By the time they found the right location, Roosevelt had been carried onboard the train and propped up on pillows, the sweat mopped from his face and his soon-to-be-trademark cigarette holder cocked upward as he prepared for the long ride to Grand Central Terminal in Manhattan.

The front page of the next day's *New York Times* carried the first announcement that Roosevelt had been stricken with polio—along with the confident assurance of Dr. George Draper, the family physician, that "you can say definitely that he will not be crippled. No one need have any fear of permanent injury from his attack." In fact, the article proclaimed, while "Mr. Roosevelt's legs and feet were affected . . . for more than a week he has been recovering the use of the affected members."[9] FDR immediately dictated a note to the paper's publisher, Adolph S. Ochs, stating that while his doctors "were unanimous in telling me that the attack was very mild and that I was not going to suffer any personal effects from it, I had, of course, the usual dark suspicion that they were just saying nice things to make me feel good." But now that the *Times* had said the same thing, he added, "I know of course it must be true."[10]

However, recovery was slow. Dr. Draper had feared that "when we try to sit him up, he will still be faced with the frightfully depressing knowledge that he cannot hold himself erect." Indeed, he wrote, "it will take all the skill which we can muster to lead him successfully to a recognition of what he still faces without crushing him." Roosevelt's arm and chest muscles gained strength, but his legs remained weak and continued to atrophy. After six weeks at Presbyterian Hospital, he was able to pull himself up and into a wheelchair, which made him eager to try standing with crutches. But, as Draper noted, "I am not encouraging him."

As it became clear that, despite his personal optimism and the rosy stories that Howe was planting in the press, Roosevelt was not regaining the use of his legs, a fierce and bitter struggle broke out within the family over his future. Sara Roosevelt was adamant that her son should abandon any thought of resuming political life and instead spend his days as the invalid squire of Hyde Park, pursuing only his hobbies and his interests, with no need even of having to earn a living. But Eleanor, despite her initial doubts, was buoyed by Louis Howe's determined insistence that Franklin not only could, but would, eventually become president, and resisted her mother-in-law's "quiet ideas for his future existence."[11] Not that there really was any debate about it: From the outset, FDR was determined to pursue and achieve his political goals.

After six weeks in the hospital, Roosevelt was sent home to his family's East Sixty-Fifth Street townhouse, where he began an intensive exercise regimen. Initially dependent wholly on crutches, in March 1922 he was fitted with a pair of steel braces that ran from his heels to above his hips. With them, he was able to develop a technique that mimicked walking by pivoting his hips, using his upper body as leverage with a crutch (later, as he gained strength, a cane) in one hand as he tightly gripped the arm of a person walking alongside him with the other. Yet while FDR continued to gain power in his hip muscles, Draper privately advised Dr. Lovett that "below the knee I must say it looks rather hopeless."[12]

Meanwhile, FDR remained as politically active as possible; he already had assured his local Democratic chairman that "the doctors tell me I am getting along splendidly and I hope to be back in the game before very long."[13] Former Governor Alfred E. Smith, having been defeated for reelection in 1920, agreed to run again to keep ambitious newspaper publisher William Randolph Hearst, the king of yellow journalism, out of the statehouse.* Smith asked Roosevelt, the acknowledged leader of the upstate Democratic forces, to publicly call for him to run, and FDR's public appeal became front-page news. At the same time, Eleanor—at the urging of Louis Howe—overcame her innate shyness and fear of public appearances and became a party activist, essentially her husband's eyes and ears in Democratic circles.

As his legs continued to show no real improvement, Roosevelt consulted extensively with every doctor he could find who had any knowledge of polio; in the process, he turned himself into a genuine expert on the disease. He also tried virtually any remedy that was suggested to him, from ultraviolet light and saltwater baths to electric currents. Frederic Delano referred him to a local neurologist, William McDonald, whose methods and rosy prognosis made an instant impression on FDR. "Of course, I have seen the methods of practically all the other doctors in the country—the Lovett Method, Goldthwaite Method, Hibbs Method, St. Louis Method, Chicago Method, etc., etc.," he wrote Draper. "They are all good in their way, but McDonald uses what they use and goes one step further. The principle of the others is the exercise of individual muscles, primarily in the line of pull. McDonald's exercises give all this, but in addition exercises the muscles in coordination with each other, i.e., the pull outside the direct plain. . . . In other words, McDonald seeks functioning as the primary objective and certainly succeeded in dozens of others."[14]

Roosevelt showed amazing resilience in the face of his disability. Part of this, of course, was based on his firm conviction that, the experts notwithstanding, he would eventually regain the use of his legs. But even Draper had to acknowledge that FDR "has such courage, such ambition."[15] Ultimately, many of his friends and associates came to believe that Roosevelt's battle with paralysis had fundamentally changed his personality—for the better. "I was instantly struck by his growth," wrote Frances Perkins, his future secretary of labor, of what she would call his

*He then vetoed Tammany Hall's backing of Hearst for the Democratic nomination for U.S. senator.

"spiritual transformation." And it went beyond his appreciation of the struggles of people in need. According to Perkins, "He had a firmer grip on life and on himself than ever before. He was serious, not playing now."[16] And he was determined to fully recover: He spoke to friends about once again playing golf and, by 1924, actually predicted that he would "be able to walk by this time next year."[17]

Much of Roosevelt's "recovery" regimen centered on water. He was no stranger to the perceived curative power of water; as a youngster, he'd accompanied his parents on four occasions to the celebrated spa at Bad Nauheim, Germany, where his father received therapy for his ailing heart that he and his family were convinced warded off invalidism, fending off death.[18] So it is hardly surprising that Franklin, as well, put his faith in the curative power of water. After the acute phase of his illness, he took refuge in the sea, as he would for the rest of his life. He went on numerous cruises and deep-sea fishing expeditions on a series of houseboats, including the *Larooco*, which he bought in 1924 together with an old Harvard friend, John Lawrence (the boat's name comes from Lawrence, Roosevelt & Co.).* And of all the physical exercises in which he vigorously partook, he found that swimming was the most beneficial. In a remarkable 1924 letter to Dr. William Egleston of Hartsville, South Carolina, who was treating a polio patient, FDR wrote that "in the summer of 1922, I began swimming and found that this exercise seemed better adapted than any other, because all weight was removed from the legs and I was able to move the legs in the water far better than I had expected." In fact, his personal prescription for similarly afflicted patients was "swimming in warm water—lots of it."[19]

Roosevelt's letter also contains another significant recommendation, indicative of his certainty of his own recuperation: "Belief on the patient's part that the muscles are coming back and will eventually regain recovery of the affected parts." To support his assertion, "Doc" Roosevelt noted that "there are cases known in Norway where adults have taken the disease and not been able to walk until after a lapse of 10 or even 12

*Lawrence was less than pleased with their purchase, saying the leaky, run-down boat looked like a "floating tenement." Roosevelt insisted the ship had just suffered from "lots of bad luck."

years."[20] At this time, FDR almost certainly believed that he would recover the use of his legs, though the doctors all told him otherwise. More important, he not only worked to assure others that he would fully recover, he tried to convince them that he was well on the way to a full recovery—even if it meant playing with the truth. Five years after becoming paralyzed, Roosevelt went far beyond his and Louis Howe's disingenuous statements that the attack had been a mild one with no likelihood of permanent effects. In a 1926 letter written from the *Larooco*, for example, FDR assured the recipient that "the legs are greatly improved. I get around now with no brace on [my] right knee & hope to get rid of the other this summer."[21] It wasn't true then, and Roosevelt would never regain the ability to stand without the use of braces on both legs.

It was this obsession with swimming that also led FDR to the place whose name would become indelibly linked with his: Warm Springs. In 1924, the tiny Georgia town of 550 was the site of the Meriwether Inn, a once-popular, but now dilapidated, resort whose pools of magnesium-laced mineral water, naturally warmed to a constant temperature of 88 degrees, still attracted visitors. Roosevelt learned of the place from George Foster Peabody, the Georgia-born banker and philanthropist who co-owned the Meriwether and who wrote FDR to tell him about a young polio patient there who, after an intense regimen of hydrotherapy, was now able to walk with the aid of canes.

Roosevelt found the warm water instantly exhilarating; he was able to spend up to two hours exercising in the pool without feeling at all exhausted and was convinced he had begun to sense movement in his toes (polio does not impair sensation). This was particularly important, because the use of braces, which allowed him to stand, also prevented him from exercising his leg muscles. As FDR himself had noted in his letter to Egleston: "Remember that braces are only for convenience of the patient in getting around—a leg in a brace does not have a chance for muscle development."[22]* Swimming also helped him develop the tremendous upper-body strength that allowed him to "walk" on his atrophied legs and gave him a powerful, athletic image from the waist up.

---

*An additional reason for Roosevelt's intensive research on polio was the death of Dr. Lovett, his primary expert on the disease, in July 1924 while traveling in England.

One of the very few photos that show FDR's atrophied legs following his attack of polio in 1921. Here, some three years after he was stricken, he relaxes at the Warm Springs swimming pool. (Franklin D. Roosevelt Library)

In long talks with the Meriwether's other owner, Tom Loyless, Roosevelt learned of his dream of developing the inn as a European-type spa and became converted—so much so that he decided to buy it. Despite concerns by both Eleanor and his law partner, Basil O'Connor, that he was overextending himself financially, Roosevelt would not be deterred and, in April 1926, he paid $201,667.83—some two-thirds of his personal net worth—for the inn, the surrounding cottages and pools, plus 1,200 acres of adjoining undeveloped woods. He then enlisted a number of his prominent friends to form the Warm Springs Foundation, later known as the National Foundation for Infantile Paralysis.[23]*

*Despite a dramatic influx of patients from the publicity surrounding his connection with Warm Springs, the foundation remained on financially shaky grounds until well into FDR's presidency, though, by Roosevelt's own accounting, the facility was "absolutely free and clear of debt" by 1930. During his second term, FDR launched the March of Dimes campaign to fund polio research, which led to Dr. Jonas Salk's successful vaccine, news of which was announced in 1955, on the tenth anniversary of Roosevelt's death.

Meanwhile, a political opportunity was developing that would thrust Roosevelt back into the national spotlight. The sudden death of Charles Murphy, boss of Tammany Hall, had left Al Smith's 1924 presidential campaign without a functioning leader. Anxious for a prominent Democrat to take the reins, Smith's advisers turned to Roosevelt and asked him to chair the campaign. He agreed, provided that he would not actually be required to do the hard political work.[24] As the national convention opened at New York's Madison Square Garden that June, Roosevelt was taken aback when he was asked to deliver the formal nominating speech for Smith (who at first opposed the choice, considering FDR a political lightweight). Once more he agreed, this time on the condition that someone write the speech for him. Smith's top political adviser, Judge Joseph Proskauer, provided him with a text that referred to the candidate as "the Happy Warrior of the political battlefield"—a phrase Roosevelt disdained, complaining to Proskauer that the speech "will probably be a flop."

Instead, Roosevelt provided the convention—which lasted fifteen days through an insufferable 103 ballots—with a moment of high drama that moved many onlookers to tears. On June 26, an outwardly confident FDR left his seat on the convention floor and, a crutch in one arm and tightly grasping son James's arm with the other, his face soaked with perspiration, slowly moved across the floor toward the podium. As he was introduced, James handed his father the other crutch—Roosevelt was going to approach the speaker's rostrum under his own power, unaided.

Though he'd rehearsed those cautious steps for weeks, those close to Roosevelt held their breath, hoping he would not fall. So did the thousands of delegates and spectators in the vast, now silent hall. For what seemed to Marion Dickerman, Eleanor's close friend, "like an hour," FDR moved toward the speaker's stand, his pace agonizingly slow. As the noted author and historian Hendrik Willem Van Loon wrote:

> Never was present at so fine a display of high mental courage as when Roosevelt carried himself to the front of the speaker's tribune. If he would run for [president] himself, I would go and stand on the corner of every street between Washington Square and 349th Street to tell the peo-

> ple what I had seen. . . . For a moment, we were in the presence of something a million miles beyond the shoddy political claptrap which surrounds us on all sides. . . . We now have [a Roosevelt] who, with sublime courage, makes his mind triumph over that mortal matter which so often kills the spirit of our souls.[25]

For fully five minutes, the gallery roared its appreciation, until Roosevelt himself had to quiet them. Then he began to speak, and for more than half an hour his rich, vibrant voice filled the auditorium. When it was over, the assembled throng once again burst into wild cheers, launching an hourlong demonstration for the New York governor—who forevermore would be dubbed "the Happy Warrior." It was all to little avail, however; the stalemated convention finally turned for a nominee to Wall Street lawyer John W. Davis, who was swamped in November by President Calvin Coolidge. But in an otherwise disastrous year for the Democrats, Franklin D. Roosevelt came away a party hero.

Two years later, Roosevelt turned down an offer to run for the U.S. Senate, calling himself "temperamentally unfitted to be a member of [that] uninteresting body"[26] and pleading that he needed to devote more time to his "recovery" from polio. In 1928, Smith once again ran for president and this time was the favorite to win the nomination. Once more, Roosevelt chaired Smith's campaign and delivered the nominating speech. This time, however, he took an active role in writing his remarks. Moreover, his oratorical skills had improved dramatically; it was a far more confident Roosevelt who took to the podium and once again electrified the assembled Democrats. The *New York Times* editorialized that "it is seldom that a political speech attains this kind of eloquence," calling Roosevelt's address "a model of its kind."[27] Ironically, some of the strongest praise for FDR came from Col. Robert McCormick's *Chicago Tribune*, which during his presidency would become the leader of the anti-Roosevelt forces. For now, however, McCormick loved what he saw, hailing FDR in an editorial as "The Last of the Silver Tongues."[28]

The acclaim led Smith and New York state party leaders to press Roosevelt to run for governor, believing he was the only Democrat capable of holding the statehouse against the strong GOP opponent, New York state Attorney General Albert Ottinger. But Roosevelt refused, just as he had earlier resisted the Senate nomination as well as Smith's offer that he become Democratic national chairman. Under mounting pressure, he said he could not afford to run, given his substantial financial investment in Warm Springs. "Damn Warm Springs," replied John J. Raskob, who held the top financial positions at both DuPont and General Motors and was a key Smith backer. Raskob promised to personally underwrite Roosevelt's losses at Warm Springs and actually sent a check for $250,000, which FDR returned. (Over the next four years, however, Raskob became Warm Springs's leading outside benefactor.)[29] For once, Roosevelt did not listen to Louis Howe, who opposed his running, and agreed to accept the nomination.

News articles over the previous two years had portrayed Roosevelt as making a near-total recovery from polio. Typical was a report from 1927 declaring that he had "discarded the crutches" he'd needed at the convention three years earlier, adding: "a brace and a cane is all he needs to lead his active life."[30] Roosevelt clearly encouraged such optimistic coverage and suggested to voters that he'd fully recovered from polio. As he told one audience:

> Seven years ago, in the epidemic in New York, I came down with infantile paralysis, a perfectly normal attack, and I was completely, for the moment, put out of my useful activities. By personal good fortune, I was able to get the very best of care and the result of having the best kind of care is that today I am on my feet.[31]

Nevertheless, the Republicans raised Roosevelt's health as a campaign issue. And despite assurances by supporters like Smith, who declared that "a governor doesn't have to be an acrobat," campaigning proved difficult for FDR, who—to allay fears about his health—maintained an unusually vigorous schedule. As his speechwriter, Sam Rosenman, recalled: "It was not easy for a crippled man to carry on this kind of campaign. He could not climb stairs, and often we had to carry him up some backstairs to a hall and down again. He always went through this harrowing experience smiling. He never got ruffled. Having been set down, he would adjust his coat, smile and proceed calmly to the platform for his speech."[32]

Roosevelt himself made light of his disability: "Most people who are nominated for the governorship have to run, but obviously I am not in condition to run, and therefore I am counting on my friends all over the state to make it possible for me to walk in."[33]

He also had the cooperation of a sympathetic press corps, which even then largely obeyed his instructions not to portray his disability. "No movies of me getting out of the machine, boys," he told photographers as his car arrived at the Hyde Park polling station on Election Day. And, in fact, the cameramen dutifully waited until he had been lifted from his auto and adjusted his braces, whereupon he gladly posed for photos.[34] According to one account, throughout the '20s news photographers actually "voluntarily destroyed their own plates [if] they showed Roosevelt in poses that revealed his handicap."[35]

Even as Smith was going down to a landslide defeat nationally, Roosevelt won the governorship, albeit by a close margin. Before his election was confirmed, however, Roosevelt left for a month's stay in Warm Springs, "resting and taking treatments there" so as to be "in fit condition to assume the duties of Chief Executive."[36] As he arrived in Georgia to a tumultuous welcome, the *New York Times* already was declaring him "the heir apparent to the leadership of the Democratic Party."[37] Not surprising, Roosevelt moved quickly to distance himself from Al Smith, refusing to reappoint the outgoing governor's key aides and making clear that Smith's expectation of calling all the shots in the new administration from the sidelines would never be realized. As a result, relations between the two men—never overly warm to begin with—cooled perceptibly. Still, Roosevelt was fortunate to inherit a well-run government from Smith, and his first term was without major incident until the Wall Street crash in late 1929. Though President Herbert Hoover and most state governors failed to recognize the impending economic disaster, Roosevelt became one of the first state executives to take action against rising unemployment.[38]

Even as Roosevelt was preparing to face the voters again in 1930 (New York's governor then served two-year terms), his name was floated by Senator Burton Wheeler of Montana as a presidential hopeful in the next campaign. But *New York Times* national political correspondent Richard V. Oulahan reflected the conventional wisdom, writing that

Roosevelt preferred to wait until 1936 in order "to test fully his conviction that he will be able to regain the use of his crippled limbs."[39] Oulahan couldn't have been more wrong: From the moment FDR won the governorship, Louis Howe began working to ensure that Roosevelt would be the Democratic presidential standard-bearer in 1932, which meant, as both men realized, that he needed to win reelection by an overwhelming margin, so as to attract national attention and prove his vote-getting abilities. That also meant tackling the health issue head-on for a national audience.

This they did on October 18 in a dramatic press conference in Albany, during which Dr. E. W. Beckwith, medical director of the Equitable Life Assurance Society, pronounced the governor remarkably fit and announced that his company and twenty-one others had agreed to insure his life for $560,000, payable to the Warm Springs Foundation. "It has rarely been my privilege . . . to see such a remarkable physical specimen as yourself," declared Beckwith, "and I trust that your remarkable vitality will stand you in good stead throughout your arduous campaign." Indeed, said the doctor, "his examination disclosed conditions which were comparable to a man of thirty" (Roosevelt was forty-eight), including a blood pressure reading of 128/82. Given that the exam took place in the same week as the Democratic state convention, said Beckwith, "he has been under very great strain, and it was an astonishing fact that his heart and blood pressure were absolutely normal, and he passed an unusually good examination for a man who has just been through such a trying ordeal." As for FDR's paralysis, Beckwith disingenuously responded: "Frankly, I have never before observed such a complete degree of *recovery* in organic function and such a remarkable degree of *recovery* of muscles and limbs in an individual who had passed through an attack of infantile paralysis such as yours" (emphasis added).[40] For his part, Roosevelt boasted that he kept fit with daily swims and horseback riding, adding that "I watch my weight carefully. I don't want to weigh more than 175 pounds," seven pounds less than his current weight.[41]

With the health issue seemingly put to rest, and Republican fortunes continuing to wane as the nation's economic woes mounted, Roosevelt coasted to victory by an astonishing, and unprecedented, margin of 725,000 votes, carrying counties and precincts that had not gone Democratic since anyone could remember.[42]* Over the next year, Roosevelt would have to contend with a messy political scandal involving corruption in the New York City courts that eventually spread to the entire government apparatus controlled by Tammany Hall, the powerful city Democratic organization. Roosevelt appointed Judge Samuel Seabury as an independent investigator, whose probe resulted in the resignation of New York's flamboyant Tammany mayor, James J. Walker. FDR, in turn, won plaudits for his forthright handling of the scandal.

His vote-getting prowess firmly established, his position in the Democratic Party's top national leadership widely acknowledged and the party's electoral prospects looking increasingly bright, Roosevelt and Howe now set out to capture the ultimate prize—president of the United States—on which they'd first set their sights two decades earlier. It would not be an easy fight.

*President Hoover, keenly aware that Roosevelt would be a leading candidate to oppose him two years later, sent three members of his cabinet to New York to campaign against him.

Is Franklin D. Roosevelt Physically Fit to Be President?

CHAPTER 4

Franklin Roosevelt's assault on the White House began in earnest two full years before he successfully captured the presidency—on the very day after his reelection as governor, in fact, when James A. Farley, his campaign manager and state Democratic chairman, told a hastily arranged press conference: "I do not see how Mr. Roosevelt can escape becoming the next presidential nominee of his party, even if no one should raise a finger to bring it about."[1] In point of fact, more than a few fingers *were* raised against it, and though he was the heavy favorite from the outset, FDR's claim on the nomination was far from the sure thing that the confident Farley had predicted.

During 1931, Farley toured the country, gauging support for Roosevelt, while the still-undeclared candidate himself wooed Southern Democratic leaders at Warm Springs. He had a formidable hurdle to overcome: Back then, the nominee had to win two-thirds of the national convention votes, rather than a simple majority, which meant that any major bloc of delegates effectively enjoyed veto power.

Prohibition, in force since 1920, remained a significant issue, particularly in the Midwest and the Bible Belt. And while its importance had waned, given the national economic crisis, the issue had proved insurmountable for Al Smith four years earlier. Foreign policy also was a sore point in some quarters, notably to publishing tycoon William Randolph Hearst, still an influential figure and a devout isolationist. On New Year's Day 1932, in fact, Hearst endorsed John Nance Garner of Texas, the Speaker of the House, for the Democratic nomination, calling on the party to reject Wilsonian internationalists.[2]

Meanwhile, Roosevelt assembled the team that would be known as his vaunted "Brains Trust"—people like Raymond Moley, Rexford Tugwell, Harry Hopkins, and Adolf A. Berle. Yet even with that intellectual star power, Roosevelt was viewed in some circles as a vacillating lightweight, particularly as he avoided going too far out on a limb on contentious issues. Chief among his critics was the nation's leading newspaper columnist, Walter Lippmann, of the *New York Herald Tribune*. FDR, wrote Lippmann, lacked "a firm grasp of public affairs. . . . He is a pleasant man who, without any important qualifications for the office, would very much like to be President."[3]

Going into the Democratic convention, Roosevelt—following a string of primary victories—was the favorite, but not prohibitively so. His onetime ally, Al Smith, mobilized a "Stop Roosevelt" campaign that nearly succeeded: FDR led on the first day of balloting with a clear majority, but it appeared that he would be unable to win the two-thirds needed for nomination. Finally, Roosevelt cut two deals: He offered Garner the vice presidency, ensuring the support of Texas's delegates, and gave former Treasury secretary William G. McAdoo, Woodrow Wilson's son-in-law, who controlled the California delegation, veto power over his cabinet choices at State and Treasury.

Those two switches put Roosevelt over the top on the fourth ballot. In a move that electrified both the delegates and those listening on the radio, Roosevelt broke with tradition and flew to Chicago to personally accept the nomination in a speech that closed with the historic vow: "I pledge you, I pledge myself, to a New Deal for the American people." To the strains of "Happy Days Are Here Again," a song from the otherwise obscure 1930 film *Chasing Rainbows*, the convention hailed its new standard-bearer.[4]

But while FDR had already disposed of the health issue as far as New York voters were concerned, doubts remained elsewhere about his physical fitness for office. And the Republicans were quick to capitalize on those fears. So were elements within his own party: As early as April 1931, Mrs. Jesse W. Nicholson of the National Women's Democratic Law Enforcement League, which opposed the repeal of Prohibition, told her assembled members in widely quoted remarks that Roosevelt, "while mentally qualified for the presidency, is utterly unfit physically."[5] Such sentiments, though rarely voiced publicly, continued into the fall campaign—so FDR, Farley, and Howe decided to tackle them head-on.

Roosevelt himself never addressed his health in the kind of comprehensive speech that a presidential candidate today might be expected to make. Indeed, after being told of widespread rumors that he'd been brought to Warm Springs on a stretcher to be treated for an undefined "very serious illness," Roosevelt declined to engage in any "propaganda stunt" to prove he was healthy.[6] But neither did he avoid the issue. During a September campaign swing through Portland, Oregon, FDR made a point of visiting a hospital for crippled children, where he told the patients, "It's a little difficult for me to stand on my feet, too."[7] Mostly, however, the issue was handled by surrogates, both medical and political. U.S. Senator Royal S. Copeland of New York, a former professor of homeopathic medicine, pronounced Roosevelt perfectly fit, saying he had "shak[en] off every temporary vestige of his serious illness." Indeed, he added, Roosevelt's "lameness . . . has proved to be no more than a trifling physical handicap to a very active person."[8] Another Roosevelt medical friend gave an even more misleading reassurance: Dr. Francis E. Fronczak, city health commissioner of Buffalo, New York, insisted the candidate had been "the victim of an illness, not so rare, which resulted in temporary, partial disability of the leg muscles." Moreover, said Fronczak, "by proper therapeutic measures the disabilities gradually disappear, as they have in Mr. Roosevelt's case."[9]

While Roosevelt campaigned on the issues, Farley took the attack directly to the Republicans. Appearing on a New York radio station, he accused the GOP of waging a "whispering campaign" about FDR's health. "In various parts of the country," he declared, "are cropping up hateful stories in regard to our candidate's physical and mental health." In fact,

The lengths to which Roosevelt went to disguise his ongoing physical disability can be seen in these two photos. On the left is the one that was distributed to the press; it shows FDR confidently standing, needing only a cane for support. On the right is the original, uncropped picture, which clearly shows him using a second cane to precariously balance himself against a wall. Even with the two canes, he was incapable of standing or walking unassisted after 1921. (AP Worldwide)

Louis Howe had spent the past two years carefully keeping track of any and all news articles discussing Roosevelt's health, firing off angry letters to refute those that questioned FDR's physical fitness. Often the responses were written by the governor's secretary, Guernsey Cross, such as when the *Newark Call* claimed that Roosevelt's "indispositions" had forced him to transfer some of his duties to Lieutenant Governor Herbert Lehman. "Governor Roosevelt has had no 'indispositions' and is in extremely good health," wrote Cross, demanding a correction.[10] Similarly, when the *New Orleans Item* reported that Roosevelt's health had "much improved . . . in recent years" but ascribed his incapacity to "a tragic paralytic stroke," Cross again demanded—and got—a published correction.[11] Sometimes Roosevelt responded personally, as when the *Danville (Virginia) Register* published an item in December 1930 stating that his health "is still poor." "My health is excellent," he wrote the paper's editor, "though as you know I still have to wear braces following infantile paralysis."[12]

As the presidential campaign picked up steam, Howe did not relent when it came to confronting suggestions of Roosevelt's unfitness for office. Now, however, he had stronger ammunition than just his or the candidate's denial. There was the 1930 insurance policy examination, of course, and another medical evaluation that had been conducted six months later in which, Howe reminded a radio audience, a trio of distinguished doctors had pronounced Roosevelt's "lameness"—again, deliberately downplaying the true effect of FDR's paralysis—to be "steadily getting better," adding that it "had no more effect on his general condition than if he had a glass eye or was prematurely bald."[13] Indeed, that examination declared that Roosevelt was showing "progressive recovery of power in his legs." Moreover, it concluded, he "can walk all necessary distances and can maintain a standing position without fatigue"—a conclusion that was misleading at best, and flatly deceptive at worst, but like the earlier exam, was reported virtually without challenge in the press.

Yet that evaluation—as most FDR biographers now recognize—was a brilliant publicity stunt. It had originated in 1930 with Earle Looker, a freelance writer with connections to the Republican branch of the Roosevelt family. A letter from Looker to Eleanor Roosevelt in December 1930 disclosed his plans, already well under way, to write a book about FDR for use in the upcoming campaign. His unidentified backers, Looker informed Eleanor, "understand exactly what I have in mind" and "are so practically and enthusiastically for you and with me."[14] What he had in mind, he later wrote, was a "challenge" to Roosevelt to allow a complete and independent medical examination of his health. The challenge was issued in a "brutal" letter he sent to FDR on February 23, 1931, and which was accepted five days later, with Roosevelt's promise of complete cooperation "without censorship from me." Not surprisingly, Looker's account made no mention of his earlier correspondence with Eleanor, or that his backers, far from being critical Republicans, actually were "enthusiastically" supporting Roosevelt. As a result, he would later falsely claim, the letter demonstrated clearly that "I belonged to the opposition."

Looker arranged for three prominent physicians—Samuel W. Lambert, former dean of Columbia University's College of Physicians and Surgeons; Russell A. Hibbs, a prominent orthopedist; and Foster Kennedy, the chief neurologist at Bellevue Hospital—to examine Roosevelt at his home on April 29. Their findings were featured in an article Looker wrote for the July 25 issue of the popular weekly magazine *Liberty*, under the title "Is Franklin D. Roosevelt Physically Fit to Be President?" and their conclusion was an unambiguous yes.*

The article itself was written in a highly melodramatic style typical of the times with clearly embellished quotations: "Do I understand," FDR asks at one point, "that as a Republican you are making a political thrust, with the thought that any admissions I might make will be used against me and my party?" Yet the piece was surprisingly candid about the extent of Roosevelt's disability, concluding at one point that "his legs [are] not much good to him." Significantly, it also included two photographs that would never be published again in FDR's lifetime: one showing him in a chair in his office, his leg braces clearly visible (after he became president, they were painted black to ensure they could not be seen in any photo), and the other—even more remarkable—in which he sat in a bathing suit by the swimming pool at Warm Springs, making no effort to hide his visibly atrophied legs.[15] Even before the issue hit the stands, Howe had sent thousands of copies of the article to Democratic political officials and previously skeptical journalists.[16] Jim Farley pronounced the piece "a corker," adding that it "answers fully [a] question that was put to me many times."

Unlike the insurance exam six months earlier, the three doctors Looker hired did not release their specific findings (in fact, they did not become public until five years after Roosevelt's death). Had they done so, at least two of the test results might have raised some eyebrows. FDR's blood pressure reading was 140/100, a significant elevation over his 128/82 reading from the previous October (a normal level for a man of forty-nine was 120/80) and certainly cause for concern. Moreover, his

*Lambert, who disagreed with Roosevelt's politics, had to be pressured into signing any endorsement of FDR's health beyond the effects of his bout with polio. Ultimately he agreed but said, "Remember, as far as I'm concerned, this doesn't go for above the neck." (Arthur Krock, *Sixty Years on the Firing Line*, New York: Funk & Wagnall's, 1968, p. 152)

EKG tracing was abnormal, suggesting enlargement of the left side of the heart and a decreased blood flow—both signs of incipient hypertensive cardiovascular disease.[17]*

Looker's account did not go entirely unchallenged. Indeed, there were suspicions in some quarters that both the piece, and the medical appraisal on which it was based, were less than impartial. The *Springfield (Massachusetts) Republican* published Looker's denial that he was "hired by politicians to hush a whispering campaign." Looker insisted that "the topic was dug up by him and no one else" and added his denial that he'd received "any financial compensation from Roosevelt, the Democratic party or anyone else." In fact, the paper reported, "Mr. Looker himself paid for the medical examination."[18]

But Looker's private correspondence with Roosevelt, as demonstrated by historians David W. Houck and Amos Kiewe, tells an entirely different story. "Well, sir," he wrote FDR, "we got away with the *Liberty* article, despite all obstacles," noting that "at least seven and a half million readers are sure you are physically fit!" He sent an even more revealing letter after the *Springfield Republican* interview appeared: "The question of who paid for the physical examination was, and still is, between us, frightfully embarrassing." Nonetheless, wrote Looker, "it had to be answered as I answered it."[19] The implication—that Roosevelt actually underwrote the cost of the exam—is clear. Looker then discussed arrangements, already in the works, for him to pen a series of articles, in Roosevelt's name, on world affairs for the McClure newspaper syndicate. "The fact that I am the 'ghost-writer' is secret," Looker reminded FDR.[20]

Looker eventually expanded the *Liberty* article into a full-length campaign biography titled *This Man Roosevelt*, which discussed FDR's health in glowing, but highly inaccurate, terms. Typical was this account: "I walked with him many times from the entrance hall into the Capitol, some fifty paces. . . . Walking some twenty paces more from the desk, he eases himself into his big Governor's chair and flexes his leg braces so that his knees bend under the edge of his desk. He seems

*Significantly, given Roosevelt's future extramarital romantic relationships, most prominently with Missy LeHand, the doctors reported "no symptoms of *impotentia coeundi*."

unfatigued." In fact, wrote Looker, "the only reason for his braces is to insure his knees locking."[21]

Looker's efforts did not silence the whispers about Roosevelt's health, but they went a long way toward discrediting them. And the candidate himself, hoping to emphasize his fitness and vitality, conducted a very public and vigorous campaign in which he traveled over 25,000 miles by train, despite the very real risk that he might fall in public. With the Depression showing no signs of abating and other developments—particularly the deadly rout by troops of the so-called Bonus Army of veterans in Washington, D.C.—working against Hoover, the results were no surprise: Roosevelt was elected in a landslide with 57 percent of the vote, carrying 42 of the 48 states and winning 472 electoral votes to just 59 for Hoover.

Once the election was over, Roosevelt decided he had no further need of Earle Looker. "Things have moved fast in this week since November eighth," FDR wrote the author, "and it has become perfectly clear to me that future articles—at least for a long time—are taboo." Yet Looker continued to press Roosevelt—though for what isn't exactly certain. Over the next year, he would complain that the press was dismissing him as a Roosevelt "apologist when the need arises." "I get it in the neck for being loyal to you," he wrote the president in November 1933, adding: "Hah! That is not a laugh."[22]

Roosevelt's dismissive reply is astonishing, given the immense help Looker had provided: "Dear Earle: 'Hah! Hah!' and again 'Hah!' said the duck laughing. However, being a practical business man, I suggest stirring up some Foreign controversy over your opus. This will sell a million copies. Yours in misery."[23]

* * *

As the time for Roosevelt's inaugural drew closer,* the president-elect—his cabinet chosen, the plans for his dramatic first hundred days in office

*Before 1937, presidents took office on March 4, some four months after Election Day. The date was changed to January 20 under the Twentieth Amendment to the Constitution and took effect with FDR's third term.

mostly set in place—embarked, not surprisingly, on his favorite form of relaxation: an eleven-day Caribbean sea cruise aboard financier Vincent Astor's yacht, accompanied by a retinue of old Harvard and political friends. It was, he wrote his mother, "a marvelous rest—lots of air and sun," adding that "I shall be full of health and vigor—the last holiday for many months."

But upon landing in Miami on February 15, Roosevelt faced a wholly unexpected threat that might have ended his presidency before it even began. After speaking at a rally to 20,000 well-wishers at Bay Front Park, he sat in his car with Chicago Mayor Anton Cermak, a former Al Smith supporter who had met the president-elect in a bid to make political peace. Suddenly an Italian-born bricklayer named Giuseppe Zangara, standing some forty feet away, opened fire with a pistol. After the first shot, which struck an onlooker, two other crowd members—Lillian Johns Cross, the wife of a local doctor, who was standing in front of him, and Thomas Armour, a contractor, in the row behind—grabbed Zangara's arm as he continued shooting. None of the five shots hit Roosevelt, but one struck Cermak, who was gravely wounded.

Roosevelt, with remarkable calm, immediately took charge, overruling a Secret Service order that the president-elect's car immediately leave the scene. Without hesitation, he once again became "Dr. Roosevelt":

> I saw Mayor Cermak being carried. I motioned to have him put in the back of the car, which would be the first out [of the park]. . . . I put my left arm around him and my hand on his pulse, but I couldn't find any pulse. He slumped forward. . . . After we had gone another block, Mayor Cermak straightened up and I got his pulse. It was surprising. For three blocks I believed his heart had stopped. I held him all the way to the hospital and his pulse constantly improved. That trip to the hospital seemed thirty miles long. I talked to Mayor Cermak nearly all the way. I said, "Tony, keep quiet—don't move. It won't hurt you if you keep quiet."[24]*

*Though Cermak appeared to be recovering, septicemia set in and he died on March 6. A defiant Zangara, whose constant abdominal pains apparently had unhinged him, expressed no remorse for the shooting, saying he would gladly kill "all presidents, kings and capitalists." Within just two weeks of Cermak's death, Zangara was tried, convicted, and executed.

The assassination attempt actually bolstered Roosevelt's political stature. He'd won election not so much on the force of his personality or his record as governor as much as the fact that, simply, he wasn't Herbert Hoover at a time when Depression-weary voters desperately sought change in Washington. But doubts still remained about his capacity to seize the reins of government and lead the nation through the ever-worsening economic crisis. Now, FDR's calm, measured response throughout the shooting, and the quick-thinking, yet commanding, way in which he immediately exerted control, actually boosted the nation's morale and elevated Roosevelt's standing, particularly the public's perception of him as a take-charge leader.[25]

Thus it was on March 4, 1933, that millions of Americans, one in four of whom were now unemployed, and many more increasingly anxious over the virtual collapse of the nation's banking system, cheered as they listened, either in person or over their radios, to the clarion sound of Franklin Delano Roosevelt's voice reassuring them, with perfect and dramatic timing, that "the only thing we have to fear is fear itself."

A Career Navy Medical Officer of No Particular Distinction

CHAPTER 5

Amid all the focus on Roosevelt's new cabinet members* and top personal staff, little public notice was taken of another presidential appointment: his selection of a new White House physician. The position has been an official one since James Buchanan's presidency just before the Civil War, and, beginning even earlier with James Monroe, the military had been called on to provide presidential medical care. Some had been picked for reasons wholly unrelated to medicine: Grover Cleveland chose Colonel Robert M. O'Reilly because, like the president, he was an avid fisherman, while Theodore Roosevelt retained predecessor William McKinley's doctor, Presley M. Rixey, who also became a close personal companion, because Rixey loved hunting and was a first-rate horseman.[1]

*Sen. Thomas J. Walsh of Montana, who a decade earlier had exposed the Teapot Dome scandal of the Harding administration and was FDR's choice for attorney general, died suddenly of a heart attack two days before the inauguration (and just five days after marrying a woman thirty years his junior). He was the first in a surprisingly long line of top FDR appointees and personal aides who died in office.

When FDR took office, the official White House physician was Navy Vice Admiral Joel T. Boone, who had treated presidents Warren Harding and Calvin Coolidge (both as deputy physician) and Herbert Hoover. Boone, a homeopathic physician, came to the White House with a brilliant military record during World War I, during which he won the Medal of Honor (the nation's highest military decoration), a Purple Heart, the Silver Star, the Bronze Star, and the French Croix de Guerre. Like his immediate predecessors, Boone enjoyed a close personal relationship with the presidents he served, teaching Florence Harding to dance and attending baseball games with the Coolidges.[2]

When the new president took over, Boone hoped—and expected—to stay on.[3] But Roosevelt had other ideas. And so did Admiral Cary T. Grayson.

It was to Grayson—to whom FDR had grown so close that he was named to chair Roosevelt's inauguration ceremonies, as he would again in 1937—that the president turned to recommend a new White House physician one month into his term. The man Grayson pressed Roosevelt to select was Ross T. McIntire, a forty-three-year-old career Navy medical officer of no particular distinction.

McIntire, a native of Salem, Oregon, had received his medical education at that city's Willamette University, from which he graduated in 1912. After five years in private practice, he joined the Navy Medical Corps as a lieutenant (j.g.) upon America's entry into World War I, serving aboard the cruiser USS *New Orleans*, which escorted transatlantic convoys and, after the armistice, was the U.S. station ship in Vladivostok, Russia. Eventually he was transferred to a naval hospital in the Philippines.

McIntire returned stateside in 1920 and, after postgraduate studies in ophthalmology and otolaryngology, was made head of the eye, ear, nose, and throat department at the naval hospital in San Diego. In 1924 he returned to sea duty aboard the USS *Relief*, the first U.S. vessel designed and built as a hospital ship, and served the Pacific Fleet. The very next year, however, he was assigned to the U.S. Naval Dispensary in Washington, whose commanding officer was Cary Grayson.[4]* During that

*Grayson had been given this assignment in 1921 with the understanding that he would be allowed to remain as Woodrow Wilson's private physician at government expense.

time, McIntire would later write, Grayson repeatedly "came to me with poor devils in need of an operation, begging to know if I could do the necessary surgery outside and away from my regular duties. And always the hospital bills came out of his private purse."[5]

After another round of sea duty, McIntire, now a lieutenant commander, in 1931 was assigned to the U.S. naval hospital in Washington with additional duties as an instructor at the Naval Medical School. During this time, he renewed his connection with Grayson, who took an interest in research that McIntire was performing on tropical diseases.[6]

McIntire's selection as FDR's physician, which he later called "a complete surprise," was based on two factors. The first was his specialty: As he said Grayson explained to him, "The president is as strong as a horse, with the exception of a chronic sinus condition that makes him susceptible to colds. That's where you come in."[7] Indeed, McIntire disclosed, this susceptibility was so strong that "if it happened that a caller presented himself with a drippy nose, [appointments secretary] Pa Watson invariably found an excuse for postponing the appointment."[8] (That Roosevelt apparently had no interest in a doctor who specialized in the aftereffects of polio is hardly surprising: "Dr." Roosevelt clearly felt himself as competent and knowledgeable as any specialist in that field—and probably was. Besides, if needed he had the staff at Warm Springs on which to rely.)

The second reason, however, was equally important—if not more so: Ross McIntire knew how to keep his mouth shut. McIntire himself made no bones about what he understood was expected from White House physicians and explained why they invariably were selected from the military ranks. "The health of the chief executive . . . is his own private business," he wrote. "These men are officers as well as physicians, and being subject to the iron discipline of the armed services, they can be counted on to keep a closed mouth about what they see and hear."[9]*

---

*This attitude also extended to the rest of the president's staff. As Press Secretary Stephen T. Early once told a reporter for the *Washington Post*, "There is every disposition at the White House to keep secrets. People working here are not given to loose talk—or else they wouldn't be here." (*Washington Post*, August 21, 1942)

He also understood from Grayson that even more important than protecting the president's physical well-being was his role in ensuring Roosevelt's political health.[10] Yet this same unwavering loyalty to the president raises serious—and still largely unresolved—issues of medical confidentiality versus the public's right to be kept informed of the chief executive's health. These issues are complicated by the unique relationship that exists between presidents and their doctors, one entirely unlike the normal physician-patient relationship and further complicated by the doctor's additional status of military subordinate attending to someone who is not only his superior officer but the commander in chief, as well.

Over the years, this has put White House physicians wholly at the president's beck and call. They have been called upon to attend to cabinet members and their families, even the president's personal friends (Boone, for example, treated both Marie Curie and Thomas Edison at Hoover's request), and "loaned out" in the national interest (Harry Truman's doctor, General Wallace H. Graham, removed an esophageal tumor from King Ibn Saud of Saudi Arabia).[11] And it leaves the physician open to any number of conflicts of interest—especially if, as with Grayson and McIntire, they develop a close personal relationship with their patient. Indeed, this close rapport—on which the physician's prestigious government position and access to the innermost circles of power wholly relies—can erode the professional detachment normally required in a healthy doctor-patient relationship.[12] Moreover, it raises the very real question of what the physician can, and should, do if his prestigious patient refuses to follow doctor's orders.

Save for Cary Grayson's deliberate cover-up of Woodrow Wilson's precarious health, never have these issues been as seriously tested as they were during the twelve years in which Ross McIntire maintained a vise-like grip, virtually unchallenged by the president's staff or family, over Franklin D. Roosevelt's health.

By McIntire's own account, his relationship with Roosevelt developed slowly but steadily. For one thing, he saw the president more than anyone else on the White House staff, and conducted twice-daily "examinations"—though the very informal way he went about it has raised many critical eyebrows over the years. As McIntire himself described it:

> In accordance with the routine decided on, I parked my car before the White House every morning around 8:30 and went to the President's bedroom for a look-see. Neither the thermometer nor stethoscope was produced, there was no request for a look at the tongue or a feel of the pulse, and only rarely was a direct question asked. Finding myself a comfortable chair, I sat a bit while breakfast was being eaten or the morning papers looked over.
>
> A close but seemingly casual watch told all I wanted to know. The things that interested me most were the President's color, the tone of his voice, the tilt of his chin, and the way he tackled his orange juice, cereal and eggs. Satisfied on these points, I went away. . . .
>
> In the afternoon, promptly at 5:30, I made a second call, parking outside the executive offices. This time my approach was more direct, for I was there to see that the President shut up shop and trundled over to the White House, either for a swim in the pool or a rest before dinner. . . . On his trips, both at home and abroad, I usually gave the President the "once over" at bedtime.[13]

Though he didn't even mention it in his memoir, McIntire also gave the president daily sinus treatments, consisting of nasal sprays that included adrenaline and cauterization of the sinuses with a thin wire, which helped relieve the built-up pressure.[14] The comprehensive daily log of Roosevelt's every movement as president is replete with multiple visits each day to the "doctor's office." Years later, Eleanor Roosevelt would write that she "always worried about the constant treatment, for I felt that while this might help temporarily, in the long run it might cause irritation."[15] Clearly, though, the treatments made Roosevelt feel better, though he was plagued throughout his first few years in office by numerous head colds and repeated bouts of sinusitis and bronchitis, as well as "not infrequent" attacks of intestinal flu.[16]

Before long, McIntire had become one of the closest members of FDR's inner circle of advisers and confidantes, which earned him a coveted seat at the president's poker table.* In 1938 Roosevelt named him surgeon general of the Navy and head of the service's Bureau of Medicine and Surgery; included in the appointment was a promotion to rear admiral, "jumping" him ahead of six officers who outranked him and had been longer in line for the higher rank.[17]

The first signs of any serious concerns about the president's health emerged in 1937, the first year of his second term. In March he was laid up for nearly a week at Warm Springs nursing a sty in his left eye and, according to news reports, "avoiding photographers."[18] That summer, Secretary of the Interior Harold Ickes confided in his diary that "Roosevelt has paid a heavy toll during these last four years. His face is heavily lined and inclined to be gaunt . . . and he is distinctly more nervous."[19] In mid-November, FDR was wracked with pain from the combination of an abscessed tooth and a gastrointestinal disorder; after the president's temperature reportedly reached 103 degrees (though McIntire insisted that "at no time has his temperature been more than one degree above normal"), the tooth was removed, while Roosevelt lay in bed, by Dr. Walter Yando, a Navy dentist.[20]

Among the visitors in his bedroom that day before the operation was Postmaster General James A. Farley, who needed to discuss some pressing political business involving freshman Senator Harry S. Truman of Missouri. "I was shocked by his appearance," he would later write. "His color was bad; his face was lined and he appeared to be worn out. His jaw was swollen. . . . During the entire interview he kept an ice bag to his jaw to relieve pain." Still, added Farley, Roosevelt's

---

*Fishing may have been Roosevelt's favorite outdoor activity, but marathon poker sessions, often lasting till dawn, were his preferred source of indoor relaxation. Regulars at the table, besides McIntire, included the closest members of his inner circle, Harry Hopkins and General Edwin "Pa" Watson, as well as other staff members and White House reporters. "Roosevelt was a great bluffer and a driver in command of the game," recalled Walter Trohan of the *Chicago Tribune*, "calling on this one to ante up, bet or fold up. Nothing delighted him more than a successful bluff. . . . He was most unhappy when one of his bluffs failed." If behavior at the poker table can be an unguarded and telling reflection of the player's personality, FDR's poker proclivities may signal how he approached the delicate question of his own health. (Walter Trohan, *Political Animals*, p. 68)

"spirits were excellent," and the president insisted he'd "be all right if I can get away," hopefully to Warm Springs, "if the doctors let me go. What I need is a bit of rest."[21]

Clearly Farley believed the president's condition involved far more than an infected tooth. He was so concerned, he wrote, that he "had a long talk five days later" with Cary Grayson, who "told me he was in daily touch with Jimmy Roosevelt on his father's condition." Farley, apparently unaware of Grayson's close connection with McIntire, urged him to go above the White House physician's head and bring in "some prominent physician . . . to go over the President thoroughly." Grayson agreed, said Farley, but stressed that it would have to be someone "who would not talk, recalling that when Wilson was ill, some outside doctors were called in for consultation and some of them talked."[22]

Writing nearly a decade after Roosevelt's death, Farley said he surmised from their conversation that Grayson "was aware of the worry regarding the President's heart" and had told him that while there was "no immediate concern," it "might become serious." Farley was the only one to suggest any concern over Roosevelt's cardiac health this early, though the only lab slip surviving from this period shows a sharp elevation in the president's blood pressure: A reading on April 22, 1937, was 162/98; less than two years earlier, it had been 136/78.[23]

Farley's conversation with Grayson notwithstanding, there is no evidence that any outside doctors were called in. Nor did Roosevelt quickly bounce back from his dental surgery, as he had from all of his many other ailments. On December 5, nearly three weeks after the tooth's removal, the president still was in obvious pain, telling reporters at his regular press conference who'd asked how he was feeling that "it is still there," and that "if anybody punched me there I would be sore." Said Roosevelt: "Putting it as a layman, I would say that it has not healed, and if it does not heal very quickly, they will probably curette it"—to which McIntire interjected that "scrape would be [a] better" word, adding that "it just has not healed the way we think it should, so we think we had better get back to where it can be looked over."[24]

At this stage in Roosevelt's presidency, such direct questions from the press about his health were highly unusual. During his first term, in fact, only nine health-related questions were asked during his hundreds of

Navy Surgeon General Ross T. McIntire (left), Roosevelt's personal physician and confidant, who never wavered from his public insistence that the president was in "terrific health." On his right is McIntire's right-hand man, Lieutenant Commander George Fox, who first joined the White House as Woodrow Wilson's physical therapist after his devastating stroke in 1919 and attended to FDR daily. (Franklin D. Roosevelt Library)

news conferences, and fourteen in his second term.[25]* Most reporters and commentators simply relied on whatever information was released by the

*Unlike today's presidential news conferences, which are broadcast live, Roosevelt's sessions took place in the Oval Office. No taping was allowed, nor could the president be quoted directly in any subsequent news stories. Still, this represented a considerable loosening of the rules; under previous presidents, all questions had to be submitted in writing and were answered in the same fashion.

White House; others, including some of the nation's most powerful journalists, felt too intimidated even to ask. For example, Franklin P. Adams, whose nationally known column "The Conning Tower" appeared for years in the *New York Herald Tribune*, wrote Stephen Early in 1936, asking for an "audience" with the president to ask about his health. According to Early's file memo, Adams said he'd wanted to raise the issue with Roosevelt at a recent press conference "but lacked the nerve." Early discussed the request directly with FDR, who agreed to the interview, provided he wasn't quoted directly—but added that Adams would need to "submit anything that he writes about his (President's) health" for approval before publication.[26]

Such rules were standard procedure in the Roosevelt White House. Indeed, they were part of a long list of restrictions laid down by Early, many originating with the president himself, that kept a tight lid on what could be reported about Franklin Roosevelt. Despite some chafing from the affected journalists, the White House press corps was largely cooperative—to the point of actually interfering with any reporter or photographer who tried to violate the rules.

At first these strictures were set down primarily to keep the American people from being reminded on a daily basis that their president could not walk normally. Most pictures, carefully choreographed by the White House,* showed him only from the waist up. No photos were allowed of Roosevelt in a wheelchair or of him being lifted into and out of his automobile, nor were reporters even allowed to mention that such things had taken place.** By and large, the press was wholly cooperative. Indeed, on the rare occasions when someone would try to sneak a photo of FDR in his wheelchair, other lensmen would "accidentally" block the shot or knock the camera to the ground. And if that didn't work, the

*Early, Roosevelt's assistant secretary in charge of press relations, joined the White House after a six-year stint as head of Paramount Pictures's newsreel bureau. Likewise, the president's confidential secretary, Marvin H. McIntyre, had been head of the Washington office of Twentieth-Century Fox Newsreels.

**Of the many thousands of photographs taken of FDR over the years, only three show him in his specially constructed armless wheelchair, and two of those were taken by close friends and not published until after his death.

president himself would point to the offending photographer, whereupon the Secret Service would move in, snatch the camera, and expose the film.[27]

Even political cartoonists—including those who opposed Roosevelt politically—invariably portrayed him "running, jumping or even fighting in a boxing arena."[28] Still, the White House did not always rely on journalistic generosity: At state dinners, for example, the president was always wheeled in and seated before his guests arrived. The deception worked, much better than the president and his handlers might have imagined. As J. B. West later recalled of his second day as chief usher at the White House in 1941, fully eight years into Roosevelt's presidency:

> The door opened and the Secret Service guard wheeled in the President of the United States. Startled, I looked down at him. It was only then that I realized that Franklin D. Roosevelt was really paralyzed. Immediately I understood why this fact had been kept so secret. Everybody knew that the president had been stricken with infantile paralysis, and his recovery was legend, but few people were aware how completely the disease had handicapped him.[29]

Journalist John Gunther, author of the celebrated "Inside" book series, recalled that when he lived in Europe in the decade before World War II, "I repeatedly met men in important positions of state who had no idea that the President was disabled."[30]*

Soon enough, the FDR-Early edicts were being toughened to include all negative depictions of the president, not just those involving his disability. When a photo that showed him frowning as he shielded his eyes from bright lights was widely published on January 30, 1936, along with a caption that suggested FDR's expression reflected his concern over agricultural problems, a furious Roosevelt ordered Early to ban all camera-

---

*One of the only occasions on which Roosevelt did not take pains to hide his disability came during a 1944 wartime tour of the Hawaiian Islands. In his visits with wounded soldiers in local military hospitals, the president made a point of moving through the wards in his wheelchair, so that the soldiers could see that, like many of them, he suffered from a physical handicap. (McIntire, *White House Physician*, p. 201; Gallagher, *FDR's Splendid Deception*, pp. 172–173)

men from photographing him "when he is unaware of them." Under new regulations, photographers were required to use tripods and to shoot their photos simultaneously—and then, "only when the President is ready to be photographed."[31] Surprisingly, newspapers and magazines on both sides of the political spectrum did not object; some, such as the *New York Times* and the *New York Herald Tribune*, actually endorsed the new restrictions.[32]

At a certain point, however, the patience of photographers, frustrated by their inability to shoot anything but staged pictures, grew thin. When Roosevelt traveled to Manhattan for a speech at the Museum of Natural History, photographers were told they could shoot only while the president was speaking; by mutual agreement, they did not turn in any pictures for publication.[33] At other times, they came up with ingenious ways of circumventing White House regulations: When Early banned cameramen from a Democratic conference in Chesapeake Bay in the summer of 1937, two leading photo agencies—Acme and the Associated Press—bought some snapshots taken by an unidentified congressman in attendance and distributed them. When the photos were published, Early ordered the two agencies barred not only from the rest of the conference but also from Hyde Park, before relenting several days later.[34]

But there was little, ultimately, that the photographers could do without endangering their own livelihood. As Myron Hoff Davis, a staff photographer for *Life* magazine, recalled, "Most newsmen made no attempt to take such pictures because (1) they supposed the Secret Service might revoke their White House passes for doing so, (2) nothing could be gained by showing the extent of Roosevelt's infirmity."[35]

Roosevelt also did not hesitate to "suggest" to the press corps how he felt their stories should be written, often "interviewing" himself and providing both the questions and answers he wanted; this practice of lecturing reporters was done so frequently that the president took to calling himself "Dean of the White House School of Journalism."[36] At a certain point, he also began taking "an active part in the wording" of photo captions distributed by White House photographers.[37] Later on in his presidency, he became more active still: Returning from a trip to Warm Springs in late 1944, he instructed the three wire service reporters who'd accompanied him to "submit their stories to him for review," whereupon he "suggested a few minor changes." This, the Associated Press correspondent noted, "has been the custom on several 'off-the-record' trips by the Chief Executive," joking that Roosevelt had "turned editor on his way back to Washington."[38]

During the president's first seven years in office, apart from his paralysis, there was little about FDR's health that actually needed covering up. But that was about to change.

The Brown Blob

CHAPTER 6

A photograph on the cover of an early issue of *Time* magazine in the spring of 1923 showed a barely visible dark spot above Franklin Roosevelt's left eyebrow.[1] No one took any notice of it; there was no medical reason to.[2] The tiny dot, familiar to dermatologists as a macule, or a simple change in skin color, was flat and could not be detected if anyone ran their fingers across it, not unlike many lesions commonly seen on the exposed skin of those who, like Franklin Roosevelt, enjoy spending time in the sun.

Over the next decade, however, this particular lesion slowly expanded and darkened; by the time Roosevelt was first inaugurated as president in 1933, it was far more noticeable. During his first term, the development hastened considerably, and, as the decade ended, the still-expanding lesion—which now stretched from the lower part of FDR's forehead to the base of his eyebrow—was exhibiting ominous signs that today would prompt a physician to suspect a highly malignant skin cancer called melanoma.

Even now, with modern advancements in diagnosis and treatment, melanoma remains one of the most feared of all cancers. The medical literature of FDR's day describes melanotic sarcoma, as it was then known, as "the most malignant of all tumors,"[3] with a prognosis "more unfavorable than that of any other type of malignant neoplasm."[4] And melanoma, like many other cancers, tends to metastasize, or spread, to many different areas of the body—particularly the brain and the gastrointestinal tract. Indeed, melanoma metastasizes to the brain more than any other cancer: Of all patients who die from the disease, 90 percent have brain metastases. Despite its relative rarity, it is the third most common cancer causing brain metastases in the United States, and even today patients who develop them have an especially poor prognosis, with less than one in six surviving as long as one year.[5] Moreover, brain metastases from melanoma are notoriously prone to spontaneous hemorrhage, which is the immediate cause of death of between one-quarter and half of all patients with melanoma.[6]

Melanoma also metastasizes to the gastrointestinal (GI) tract more than any other tumor; studies have shown that three cases in five metastasize to the small bowel. Current oncologists suspect bowel involvement in any melanoma patient who develops acute gastrointestinal pain. This propensity for both brain and GI metastases is particularly pertinent in Franklin Roosevelt's case, for their presence plays a key role in establishing a highly probable clinical scenario that he had melanoma.

Little public notice was taken as the lesion expanded, or when it began to disappear, beginning in mid-1940. The few published references to the skin patch invariably treated it as just another of the president's physical quirks. *Time* magazine, for example, wrote of FDR's 1936 State of the Union address to Congress that "the glare of klieg lights . . . made the mole over his left eye stand out in pitiless relief."[7] Four years later, a wire service assessment of the president's health spoke of his "great smiling face, made manly, perhaps, by its blemishes," adding: "Looking closely, you notice the brown blob over his left eye."[8] A few other newspaper and magazine articles of the day also matter-of-factly mentioned the "mole over his left eyebrow."[9]

But while reporters may have considered the "brown blob" harmless, one prominent doctor who had never treated Franklin Roosevelt *was* looking closely—and was concerned enough to contact the president directly.

At seventy-eight, Reuben Peterson enjoyed a national reputation as an astute clinician and veteran medical educator, having received his medical degree at Harvard. For over half a century, he taught obstetrics and gynecology at leading medical schools, including the University of Michigan, where he'd also been the hospital medical director, and wrote several of the standard textbooks on obstetrics. He was one of the founders of the American College of Surgeons and had served as president of the American Gynecological Society.[10] Significantly, Peterson had long been involved in the war against cancer; in 1913, he helped organize a nationwide campaign of doctors aimed at eradicating cancer and educating Americans about the dread disease.[11] So from his retirement home, Powder Point, in Duxbury, Massachusetts,* Peterson took up his pen on January 17, 1940, and wrote a letter to Franklin D. Roosevelt about that "brown blob" above his left eye.

He didn't call it that, of course. Most likely (his original letter has been lost), he advised the president to ask his doctors to take a close look at the lesion. Given Peterson's stature, the letter was passed to Ross McIntire, who replied just a few days later: "I will say to you, in confidence," the president's physician told his colleague, "that the pigmented area above the President's eye is very superficial and has never shown any sign of an inflammatory nature. You can rest assured that it is under observation at all times."[12] This is the only recorded comment, public or private, that McIntire ever made about the lesion, and it suggests his awareness that there were grounds for continued inspection. But was McIntire telling the truth when he told Peterson that he was on top of the situation, and that the lesion was utterly harmless?

The late Dr. A. Bernard Ackerman, widely considered one of the world's leading experts in the diagnosis of melanoma—a profile of him in a leading dermatology journal on the occasion of his seventieth birthday referred to him simply as "the legend"[13]—examined hundreds of photos of the lesion together with the authors of this book over a period of several weeks and concluded, in a paper for the *Archives of Dermatology*, that "it is impossible, despite the imponderables, to exclude melanoma."[14] The editors of that respected journal went even further,

---

*A street, Peterson Road, has been named for him in Duxbury.

stating in their abstract that "when fully formed [Roosevelt's lesion] resembled most closely a melanoma with signs of regression."[15] Ackerman himself later expanded on the paper, stating that while "I'm not stating unequivocally that he had melanoma . . . it sure looks like it." Moreover, he said, the lesion "is something that any competent doctor today would look at and say reflexively it's melanoma."[16]

As Ackerman explained, there are five criteria for diagnosing a slightly raised lesion like Roosevelt's as melanoma, known as the "ABCDEs": Asymmetry, Border irregularity, Color variability, Diameter greater than 6 millimeters, and Elevation. But these same criteria can be seen, albeit less frequently, in an exceedingly common, noncancerous growth called a solar lentigo or seborrheic keratosis, medical terms for what is commonly known as a "sun spot." Based solely on photographic evidence, he said, FDR's lesion "could be either a melanoma or a solar lentigo/seborrheic keratosis"—the only way to be certain, of course, would be to take a sample of tissue from the lesion and biopsy it.[17]* Furthermore, there were a number of factors that argued against melanoma, said Ackerman, such as the size of the lesion, which was smaller than would be expected in a cancerous growth, and the fact that it appeared to have regressed, or disappeared, entirely in a short period of time; melanomas typically do not regress completely.[18] Still, the venerable authority added, a number of other factors tipped the scales in favor of melanoma: The lesion had different shades of color—the "C" in ABCDE—and it was an

---

*In 1991 Dr. William Ober, a New Jersey pathologist and author, wrote to medical historian Dr. Hugh L'Etang and informed him that in 1949, while serving at the Naval Medical Center in Bethesda, Maryland, he saw a tissue slide from Roosevelt's lesion and that it showed a benign seborrheic keratosis with a fair amount of melanin in the basal layer. However, it's not at all certain that the slide he saw was from the lesion over FDR's eye; Roosevelt had numerous pigmented age spots on his face that were removed over the years, and he may have been looking at a slide of one of them. Ober's account is suspicious for another reason. He had to have seen the flood of national attention that greeted the 1979 publication of Dr. Harry Goldsmith's paper suggesting FDR had melanoma, especially since Ober's close friend and neighbor, Dr. George Pack, was prominently mentioned in it. The notion that Ober waited twelve years to disclose that he'd seen evidence that debunked this widely publicized theory makes no sense. (Hugh L'Etang, *Ailing Leaders in Power, 1914–1994*, p. 40; phone interview with Ober's daughter, Elaine Ober Skagestaad)

isolated patch; benign growths normally are uniform in color and are seen in multitude on sun-exposed skin.

What Ackerman chose not to address was that Ross McIntire was regularly reducing the lesion at the margins for cosmetic reasons, most likely using cauterization with electricity and curettage (scraping). His differential diagnosis was narrowed to two possibilities—neither of which was possible unless the lesion had been intentionally removed. Moreover, doctors of Roosevelt's time—even trained dermatologists—rarely diagnosed a lesion such as FDR's as melanoma. Instead, according to Ackerman, it was "considered to be benign . . . or, at worst, a pre-malignant neoplasm designated as a Hutchison's melanotic freckle." Even well into the 1950s, he wrote, "such a lesion was deemed to be a precursor of melanoma, not a melanoma per se."[19]

Just when a biopsy specimen of the lesion first revealed that it was malignant is unknown; not surprisingly, none of the surviving medical records indicate any treatment of the spot, and McIntire would always insist that the only invasive medical procedures FDR underwent as president were for the removal of a wen, or sebaceous cyst, on the back of his head (see Chapter 8) and an abscessed tooth. But the Peterson letter likely was a signal to the president and his physician that the lesion was raising concerns among other doctors and acted as a wake-up call that prompted McIntire to start taking more aggressive measures to reduce its visibility.

The timing could not have been more politically complicated. For all his private dissembling to aides and cabinet members that he wanted to leave public life, Roosevelt had long been laying the groundwork for an unprecedented third term as president. The long-expected war in Europe had broken out in September 1939 with Hitler's invasion of Poland. Roosevelt remained convinced that despite the nation's strong isolationist trend, America could not remain aloof from events across the Atlantic. No doubt that is why Secretary of the Interior Harold Ickes had written in his diary that same month that FDR "did intend to be a candidate if he had control of the convention and if the foreign situation had assumed a serious aspect."[20] By January 1940, Roosevelt's top aide and political alter ego, Harry Hopkins (who himself harbored presidential ambitions), was telling presidential speechwriter Robert Sherwood he was certain Roosevelt would run.[21] At the same time, FDR himself was telling Treasury

Secretary Henry Morgenthau that "I do not want to run *unless between now and the convention things get very, very much worse in Europe*" (emphasis added).[22]

FDR was by no means a shoo-in for reelection. Despite his historic landslide win over Alf Landon in 1936, the most one-sided contested presidential election in U.S. history, he was running almost neck-and-neck with his prospective GOP opponents: As late as May, he led the Republican front-runner, Manhattan District Attorney Thomas E. Dewey, by just 48–44 percent in the Gallup poll.[23] Besides the huge political divide over fears of involvement in the European crisis, Roosevelt had suffered several key defeats over the previous four years, such as the divisive battle over his proposal to expand ("pack," his opponents charged) the Supreme Court. And, of course, there was decided resistance, even among some FDR supporters, to breaking the traditional two-term limit. Even the slightest hint that the president had a malignancy surely would have spelled political disaster.

It is difficult to overstate the fear cancer inspired in Americans of this period; the medical community had even diagnosed a condition called "cancerphobia" to describe a hysterical fear of the disease.* In Roosevelt's day, many Americans considered cancer a stigmatizing illness to be kept quiet at all costs; many doctors deliberately withheld a cancer diagnosis from their patients, while others were pressured by family members (and ultimately agreed) to falsify death certificates to keep a patient's fatal cancer from becoming known.[24] And this doctor-imposed secrecy was not reserved solely for average patients or for those without the means to afford intensive treatment. As late as two months before his death in 1948, the great baseball slugger Babe Ruth was deliberately kept in the dark about the naso-pharyngeal cancer that would take his

*At least one of FDR's predecessors, Grover Cleveland, had taken great pains to conceal his cancer from the public, undergoing two secret operations onboard a private yacht in 1893 to remove a malignant growth from the roof of his mouth. One of his successors, Lyndon Johnson, underwent similarly secret surgery in 1967 to remove a basal cell epithelioma, a less dangerous skin cancer, from his ankle. Even after LBJ's death, his family and doctors denied that cancer was involved, because of fear that public reaction to the word "would far exceed the seriousness of the situation." Eventually, the Navy received permission to confirm the operation. (*New York Times,* June 29, 1977)

life at fifty-three.* Argentina's legendary first lady, Eva "Evita" Peron, was told that the vaginal bleeding from the cervical cancer that eventually killed her at age thirty-three was caused by the dye she was using on her pubic hair.[25] Indeed, Neil Simon's depiction in his play *Brighton Beach Memoirs* of people whispering the word "cancer" out of fear is only a slight exaggeration. When a 1939 Gallup poll asked respondents which disease they most feared, 66 percent said cancer, citing as reasons that it "always kills," that it was a lingering disease, and that its patients suffered more.[26] With such prevailing public attitudes, it is quite clear that Roosevelt could not risk disclosing even the slightest hint that he was being treated for a malignancy. Nor could he allow it to be treated in any way that would call attention to it—even if that treatment ultimately might improve his chances of survival.

It was during this time that a touch of fatalism began to creep into Roosevelt's conversation, according to Jim Farley (who would permanently break with the president over the third-term issue). During a heated discussion at Hyde Park about the upcoming race, Roosevelt responded to Farley's insistence that he issue a Shermanesque statement flatly refusing a third term by saying: "Jim, if nominated and elected, I could not in these times refuse to take the inaugural oath—even if I knew I would be dead within thirty days."[27] Later, as the two debated the merits of possible running mates, the president said: "The man running with me must be in good health because there is no telling how long I can hold out. . . . While my heart and lungs are good and the other organs functioning along okay, nothing in this life is certain."[28] Such statements, though they would become more frequent as the years went on, and despite Roosevelt's well-known penchant for intrigue, seem highly unusual for a man in his late fifties.

Farley, who hoped to succeed Roosevelt in the White House, privately expressed doubts about FDR's health. "I am really fearful that if the president is elected for a third term," he'd written in a private memo two

*Ruth's wife, Claire, wrote of the time he entered Memorial Hospital, as New York's Sloan-Kettering Cancer Center was then known, and nervously asked his doctor, "This is a cancer hospital. Why are you bringing me here?" Not everyone at Memorial has cancer, the doctor replied truthfully—if disingenuously. (*New York Times*, December 29, 1998)

Roosevelt with his first vice president, John Nance Garner (left), and Postmaster General James A. Farley (right) at the Jefferson-Jackson Day dinner in January 1939. "I doubt if he can stand the strain of another four years," Farley—who'd hoped to replace the president—told Garner, who would himself be replaced on FDR's third-term ticket by Henry A. Wallace. (Bettmann/CORBIS)

months before their Hyde Park chat, "he may not be able to stand up physically under the strain and he will let those around him get into a situation that will be bad for the country and himself."[29] And, to Vice President John Nance Garner, he confided that "I doubt if he can stand the strain of another four years, particularly war years."[30]

Clearly, though, the decision to run despite a looming fatal illness was Roosevelt's alone—notwithstanding the myth that has been propagated since his death that FDR was disinterested, aloof, and uninvolved when it came to his health. Despite the propensity by doctors of the era to sometimes withhold a cancer diagnosis from their patients, it is simply irrational to believe that McIntire would be so presumptuous when it came to the president of the United States. The doctor, after all, was a dedicated and intensely loyal career naval officer and Roosevelt was his commander in chief; McIntire's prestige and influence flowed from his proximity to the president, and it defies logic that he would jeopardize that relationship by keeping such critical information hidden from him—even, as others would contend, if he later did so with respect to FDR's cardiac condition.

But, above all, FDR's take-charge personality argues against anyone but "The Boss" being in complete control when it came to matters as vital as his own well-being and his ability to remain in office. Despite his generally high regard for the medical profession, FDR took charge of his polio to the point of near-obsession, educating himself to a level of expertise that was equal to, or better than, that of the leading specialists of the day. Moreover, he refused to accept that any problem was insurmountable.

His speechwriter, Robert Sherwood, tells how in 1939, Harry Hopkins was undergoing treatment at the world-renowned Mayo Clinic in Rochester, Minnesota, for a life-threatening gastrointestinal disorder; the White House aide's family had been told that he had four weeks to live, and FDR himself was telling friends that "the doctors have given Harry up for dead." But the president, indignant over what he considered the doctors' defeatist attitude, seized control of the case himself and ordered McIntire to do whatever was necessary to save Hopkins. McIntire immediately brought in one of his predecessors as Navy surgeon general, Admiral Edward R. Stitt, a leading expert on tropical diseases. Together with his Navy colleagues, Stitt subjected Hopkins to a barrage of biochemical experiments that turned a dire four-week prognosis into an additional six-plus years of active and productive life.[31]

In short, Roosevelt's grit and determination, so evident during his struggle with polio, had not changed one iota. And if he was unwilling to surrender to what he'd been told was the inevitable when it came to his closest aide—to the point where he took charge of the case himself—why would he have been any less willing to do so when it came to his own life? While the time constraints and responsibilities of the presidency, particularly in the midst of a rapidly escalating world crisis, may have prevented him from studying his own dire situation as intensely as he had two decades earlier, there is no reason to believe that, ultimately, anyone other than Franklin Roosevelt was calling the shots.

If Roosevelt and McIntire were dismayed by the knowledge that melanoma has a worse prognosis than any other type of malignant neoplasm, as the contemporary medical literature indicated, there also were grounds for some hope—a time frame, at any rate, that might afford FDR an opportunity to accomplish what he saw as the most important task before him: taking the United States into and through the conflict with Germany and Japan, which he believed was both inevitable and necessary to combat the most dangerous global threat in history. A 1935 paper published in the respected British medical journal *The Lancet* described how, while melanoma inevitably was fatal, it didn't necessarily kill quickly. While melanoma is "the most malignant of all tumors," the author wrote, "it is certainly not the most rapidly fatal. The average duration of a case . . . is about three years." Even more significant, he added, "up to within a few months of the end, the patient remains free from pain and able to get about."[32] Nor was this an isolated judgment: A 1932 paper by Dr. Hubert J. Farrell of the Mayo Clinic reported that it took between "five and twelve years" after the removal of a malignant melanotic lesion for "demonstrable evidence of metastasis" to appear, even though the cancer likely had already begun to spread at the time of removal. Moreover, he suggested, "some persons seem to possess unusual resistance to invasion of the internal organs by these growths."[33]

There were only two prescribed courses of treatment for melanoma: removal of the entire lesion in one surgical procedure—known as wide excision—or concentrated doses of radiation. Neither of these was acceptable in Roosevelt's case, however, because the effects would have been immediately and unavoidably visible; radiation would have caused the loss of FDR's eyebrow and most probably the scalp hair, as well as damaging the eye itself. Instead, it appears that McIntire began (or continued) treating the lesion to effect a gradual, purely cosmetic, removal—this despite the warning of at least one contemporary melanoma specialist that "partial removal . . . constitute(s) a serious danger."[34]

Particularly after August 1940, when Roosevelt accepted renomination for a third term, the lesion over his eye began to undergo a dramatic and unusually rapid change. By October, what the press just months earlier had described as a "brown blob" had faded considerably. Film of the victorious president delivering his historic "Arsenal of Democracy" speech on December 27 shows more of a faint shadow than the intensely dark lesion seen just ten months earlier. By September 1941 the patch was barely distinguishable, and by the middle of 1942, it had virtually disappeared completely. It is medically possible, though rare, for lesions such as Roosevelt's to vanish, or regress, entirely on their own. But it is highly unusual for a malignant melanoma, or any pigmented lesion of the size and character of the one over FDR's eye, to do so as rapidly; even stretching the period of total regression to four years would be most uncharacteristic.[35]* Clearly, then, Roosevelt's lesion could not have disappeared as it did without the help of a trained eye, ear, nose, and throat surgeon like Ross McIntire.

The change becomes dramatically apparent when examining a series of photo portraits taken of the president at the White House on August 16, 1940, as he prepared for what was shaping up to be a heated election campaign against the surprise Republican nominee, Wendell Willkie. As with all Roosevelt photos, these were meticulously staged by Press Secretary Steve Early: The president, wearing a blue seersucker suit and plaid tie, was seated at his Oval Office desk, a serious but strong expression on his face befitting the critical times. Behind the cameras that day were photographers from some of the leading portrait studios, including Harris and Ewing, Underwood, and Hessler. One of the color photos that came out of that session was destined for *Fortune* magazine's October issue, just before the election; another appeared that same month on the cover of newspaper photogravure sections across the country. Yet these portraits, which were meant to afford FDR four more years in the office he so coveted, also provide a lasting record of the secret he was so desperately trying to hide.

Making medical deductions from photographs is complicated, not only because of varying factors such as lighting and camera angles, but also because so many of the photos—particularly posed portraits like these—were retouched by artists in the studios. But an unretouched proof of a Hessler photo, the one that was syndicated to newspapers,

*Although benign solar lentigos can, rarely, regress much more rapidly, when that happens, the lesion almost always is small, located on the chest, and accompanied by highly visible skin eruptions. (Ackerman and Lomazow, "An Inquiry into the Nature of the Pigmented Lesion Above Franklin Delano Roosevelt's Left Eye," pp. 530–531)

exists, and appears on the cover of this book; it provides solid evidence that the "brown blob" had undergone changes that can only be attributed to surgical procedures. Sparse hairs are combed over a new scar in the base of the eyebrow, and the area of pigmentation in Roosevelt's eyelid that had been expanding since 1939 has been replaced by a discreet, but definite, surgical scar. Moreover, one of the two small, circular pigmented lesions *below* FDR's left eye, seen just a month earlier on the cover of *Newsweek*, was now gone completely.[36]

How and when was this surgery—likely a series of small procedures—performed, in ways that escaped public detection? Beginning in early 1939 and continuing until his death six years later, Roosevelt's already regular visits to Ross McIntire's office increased to the point where he often made several such trips each day.[37] Some of the earlier work on Roosevelt's eye may well have taken place aboard the Navy cruiser USS *Tuscaloosa*, which hosted the president on a hastily announced and mysterious two-week cruise in mid-February 1940, just after Peterson's letter was received. Contemporary press reports initially billed the voyage, on which "official business would be kept to a minimum," as FDR's "annual vacation."[38] But the *New York Times* speculated that Roosevelt "might meet at sea high officials of the British, French and Italian governments, supposedly to consider means of ending the European war."[39] The president himself added to this air of secrecy by refusing to discuss any details of the forthcoming trip, even when one reporter suggested to Roosevelt that his vagueness "had all the elements of a mystery novel."[40]

The cruiser departed from Pensacola, Florida, and sailed for two weeks in the Caribbean, where Roosevelt spent most of his time relaxing and fishing, along with what was described as an "intensive" inspection of Panama Canal Zone defenses and consultations with the leaders of Panama, Colombia, and Costa Rica.[41] But in a letter to his cousin and confidante, Daisy Suckley, the president wrote that "we have all been laughing at the complete ignorance & gullibility of the Press!"[42] A forty-eight-minute color silent film shot onboard by a cameraman from the Navy's Recruiting Bureau for the president's private collection shows some unusual occurrences. For one thing, FDR is photographed almost exclusively from the right side, making it difficult to see his left eye. And, in footage taken late in the voyage, he is wearing sunglasses, which is most atypical for Roosevelt.[43] Ross McIntire was aboard, of course; in fact, the forty-pound red snapper he landed while fishing was the largest catch on the cruise.[44] It is not unreasonable to suspect that he used the occasion for intensive and urgent surgical work on the president's eye, confident that the two-week period away from the public gaze, as well as the camera lenses of the press corps, would provide sufficient time for Roosevelt to recuperate and any scar tissue to heal.

Whether or not the *Tuscaloosa* was the site of secret presidential surgery, it is undeniably certain that Ross McIntire continually was burning, carving, and scraping away at the malignant lesion above FDR's eye until it disappeared. Confident in the conventional medical wisdom that he had a window of opportunity of about five years before the effects of the cancer already ravaging his body would kill him, the president, with the aid of his doctor, had decided to roll the dice with history, believing he would be able to undertake the colossal challenge that lay before him.

But unexpected problems lay ahead. Within months of his inauguration, FDR would face a critical medical threat to his life that even today has gone unrecognized by historians and Roosevelt biographers—and that very nearly put Vice President Henry A. Wallace into the White House at one of the most critical points in U.S. history.

The Beginning of the End

CHAPTER 7

As Franklin Roosevelt, on January 20, 1941, became the first chief executive to take the oath of office for a third time, he brought with him a new vice president, Henry Agard Wallace. FDR's elevation of his agriculture secretary, who hadn't even enrolled as a Democrat until after the 1936 election, surprised the country—and enraged many in his own party. Besides his past political loyalty and the fact that he'd never before run for office, Wallace was regarded by most Democrats as a naive dreamer, almost a crackpot. Little did they know that he was a disciple of a White Russian émigré mystic named Nicholas Roerich, to whom he wrote dozens of letters, addressed "Dear Guru," that were filled with occult-like mysticism and references to FDR as "The Flaming One."*

Roosevelt's decision to name Wallace as his running mate, succeeding Vice President John Nance Garner, who had broken with the New Deal

*Republican presidential candidate Wendell Willkie, told of the letters, refused to make use of them, reportedly as part of a deal in which the Democrats agreed not to disclose his own extramarital affair with Irrita Van Doren, literary editor of the *New York Herald Tribune*. The letters eventually surfaced in 1948, when Wallace ran for president as a third-party candidate.

after FDR's attempt in 1937 to enlarge the Supreme Court, stunned the delegates at the Democratic convention. Yet Roosevelt was adamant—to the point of declaring that, without Wallace on the ticket, he would refuse to run. Why he was so unwavering about the Iowan has never been certain, but the president believed he needed someone who was a strong liberal—Wallace inhabited the far-left precincts of the Democratic Party—and also could help cut into the GOP's Farm Belt stronghold against Willkie. The convention delegates were far from convinced, however; Wallace only narrowly won the nomination, and then only with a considerable amount of arm-twisting by party leaders. As he prepared to ascend the podium to deliver his acceptance speech, Senator James F. Byrnes warned him, "Don't do it, Henry. You'll ruin the party if you do." Wallace returned to his seat.[1]

Roosevelt and Wallace entered the fall campaign only two points ahead of the Republicans in the Gallup poll.[2] But after adoption of the popular "destroyers for bases" deal with Britain, in which U.S. ships were exchanged for ninety-nine-year leases to British naval bases in the Western Hemisphere, they opened up a ten-point lead in a matter of weeks. Willkie's endorsement of the nation's first peacetime draft, though laudable, cost him the support of the Republicans' isolationist wing. In the end, Roosevelt coasted to an easy victory; closer than the previous two elections, but a landslide nonetheless.

On May 4, 1941, just 103 days into his third term, Roosevelt traveled to the sleepy Shenandoah Valley town of Staunton, Virginia, to speak at the dedication of the newly restored boyhood home of his former boss and mentor, Woodrow Wilson. He used the occasion to deliver a sharply militant blast at isolationism, telling his listeners that their presence demonstrated their faith in the freedom of democracy in the world. But, in sharp contrast to his rhetoric during the campaign, when he'd assured voters that "we will not send our men to take part in European wars,"[3] he now sent an unveiled warning that America had an obligation, first expressed by Wilson, to keep the world safe for democracy. "It is the kind of faith for which we have fought before," Roosevelt declared, "and for the existence of which we are ever ready to fight again."[4]

The speech "moved the crowd as few recent Presidential speeches have," wrote *Time*. "Even hardened Washington correspondents, tired of all speeches, tired of the same old faces, stood silently like the others, with heads bared, when the President had finished."[5] Privately, however, the magazine's correspondent confided, "FDR looked as bad as a man can look and still be about."[6]

Upon his return to the White House, the president complained to Ross McIntire that he had a stomachache and felt unusually tired; this prompted the doctor to immediately order a complete blood exam, which was sent to the U.S. Naval Medical School for analysis under the thinly disguised pseudonym "F. David Rolph." This was one of over two dozen aliases used to conceal Roosevelt's medical tests as well as dozens of publicly undisclosed visits to the Naval Hospital at Washington's Foggy Bottom and, from mid-1941, the National Naval Medical Center in Bethesda, Maryland.[7]* The results must have floored McIntire: Roosevelt's level of hemoglobin, the iron-rich protein that gives blood its red color, was a shockingly low 4.5 grams per deciliter. A normal value for a healthy man is between 14 and 17 grams, and FDR's last previous test for which the results are still available, taken on March 27, 1940, had shown a level of 13.5 grams.** This meant that Roosevelt had lost the equivalent of eight pints of blood, two-thirds of his body's normal supply, sometime over the previous fourteen months. And his count of red blood cells, which carry oxygen to the body's tissues, had dropped to just 2.8 million, a level far below normal, showing characteristics indicating that the blood loss was due to an iron deficiency that had occurred not suddenly, but

*The complete list of aliases was obtained by authors Kenneth R. Crispell and Carlos F. Gomez through a 1981 Freedom of Information Act request to the Naval Medical Center. They included other plays on his name and initials, such as Mr. Delano, Roy F. David, Dan F. Rhodes, Daniel F. Rhodes, Fred Rosen, Fred D. Rosen, and F. David Roy; variations on his sons' names, such as Mr. Elliott and James D. Elliott; and the actual names of aides and staff members, including Mr. Fox (his pharmacist/masseur) and John Cash, a White House police officer. The other names on the list were Mr. Ford, G. A. Forkes, Ralph Frank, Rolph Frank, Frank A. McCormack, D. Rhodes, Dan R. Rhodes, D. Rhoades, Dan R. Rhoades, Mr. Rhodes, and Mr. Rolphe. All of this essentially confirms McIntire's later admission that "journeys" to Bethesda "could be made without exciting comment."

**At the time, Roosevelt was suffering from what was described as a case of "swamp fever." McIntire ordered three bloodwork exams in the space of just six days, after the first test showed a sharply elevated white blood count.

over several months. In fact, it is unlikely that Roosevelt would have survived a rapid blood loss of this magnitude.[8]

However long it had taken, his blood level was now at a critical stage: The president of the United States was on the precipice of medical catastrophe.

Publicly, the White House reacted calmly and with seeming unconcern: Press Secretary Steve Early announced to the press corps, assembled in the Oval Office for a scheduled presidential news briefing the next morning, that after Roosevelt "finished his conference this morning with what you gentlemen call the 'War Cabinet,' [Ross McIntire] saw the President and found that he has a degree and a half of temperature. Ross believes that he has eaten something that disagreed with him; he thinks he knows what it is and that the situation will be cleared up; everything else is quite all right." Therefore, Early added, "the wisest thing is to keep him confined to his quarters . . . so we are cancelling the press conference." McIntire, making an uncharacteristic appearance at the press gathering, insisted that FDR had only a "slight gastro-intestinal upset; we will have to give him a little time to straighten out," adding that "it is nothing serious." Off the record, McIntire described it as "a nice 'stomach rolling,' and we have to give it a few hours to get cleared up."[9]

Ross McIntire had willfully deceived the press and the entire nation about the state of Franklin Roosevelt's health. It would not be the last time he did so.

Actually, the president had been ill for at least twenty-four hours; he had spent the previous day in bed, officially indisposed, with only Daisy Suckley, apart from his medical staff, at his side during the afternoon and evening hours.[10] And he was suffering from far more than a slight "gastro-intestinal upset"—FDR was bleeding from somewhere in his lower GI tract. Though never openly discussed during Roosevelt's lifetime, the official story was that he'd suffered from a bad case of hemorrhoids. Roosevelt "never had a serious illness," McIntire told *U.S. News & World Report* in 1951, "but we had one case that gave us a little concern. He developed a mild anemia. . . . We found that he had an ordinary thing that a lot of people have—he had a bleeding hemorrhoid that he hadn't noticed, and blood had been dripping from this thing for quite a little time

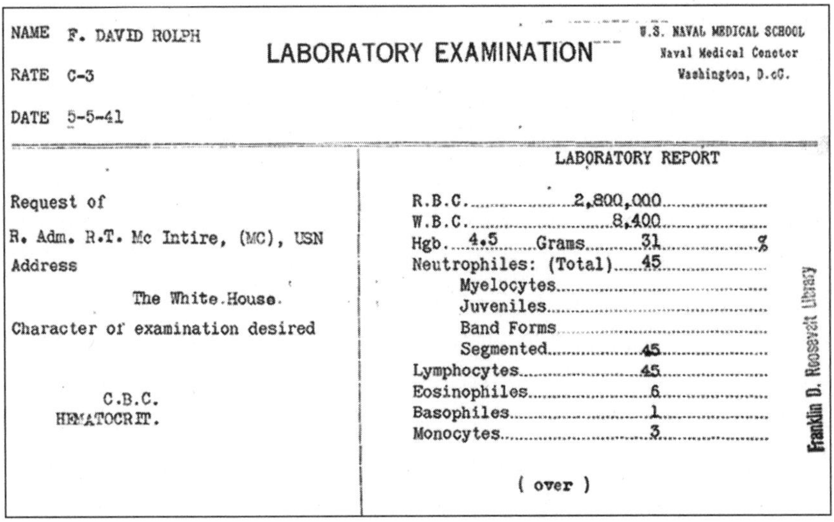

NAME F. DAVID ROLPH

RATE C-3

DATE 5-5-41

LABORATORY EXAMINATION

U.S. NAVAL MEDICAL SCHOOL
Naval Medical Center
Washington, D.C.

Request of

R. Adm. R.T. Mc Intire, (MC), USN

Address

The White House.

Character of examination desired

C.B.C.
HEMATOCRIT.

LABORATORY REPORT

R.B.C.	2,800,000
W.B.C.	8,400
Hgb. 4.5 Grams	31 %
Neutrophiles: (Total)	45
Myelocytes	
Juveniles	
Band Forms	
Segmented	45
Lymphocytes	45
Eosinophiles	6
Basophiles	1
Monocytes	3

(over)

Franklin D. Roosevelt Library

The laboratory report from the U.S. Naval Medical Center, showing Roosevelt's hemoglobin level at a life-threatening low of 4.5 grams. Note the name "F. David Rolph," one of over thirty aliases used on Roosevelt's medical records. (Franklin D. Roosevelt Library)

and brought him down some. But he picked up in no time flat. In fact, no one ever noticed that, it was just that easy."[11]

By no stretch of the imagination was FDR's case "mild": Howard Bruenn, Roosevelt's cardiologist, would later describe the anemia (which occurred at least two years before he began treating the president) as "profound."[12] Moreover, the notion that it had been caused by hemorrhoids, dilated veins in the anal area, was dubious, at best: Crispell and Gomez note that such severity of blood loss is "highly unusual for hemorrhoids alone,"[13] and, as anyone with a case of bleeding hemorrhoids knows, even a few drops of blood is enough to turn the water in a toilet bowl bright red. That Roosevelt, even with his paralysis, or anyone who physically helped him, never spotted this degree of blood loss over a period of months if hemorrhoids were involved is highly unlikely. And even if he did have hemorrhoids that caused him to lose eight pints of blood, the treatment would have been immediate surgery, and the problem would have been corrected in one fell swoop—not the four months it actually took to stabilize him. McIntire, quite simply, had been caught asleep at the wheel, failing to monitor his patient's blood count (though frequent urinalyses were performed) and allowing him to slip into such a precarious position.

McIntire and his trusted associates—cardiologist Paul Dickens and the two top officers at the U.S. Naval Hospital, its commandant, Captain John Harper, and the executive officer, Captain Robert Duncan—quickly ordered an extensive battery of blood exams, one on each of the next four days and at least ten in the two and a half weeks following the initial diagnosis. Meanwhile, as Harold Ickes wrote in his diary, Roosevelt "kept to his bed" all week with what McIntire continued to call "an intestinal disorder which is not particularly important, but which results in a temperature and leaves the President too weak to contract business. No one has seen him, except the usual coterie."[14] A week later, Roosevelt canceled a scheduled nationwide radio address because of his illness; he would postpone no fewer than five Oval Office news conferences because of ill health during 1941.[15] Though the president's hemoglobin level rose slightly, it remained critically low for more than a week, before abruptly shooting up to 8.0 grams on May 15.

There is only one explanation for such a sudden rise—his hemoglobin had been just 5.75 two days earlier—and it was not the ferrous sulfate, or iron injections, that both McIntire and Bruenn later insisted had done the trick. Roosevelt had undergone a blood transfusion, and certainly more than one. And the prolonged temperature rise that McIntire reported likely was in reaction to that transfusion, a common consequence of introducing a foreign protein into the body.* Though never disclosed by Roosevelt's doctors, even after his death, that such a procedure had taken place, it is confirmed in a letter from Eleanor Roosevelt to her daughter, Anna. "I found Pa had really been quite ill," she wrote, "& Dr. McIntire was worried because his red cells which should be up to 5,000,000, dropped suddenly to 2,800,000. He has had 2 transfusions & his tummy is cleared up & his color seems good, his blood is back up to 4,000,000."[16] This was a rare occasion in which McIntire elected to discuss the president's health with members of his immediate family, as

*In his analysis a quarter-century later of FDR's surviving medical records, Dr. James Halsted, Anna's husband, surmised that FDR had had "a transfusion reaction of a febril(e) nature," though he also accepted McIntire's explanation of bleeding hemorrhoids. (James Halsted to Howard G. Bruenn, August 6, 1967, FDRL-HP)

shown by Eleanor's knowledge of his precise blood count, though the doctor's claim of a "sudden" blood loss suggests an effort to cover up his own negligence.

But an analysis of the battery of bloodwork performed during the period, the lab slips for which survive, shows that FDR underwent far more than two transfusions. After the initial transfusions, his hemoglobin slipped back to 7.5 on May 17, only to rise again sharply to 8.75 on the 21st, again to 10.5 on the 24th, and to 12.0 on June 4. The course of Roosevelt's seesawing hemoglobin level provides unequivocal evidence that between May 15 and August 2 he continued to hemorrhage, necessitating at least eight transfusions before finally stabilizing.[17] Further evidence appears in another letter from Eleanor to Anna, this one on June 22, just two days after indications that he'd received a fresh transfusion: "Pa has had another . . . low temperature[,] which they say comes from a low grade infection, but they don't know what it is," she wrote from Campobello.[18] Clearly worried at this point, the First Lady added, "I telephone every day since I've been here & today begged him to have an outside doctor & he said he would tomorrow."[19] Whatever the cause of the bleeding, it was not quickly stanched: A stool specimen on July 15—ten weeks after the initial diagnosis—revealed the presence of a large amount of "fresh blood," according to the lab report.[20] Fiberoptic endoscopy, allowing complete inspection of the colon, was still more than three decades in the future; short of surgery, of which there is no evidence, there was no capability at the time of visually inspecting more than the lowest twelve inches or so of the colon.

Henry Wallace, who spent his days presiding over the U.S. Senate and wondering whether, as vice president, he would ever be given a meaningful assignment, wasn't even remotely aware of the acute threat to Franklin Roosevelt's life—which might have unexpectedly propelled him into the Oval Office.

If Roosevelt did not have bleeding hemorrhoids, what did cause this catastrophic blood loss? The extensive battery of lab tests that followed suggests that his team of physicians was puzzled. Most common maladies were ruled out: Tests for inflammation and hemolysis (a condition in which red blood cells spontaneously rupture), as well as routine blood chemistries,[21] did not reveal any major problems, leaving a long list of possible but unusual diagnoses that could have produced a fourteen-month history of lower GI bleeding. Colon cancer, one of the most common causes of occult bleeding, can be ruled out by a complete contrast exam he underwent of the upper and lower GI tract, which was essentially normal, excluding any large constricting mass. Diverticulitis, bleeding from an inflammation of a small outpouching of the bowel, is a possibility, though such bleeding should have been evident much earlier and, like a severe case of hemorrhoids, surely would have been treated surgically. A common diagnostic principle taught to medical students is, "If you hear hoofbeats, think of horses, not zebras." In Roosevelt's case, the clinical history and diagnostic evidence rule out virtually all of the most common possibilities, leaving a list of "zebras," including abnormal blood vessels, parasites, and exposure to various physical or chemical toxins.

One of those medical long shots, though, is the very real and intriguing possibility that Roosevelt's bleeding was the result of exposure to radiation—though not for anything having to do with his melanoma. Throughout his third term, rumors circulated widely throughout both the medical and journalistic worlds that the president had been diagnosed with prostate cancer. The noted actress Veronica Lake, in her autobiography, claimed that she'd been told this by Eleanor Roosevelt herself during a reception in the White House celebrating FDR's sixty-third birthday in January 1945 (FDR was on his way to Yalta at the time):

> The nation's First Lady turned very solemn and gazed through the window onto the green. . . . She finally broke the silence by getting up and walking across the room. . . . Then she turned to me.
>
> "The President is ill, you know." She said it so flatly, so without emotion or tone to draw attention from me. I said nothing.
>
> "The President has cancer of the prostate gland. He'll be operated on when he returns."
>
> I sat there desperately wishing she hadn't told me that. . . . "I don't know what to say," I said. "I'm sorry, I mean . . . "
>
> "And I don't know why I've told you this," Mrs. Roosevelt said with a smile. "I'm the one to be sorry. I suppose we all need to tell these things

to someone. I chose you for no reason. No one knows of this except his physician and a few close advisors. Please respect my confidence."

. . . I never repeated what Mrs. Roosevelt told me. Never. I don't know why.[22]

Hers wasn't the only report that a malignancy had been discovered in Roosevelt's prostate. Throughout 1944 and early 1945, the FBI, at J. Edgar Hoover's personal instructions and under direct orders from the top levels of the White House, furiously searched for the sources of a flood of rumors, most of them flying in medical circles, concerning the president's health and his reported prostate cancer, as will be seen in Chapter 10. But might the illness have begun even earlier?

Prior to 1941, the treatment of choice for prostate cancer was the surgical implantation of a radioactive substance—in FDR's time, radium—directly into the prostate through either the perineum (the area between the base of the penis and the rectum), the bladder, or the rectum, followed by large doses of external beam radiation with X-rays. Radiation to this area is extremely irritating, uncomfortable, and technically challenging, often producing bleeding from the adjacent colon; not surprisingly, it rapidly fell out of favor after hormonal therapy was introduced.* However, as opposed to the radiation that would have been needed to treat the lesion above Roosevelt's eye, this treatment would not have been noticeable. One of Roosevelt's prolonged absences from public view, such as the reported "swamp fever" attack in March 1940, would have been just long enough for him to recover.

Many of the widespread rumors of prostate cancer centered on Roosevelt's reported treatment by Dr. William Calhoun "Pete" Stirling, a

---

*In 1941 Charles Huggins and Clarence Hodges published a landmark paper identifying male hormonal activity, using the level of acid phosphotase, an enzyme in the blood, as an objective measure, to be an influence on prostatic cancer. The paper described the effective use of surgical and/or chemical castration with the administration of oral estrogen—the first systematic approach to the treatment of prostate cancer. This breakthrough earned Huggins the Nobel Prize for Medicine in 1966. Moreover, the Navy was then in the forefront of radiation medicine. Roosevelt's radiologist (at that time both diagnostic and therapeutic) was Charles F. Behrens, who in 1949 edited *Atomic Medicine*, the first textbook on radiation's effects on the body.

prominent Washington, D.C., urologist, a close friend and both bridge and golf partner of White House Press Secretary Steve Early, whom he'd also treated.[23] A graduate of the University of Texas and Vanderbilt University Medical School, Stirling had been practicing for two decades and teaching at Georgetown University Medical School when he first saw Roosevelt.[24] Before long, the Army Medical Corps veteran would be named by Ross McIntire to a special task force on naval medicine, as were several other physicians who treated the president.*

That the rumors of his involvement were true was confirmed by none other than Stirling himself, who—unlike nearly all of the other doctors who treated the president—apparently had less discretion about publicly discussing his famous patient, whose politics he intensely disliked. In his 1975 autobiography, the *Chicago Tribune*'s like-minded White House correspondent, Walter Trohan, confirmed that Stirling had been one of his sources during FDR's lifetime, although "he refused to authorize any quotation."[25] Word of Stirling's reported refusal to perform unspecified surgery on the president because of the fragile state of his health spread like wildfire in Washington journalistic circles in 1944 (likely begun by Trohan, based on his inside information) and were investigated by the FBI. But Trohan wrote that Stirling first saw Roosevelt as early as 1942,[26] and the doctor's daughter, Margheritta, who'd worked in her father's office, placed the date even earlier: "sometime around 1940."[27]

Rumors concerning the president's health may not have made it into the American press, but they were of intense interest elsewhere. Files of the *Abwehr*, Hitler's secret service headed by legendary spy Admiral Wilhelm Canaris, disclose that on June 19, 1941, a top-secret message from Washington was sent via a Pan-American Clipper to China, then cabled from Japanese-occupied Shanghai to Berlin. It was one of a series of regular updates on Roosevelt's health relayed by Count Friedrich Sauerma,

---

*Ironically, Stirling's father-in-law, Navy Commander Edwin Hood Tillman, had his own connection to presidential medicine. As commander of a flotilla of vessels carrying William Howard Taft down the Mississippi River, he overruled White House doctors who hoped to force the corpulent president to lose weight by limiting the food portions of everyone at Taft's table. "Let him learn to control himself," Tillman said, ordering that full rations be served to the other diners. Not surprisingly, Taft appreciated Tillman's attitude and they became good friends. (*Washington Evening Star*, March 26, 1938)

Dr. William Calhoun "Pete" Stirling, the prominent Washington urologist and close friend of White House Press Secretary Steve Early. Stirling examined the president but refused to operate on him, citing FDR's physical condition. (Courtesy of Margheritta Allardice)

an *Abwehr* agent code-named Dinter, who claimed to have a direct pipeline to the president's doctors and who picked up his information on the D.C. society circuit—of which Stirling and his family were a leading part. This particular message reported: "Reliable source confirms that Roosevelt is suffering from uremic condition causing serious disturbances of consciousness as a result of constant application of catheter in urinary tract. Recurrent announcements indicating mild soreness of throat and similar illnesses are merely to camouflage his true condition."[28] In Berlin, Nazi medical experts reading Sauerma's dispatch wrote ominously of "the morbid condition of the President's blood caused by his inability to excrete urinary matter."[29] The diagnosis may not have been entirely correct, but it contained just enough hints of the truth to suggest that the German agent was, indeed, well connected.

It was also about this time that Roosevelt began making more and more day trips to the naval hospital at Bethesda: at least twenty-nine between 1941 and his death four years later. Aside from the lab exam slips, there is no record of what else was done to the president at the facility; according to officials at Bethesda, the president never spent a night there, as McIntire often pointed out much later. But Barbara Lint, a naval nurse stationed at the hospital, recalled that Roosevelt made "weekly visitations" every Tuesday for "therapeutic swimming sessions"[30]—a surprising claim, given that there was a White House swimming pool, which had actually been built for him in 1933 and which he used regularly.[31]

Even as he was struggling to throw off the lingering effects of his brush with death, Roosevelt and his top diplomatic aides, such as Secretary of State Cordell Hull and Undersecretary Sumner Welles, were engaged in scores of conversations with the Japanese ambassador to Washington, Kichisaburo Nomura, who was trying frantically to defuse escalating tensions between the two nations and stave off what appeared to be an inexorable slide toward war.

It is also about this time that the diary of FDR's distant cousin and confidante, Margaret "Daisy" Suckley, resumes after an apparent break of nearly two years. The journal that she had kept faithfully since the day Roosevelt was inaugurated broke off in July 1939 and did not resume until May 25, 1941. That is certainly surprising, given everything that had occurred in the intervening period, including the outbreak of the war in Europe, Roosevelt's campaign for a third term, and Daisy's gift to him of Fala, the Scottish terrier who was to become the most famous presidential pet in history. But as the diary's editor, Geoffrey C. Ward, concedes, Daisy censored her material, having "destroy[ed] some of [her letters to FDR] and drastically edited others."[32] Was there a volume for this critical period that, in the more than half a century between Roosevelt's death and her own, she chose to destroy? We probably will never know.

Yet if the material is complete and Daisy did resume her entries in the midst of Roosevelt's anemia crisis, it may have been because she understood that the president was gravely ill, though she came to an entirely wrong conclusion about his ailment. As entries several years later disclose, Daisy realized FDR was experiencing "very bad trouble" with his blood. But she likely either misheard or misunderstood the precise nature of the problem: Instead of a problem with his red blood cells, she thought he suffered from "a lack of white corpuscles." Doing her own amateur medical research, she was able to "find only one disease" that matched that problem, whereupon Daisy incorrectly concluded that Roosevelt had leukemia—which, she noted fearfully, "is considered fatal over a period of time."[33]

Her entries were only intermittent for the rest of 1941, even failing to record anything on or around December 7, the "date which will live in infamy," when Japan's attack on Pearl Harbor brought America into the war and led FDR to deliver the most famous speech of his entire presidency. As for Roosevelt, America's entry into the conflict meant, as Ross McIntire put it, "our daily schedule went by the board and my protests were brushed aside."[34] It also meant that whatever progress Roosevelt had been making on rebuilding the muscles in his crippled legs "came to a standstill" as, says McIntire, he cut back on the president's exercises in order to conserve his strength.[35] According to Walter Trohan, Stirling at about this time recommended an operation (presumably on his prostate, though Trohan doesn't specify), but Roosevelt declined because of the pressures of the war.

As the new year dawned, Daisy Suckley became an active diarist, writing regular accounts of what she called her "attempt to show the P. from a personal side which does not appear through the papers, and will not attempt to describe political or world conditions, except as these things are reflected in FDR."[36] These entries, along with her exchange of remarkably candid letters and phone conversations with the president, document not only her status as Roosevelt's close confidante, but also the gradual worsening of his health. But 1942 brought no new immediate medical crises, save for an increase in the number of what she referred to as "bad nose" days and his growing inability to deal with his chronic sinus problems. As for the lesion over his eye, by the spring of that year, it had all but vanished.

In mid-January 1943, Roosevelt became the first sitting president to ride in an airplane when he flew to Casablanca, Morocco, for a summit conference with British Prime Minister Winston Churchill and the two leaders of the Free French forces in exile, Charles de Gaulle and Henri Giraud. (Soviet leader Joseph Stalin also had been invited but declined to attend.) Its purpose was to plot Allied military strategy in Europe, though ultimately it was decided not to undertake the cross-Channel invasion of France that year and to focus instead on German-occupied North Africa. But it was also at Casablanca that the Allied leaders agreed for the first time, and declared publicly, that they would settle for nothing less than the unconditional surrender of the Axis powers.

Roosevelt spent ten days abroad, and though McIntire would write that the grueling negotiations removed "any doubt as to the President's fitness,"[37] Casablanca marked a definite turning point in his health; after his return on January 31, Roosevelt found it increasingly difficult to fight off illness and to bounce back as he'd always done before. He'd been running a fever during the conference, and wrote Churchill on his return that he'd caught some "strange African bug" that put him in bed for days and left him feeling exhausted. William Allen White, noted editor of the *Emporia Gazette (Kansas)* and a key organizer of the prewar anti-isolationist Committee to Defend America by Aiding the Allies, attended Roosevelt's Lincoln Day speech at the Washington Statler-Hilton just days after his return and observed that the president seemed to grow visibly tired during the evening, his voice losing its customary fire and eventually dropping to the point where White no longer could hear him.[38]

On February 27, Daisy's diary records that Roosevelt was spending his "4th day in bed and he still feels somewhat miserable though his fever has gone. Last Tuesday, without any warning, he felt ill at about noon" and was found to have a temperature of 102. McIntire, she noted, "found it was a toxic poisoning, but they can't ascribe it to anything they know of."

The following day, she reported, "they gave him 4 doses of a sulpha drug—from which he will have to recover."[39] In fact, the medication left him so tired he could not work past 2 p.m. for some time.[40] Ten days later he still had not fully recovered—Daisy quotes him as saying he "feels like a rag & is much annoyed at himself."[41] His cousin also now noticed for the first time that "his hand sometimes shakes."[42] This intention tremor, which occurs during voluntary movement (as opposed to the resting tremor that typifies Parkinson's disease), would increase rapidly and markedly until Roosevelt's death; by June he had to ask his secretary, Grace Tully, to get him a larger coffee cup so that he would not spill the contents as he drank from it.

By the fall Roosevelt was showing visible signs of exhaustion and illness. In October, according to Daisy, he spent at least nine days at the mercy of what he ascribed to "grippe," saying he "ached all over and had fever up to 104 and ¼."[43] And there were other worrying signs, though Daisy did not recognize them, such as his falling "asleep twice while trying to write a message to Congress"[44] and "swelling in his ankles"[45]—

both of which likely were warnings of diminished cardiac function. Then there was the "pain in his side," which Daisy in September implored him to discuss with McIntire, the first evidence that the melanoma had metastasized to his abdomen. (FDR's response minimized any concern: "The pain had moved & the doctor had left.")[46]

But there was no laughing off the incident that occurred two months later in Teheran, at the first summit meeting of the three major Allied leaders, during a steak and baked potato dinner that Roosevelt was hosting on November 28. He and Stalin were discussing the question of access to the Baltic Sea when, according to his interpreter, Charles Bohlen, "suddenly, in the flick of an eye, he turned green and great drops of sweat began to bead off his face; he put a shaky hand to his forehead. We were all caught by surprise. . . . [Harry] Hopkins had the president wheeled to his room," where McIntire examined him. "To the relief of everyone, [Hopkins] reported [back] nothing more than a mild attack of indigestion." Significantly, though, "the President retired for the evening without returning to the dining room." Privately, Hopkins told Bohlen that "he was quite concerned."[47] And there was another disturbing sign: When a member of the British delegation asked Prime Minister Winston Churchill whether Roosevelt had said much during that day's meeting with Stalin, he hesitated, then replied: "Harry Hopkins said that the president was inept. He was asked a lot of questions and gave the wrong answers."[48] Clearly the president's staff was being asked to conceal much more than a case of indigestion, and they were struggling to hide the fact of his illness.

The months ahead would bring even greater, and more immediate, health crises. But the Teheran conference was the beginning of the end: From this point on, Franklin Delano Roosevelt was on an inexorable downward medical slide. He'd returned from Casablanca in early 1943 a tired and sick man. By the end of the year, the president of the United States was dying.

Enter Bruenn—But When?

CHAPTER 8

Three times during the predawn hours of February 3, 1944, Press Secretary Steve Early found himself roused from his sleep by determined reporters, all asking the same urgent question: Is it true that President Roosevelt underwent an operation out at the naval hospital in Bethesda? Each time, Early was forced to reply that he couldn't discuss it. "The president wants to tell you about it himself," he said wearily. And so the reporters reluctantly held off writing their stories until the next day's scheduled news conference in the Oval Office.

It's not surprising that the president's health was on reporters' minds. Drew Pearson had just reassured the nation in his widely read "Washington Merry-Go-Round" syndicated column that "FDR goes into 1944 with the greatest gift given to any president or any person—remarkable good health," adding that "Roosevelt, more than any other president, has mastered the art of health under strain."[1] But it was nonsense; the president was not well, as he himself confessed to the nation in his Fireside Chat on January 11, in which he explained why he was unable to deliver his annual State of the Union message to Congress, as was traditional. "Like a great many other people," said Roosevelt, "I have had the flu, and although I am practically recovered, my doctor simply would not let me leave the White House to go up to the Capitol."[2]

But the president's flu was nowhere near as mild as he was suggesting, nor was he even close to recovering. He'd come back from Teheran with a severe bronchial infection that simply refused to go away, leaving him bedridden for over a week, with coughing spells filled with "thick, tenacious mucus" that lasted fully three months and "racked him by day and broke his rest at night," McIntire later recalled. But "more disturbing than anything else," he added, "there was the definite loss of his usual ability to come back quickly."[3] Daisy Suckley, seeing him at Hyde Park on the 22nd, noted that "he looks better than I expected, but says he still gets tired very easily."[4]

On February 2, however, Roosevelt's problem was of an entirely different nature. For two decades, he'd had a wen, or sebaceous cyst, growing on the back of his head that was now causing him discomfort when his hat band rubbed against it, and he'd decided to have it removed. There was nothing urgent about the procedure and both Daisy and Roosevelt's daughter, Anna, accompanied him to the naval hospital for the routine surgery. Daisy, worried as always, nervously confided to her diary that "I think it will be more of an operation than they imply, but I hope not. Four doctors are to be there—even a *wen*, if on a P. of the U.S., is an important matter!"[5]

In fact, no fewer than seven doctors were in the operating room that day, a large number even for a supposedly minor presidential surgery: McIntire; the two top officials at the naval hospital, Captain John Harper, the chief of staff, and executive officer Captain Robert Duncan, a cardiologist; Captain Louis Gilje, chief of general surgery; Captain Winchell M. Craig, chief of neurosurgery (a position he'd held previously at the Mayo Clinic); Captain George Webster, chief of plastic surgery, who actually performed the procedure; and Captain John W. Pender, the anesthesiologist, who'd also enjoyed a distinguished career at Mayo. In a 1979 letter to Dr. Harry Goldsmith, Webster disclosed that he and Craig "did not have a chance to examine the President before his arrival but were told by Admiral McIntire that the lesion was 'about the size of a hen's egg and almost exactly in the midline where the hat band would hit the head.' The description proved to be accurate."[6]

Given that this was not an emergency procedure, it's surprising that neither of the two surgeons directly involved was allowed to examine the president before he was wheeled into surgery. Also surprising is Webster's insistence that "the President could not very well lie down for this procedure"—a number of present-day surgeons consulted by the authors all maintained that lying prone is precisely how such a procedure would have been performed, even given FDR's paralysis. But, according to Webster, Roosevelt remained seated in his wheelchair, his head positioned against a headrest he and Craig had devised especially for the occasion.[7]* There is another possibility: that FDR was unable to lie down because, as would be documented just a few weeks later, he was suffering from orthopnea, the inability to breathe without distress while lying down—a telltale sign of left ventricular cardiac failure. Craig's primary function in the room was to correctly position Roosevelt's head.

The operation, performed under local anesthetic, went smoothly and without difficulty, according to Webster, who said that a tissue sample was sent to the lab and appeared to be a "benign epidermoid cyst."[8] Daisy, who'd declined McIntire's invitation to witness the operation, declared that "everything went off beautifully," adding gleefully that "the P., by all accounts, instructed the doctors as they worked."[9] Both she and Roosevelt were surprised that the eight stitches needed to close the incision were covered by only a light local gauze dressing, Webster noted, given that "he had already concocted a story for the press about being like the Spirit of '76, with a big bandage around his head, as he had expected such a bandage."[10]

---

*Because he was seated, rather than lying prone, and also because of his having regularly taken aspirin, an anticoagulant, for his frequently elevated temperature, the blood flow from Roosevelt's scalp was unexpectedly heavy and drenched his T-shirt, which was removed during the procedure and replaced with a fresh one from the enlisted men's quarters. Webster wrote Goldsmith that "the bloody t-shirt disappeared, much to the consternation of the head nurse" and that a sweeping investigation, during which "the entire operating crew was restricted to base for a considerable length of time," failed to locate it. "Where it is, or what happened to it, we will never know," he added. In fact, the authors located the shirt: It was taken by Pharmacist's Mate R. Harry Gunnison, who kept it hidden, and remains today in his son's possession. (John Gunnison to authors, 2007)

Roosevelt, then, already was considering how to tell reporters—and, with them, the rest of the country—about his operation. That was heightened when several of the correspondents, tipped off by someone either at the naval hospital or in FDR's entourage, had begun phoning Early after midnight, demanding details. But in an effort to downplay any hint of urgency, the president waited twenty-four hours before discussing it, and then only at the tail end of his news conference.

"Steve came in yesterday morning with blood in his eye," Roosevelt said to general laughter, describing how his press secretary repeatedly had been woken after midnight "to ask if [I] had been under the knife. That was the headline desired. And I said, 'Sure, I was under the knife. I am under the knife whenever I cut my fingernails.'" He then detailed the procedure, which he called "a preventive," adding, "I don't know why I should talk about this." Whether it was the dismissively joking tone he used, or the general disinclination of the press to question Roosevelt about his health, there were no further queries about the procedure, save one: "Mr. President, did those Naval 'gims' permit you to smoke while they did their hacking?"

"No," Roosevelt interrupted, "but I yelled for a cigarette right afterward." His audience, now convulsed in laughter, quickly moved on to another political subject, and the next day's papers, if they mentioned it at all, carried only short articles like the one that appeared in the *New York Times* under a small, one-column headline: "Went Under Surgery, Roosevelt Discloses/But It Was Only For an Old Wen On His Head, He Says."[11] The account in the *Washington Post* was but two paragraphs long and ran under the headline "Roosevelt Recovers From Minor Surgery."[12] No one in the press raised any further questions about the operation.

Although the operation had been routine, Roosevelt's recovery was slow and complicated by the flu, which continued to "hang on," as Daisy put it. Her diary over the following weeks records his constant headaches and never-ending exhaustion. By the third week in March, she was fretting that "he finds it very hard to relax, unless he just falls asleep, sometimes sitting bolt upright"—another indication of continuing orthopnea.[13] (At least one medical history of FDR contends that his orthopnea was so severe that four-inch boards were used to elevate the head of his bed, but the original source of this information is not clear.)[14] Dur-

The two principal surgeons who removed a benign growth from the president's scalp in February 1944: Dr. Winchell McKendree Craig (left), who positioned FDR's head (and may also, at a different time, have performed a highly invasive imaging procedure on Roosevelt's brain), and Dr. George V. Webster, who performed the operation. (Franklin D. Roosevelt Library; U.S. Navy Bureau of Medicine)

ing this period, Roosevelt was so ill he had taken to bed and canceled all his appointments. And Daisy wasn't the only one in the president's entourage who was concerned: Anna, who after the Teheran conference had moved into the White House at her father's request as a combination secretary/personal aide, was shocked by his appearance—the dark circles under his eyes, the tremor in his hands, the exhaustion.* Bill Hassett, his personal assistant, recorded in his diary that "every morning, in response

*FDR set only one condition for Anna's coming to work with him: Under no condition was she to keep a personal diary or journal. It's not known why he made this unusual request of his own daughter—was he aware that Daisy Suckley was preserving a record of her close relationship with the president? (Anna Roosevelt to Bernard Asbell, *Mother and Daughter*, p. 175)

to inquiry as to how he felt, a characteristic reply has been 'Rotten,' or 'Like hell.'"[15] Two days later Hassett recorded that Roosevelt had taken to bed with a temperature of 104; "Boss looks ill, color bad," he wrote.[16] And FDR's secretary, Grace Tully, grew concerned by something she had never seen before: "I found the Boss occasionally nodding over his mail or dozing a moment during dictation. . . . He would grin in slight embarrassment as he caught himself . . . but as it began to occur with increasing frequency I became seriously alarmed."[17]

In fact, Tully grew so worried that she spoke with Anna about it, only to learn that the president's daughter was equally concerned, having observed unusual periods of "quietness" in her father: "When I went a step further a few days later in speaking with Dr. McIntire," Tully wrote in her memoir, "I found that she already had talked it over with him."[18] Anna would later recall that there "must have been times when the blood was not pumping in the way it should through one hundred percent of his body. I saw this with my own eyes, but I don't think Mother saw it."[19] At Anna's insistence, McIntire agreed to bring Roosevelt to Bethesda on March 27 for a complete examination. Or, as Daisy put it, "They will be experimenting on him again at the Naval Hospital—Medicines, treatments, x-rays, etc."[20]

It was at the naval hospital on that date that Roosevelt, or so the accepted story goes, was first examined by the facility's chief of cardiology, Howard G. Bruenn, who delivered a "bombshell" diagnosis—wholly unsuspected by McIntire up to that point—that the president was in acute and severe cardiac failure. This is how Bruenn himself described it in a famous paper he wrote for *Annals of Internal Medicine* in 1970 and that, up to now, has been accepted as the "true" story of Roosevelt's final illness. But there is good reason to believe that Bruenn was not seeing the president for the first time on that March day—and that McIntire had known months earlier that the president was in cardiac distress.

Most historians have described Bruenn at the time as a "young" doctor, implying that he was virtually fresh out of medical school, but in fact he was thirty-nine, a well-known specialist with at least ten published papers in medical journals to his name. He'd spent more than a decade at Columbia Presbyterian Hospital in New York, where he was a member of the faculty, and in private practice. Born in 1905, the

Youngstown, Ohio, native graduated from Columbia University and Johns Hopkins Medical School, near the top of his class. After Pearl Harbor, he sought to join the Navy. As he later explained, "I went to the enlisting office where . . . they told me to come back after my next birthday and they would make me a lieutenant commander instead of [just] a lieutenant," which he did in November 1942.[21]* Like most physicians who entered the service, he was sent to Sampson Naval Training Hospital in Geneva, New York, for his basic training. But on April 7, 1943, McIntire sent a letter as naval surgeon general asking that Bruenn be reassigned to the National Naval Medical Center at Bethesda, where he "was made [chief] cardiologist for the hospital and consultant to the Third Naval District."[22] Just how and why he received this plum assignment was something Bruenn himself never could determine, though not for lack of trying: "After the war," he told Navy historian Jan K. Herman in 1990, "I tried to find out how the Navy had obtained information about me. [But] how I got transferred from a ward officer in a boot camp to the head of the cardiology department at Bethesda is still a mystery."[23]

Walter Trohan of the *Chicago Tribune* would later claim that Bruenn (whom he misidentified as a Boston heart specialist) "had been inducted into the Navy for the specific purpose of looking after the president's heart."[24] But this does not seem credible, given Bruenn's version of his experience when he initially tried to enlist. What seems more likely is that McIntire, on the lookout for a top-notch cardiologist, had him quickly transferred to Bethesda. Why, though, would the president's personal physician want another cardiologist nearby when in Robert Duncan he already had a top-flight heart specialist?

Back in January 1943, as Roosevelt prepared to fly to the Casablanca conference—his first trip in an airplane in more than ten years—McIntire ordered the pilot not to fly above an altitude of 9,500 feet, despite wartime precautions calling for a minimum height of 13,000 feet.[25] According to Harry Hopkins's contemporary notes, McIntire "was worried about the President's bad heart"—this, more than a year before doctors

*It is not clear why Bruenn would have been told this; there is no indication that Navy officer ranks ever carried a minimum age.

were supposed to have discovered any cardiac problems.[26] High altitude provides unique stresses and the potential for cardiac decompensation in those with existing heart disease, as the thinner air provides less oxygen to the bloodstream.[27] As the body tries to send more oxygen to the brain, the heart rate increases and, at very high altitudes, body fluid can leak into the brain or the lungs, a life-threatening condition.[28] Even at 9,000 feet, Hopkins added, "McIntire was quite disturbed about the President, who was quite pale at times."[29] Later on, when McIntire heard that they would have to fly at 13,000 feet over mountains for the rendezvous with Churchill, he objected strenuously. "Something will have to be done about that in the morning," Hopkins wrote, "for the President can't stand that height."[30]

At the end of the year, as Roosevelt prepared to fly to Asia for the Teheran conference, McIntire was even more adamant, suggesting that FDR make part of the trip by train. "Nothing over seven thousand, five hundred—and that's tops," he ordered the president's son Elliott, who reluctantly promised to speak to the pilot, Captain Otis Bryan.[31] On the way back to Washington, McIntire ruled out any effort to seek protective cloud cover, placing them at 8,000 feet, even though the flight would take them close to enemy-occupied territory.[32] In his own memoir, McIntire mentions nothing of the restrictions he'd imposed; on the contrary, he wrote that FDR could tolerate "a good ceiling."*

Clearly, then, McIntire was raising concerns about the president's heart as early as the beginning of 1943, shortly before Bruenn arrived at Bethesda. And just after his arrival, Bruenn saw a famous patient: Eleanor Roosevelt, who underwent a battery of tests—basal metabolism, EKG, complete blood work—at Bethesda on May 11, at the request of Dr. George Calver.[33] Part of the complete multispecialty medical workup was a cardiac consultation, performed by Bruenn, who also read her

*After publication of Elliott's book, McIntire wrote the editor of his hometown newspaper to claim that "there were many times when it was necessary for us to go well above 10,000 feet" and to charge that "Elliott must have picked some figures out of the air." However, Robert Sherwood's book, which contains Harry Hopkins's diary entries and was published the following year, confirms Elliott's account. (Ross McIntire to Richard Neuberger, January 17, 1947, Ross T. McIntire papers, FDRL-HP)

EKG results.[34]* Bruenn never mentioned, either in his 1970 paper or in the numerous interviews he later gave, ever having examined the First Lady, and it is not known whether he saw her subsequently. Strangely, there is no evidence he ever mentioned this fact to the president when, he says, he first saw him nearly a year later.

But on several occasions over the years, both Bruenn and McIntire placed the beginning of his treatment of FDR much earlier than the date he subsequently would assert. According to his account in 1970, Bruenn treated the president for a period of one year and two weeks. Yet, in 1946 he and McIntire exchanged letters, in preparation for the latter's book, which set another timetable entirely. "Your excellent judgment and cooperation *for a period of over two years* unquestionably helped keep the President in physical condition to perform his tremendous duties," McIntire wrote (emphasis added).[35] Bruenn's response contained only a slight correction: "As you know, it was my good fortune to be with the President *for almost two years* before he died" (emphasis added).[36] In a 1951 interview with *U.S. News & World Report*, McIntire matter-of-factly declared that "in the last couple of years, I used Howard."[37] Nearly two decades later, meeting with Anna's then-husband, Dr. James Halsted, to discuss depositing his records at Hyde Park, Bruenn gave a similar story: "He told me," Halsted wrote in his notes of their conversation, "that when he *first saw the President in late 1943* he was appalled at his condition" (emphasis added).[38] One mistake could be ascribed to a slip in memory; three, involving two different people, over a period of two decades, is much more telling.

Bruenn would later say that he examined the president with little advance notice or explanation, being told only that Roosevelt had a racking cough and an upper respiratory infection. Nor was he provided, until he insisted on them, with FDR's medical file. Observing his patient, Bruenn noted that simply "moving about caused breathlessness and puffing." Indeed, he would later recount, "I suspected something was terribly wrong as soon as I looked at him. His face was pallid and

*His findings: "No evidence of organic heart disease. Edema of extremities [swelling in her legs and/or ankles, which probably was the reason for the exam] does not appear to be of cardiac origin." (Report of Cardiac Consultation, May 11, 1943, Anna Roosevelt Halsted papers, FDRL-HP)

there was a bluish discoloration of his skin, lips and nail beds. When the hemoglobin is fully oxygenated, it is red. When it is impaired, it has a bluish tint. The bluish color meant that the tissues were not being supplied with adequate oxygen."[39]

Bruenn himself sketched out his findings in preparation for writing a paper on the president a quarter-century later. Written almost like a screenplay and titled "Scene 1," his notes read:

> Appeared slightly cyanotic [the bluish discoloration] . . . Heart enlarged, normal rhythm, no murmurs, B.P. 180/90–170/110. . . . Some rales [crackling noises indicating fluid in the lungs] throughout both bases. Under fluoroscopy—heart was "enormous." Aorta somewhat widened and torturous. . . . Appalled at what I found . . . spoke to S.G. [Surgeon General] that P. was in left ventricular failure.[40]

In his 1970 paper, Bruenn added that Roosevelt "appeared to be very tired" and that he coughed frequently during the examination but produced no sputum."[41]* The president, Bruenn declared, was in acute con-

---

*That he expressed no apparent concern over the president's elevated blood pressure is not surprising. By 1944, doctors were only beginning to understand the dangers of hypertension. Even the eminent cardiologist Paul Dudley White, who would later work with Bruenn in treating Navy Secretary Frank Knox, and who became President Dwight Eisenhower's personal physician following his heart attack, wrote in his classic 1931 textbook, *Heart Disease*, that "hypertension may be an important compensatory mechanism which should not be tampered with, even were it certain we could control it." Charles K. Friedberg, writing one year after FDR's death in his textbook *Diseases of the Heart,* declared that "people with mild benign hypertension with levels up to 210/110 need not be treated." If the issue was addressed at all, doctors usually prescribed remedies like watermelon and cucumber seeds, mistletoe, and garlic. Needless to say, there was no available medication at the time for hypertension. This contemporary misunderstanding of hypertension puts the often-criticized McIntire's failure to appreciate the consequences of the steady elevation of Roosevelt's blood pressure in a different perspective. However, 1944 also saw the publication of *Cecil's Textbook of Medicine*, which observed: "In malignant hypertension, the systolic blood pressure is exceedingly high, 200 to 250 mm, and the diastolic pressure is correspondingly elevated. . . . Congestive heart failure commonly complicate(s) the clinical picture. . . . The condition is invariably fatal." (Beeton et al., *Cecil's Textbook of Medicine,* p. 1037, quoted in Park, *The Impact of Illness on World Leaders*). Beginning on March 31, the president's systolic pressure was regularly over 200.

gestive heart failure, suffering from an enlarged heart, hypertension, and hypertensive heart disease. McIntire's response to this diagnosis, he added, was "somewhat unprintable," but he instructed Bruenn to write out a formal report with a list of recommended therapy.[42] This he did (without ever naming his patient) and addressed it to Captain Harper, Bethesda's commandant and Bruenn's superior officer. It called for

(1) Rest with nursing care for a period of 1–2 weeks.
(2) Digitalization. ¼ gram digitalis every day for 5 days; subsequently /1 gram every day.*
(3) A light, easily digestible diet. Portions are to be small and salt intake is to be restricted. Potassium Chloride in a salt shaker may be used as desired for seasoning.
(4) Sedation should be employed, to insure rest and a refreshing night's sleep.[43]

Harper's reaction to this list, Bruenn wrote in his notes, was "extraordinary"—and not in a good sense. The chief of staff pressed his top cardiologist on whether he understood the personal implications for both of them of the drastic course of treatment he was recommending—"i.e., what it might mean to my (his) future, etc."—and that Bruenn obviously was expecting his superior to endorse.[44] Clearly, though, Bruenn understood that Roosevelt's cardiac problems had grown so acute that unless he was digitalized immediately, he might not even survive until the end of his current term.

As Harper must have predicted, McIntire's reaction to Bruenn's recommendations was pretty much the same as to his diagnosis: "Summarily rejected," Bruenn wrote, with FDR's doctor telling him, "You can't do that, this is the president of the United States!"[45] On each of the next two days, Bruenn examined the president at the White House and found his symptoms "essentially unchanged." So during a group consultation, McIntire presented Bruenn's findings to Harper, Duncan, chief radiologist Charles

*Digitalis, a drug derived from the foxglove plant, strengthens the contraction of the heart muscle, slows the heart rate, and helps eliminate fluid from body tissues. It is commonly prescribed for congestive heart failure.

Behrens, and Dr. Paul Dickens, a clinical professor of medicine at George Washington University, along with an expanded list of suggestions:

> Limitation of daily activity must be emphasized.
> Cigarettes [FDR smoked two packs a day of unfiltered Camels] were to be curtailed.
> Trial of aminophylline [a drug for treating bronchial asthma], Grains, iii 1 tablet, enteric coated, three times a day, after meals. [This was never given, for fear of causing even higher blood pressure.]
> Phenobarbital [a barbiturate to help him sleep], Grain, ¼ of Thesodate [theoboromine for bronchitis], three times a day.
> Period of rest for 1 hr. after meals.
> Light passive massage.
> Dinner in quarters at White House (i.e., no guests or working dinners).
> A minimum of 10 hr sleep.
> No swimming in the pool.
> Diet: 2,600 calories, moderately low in fat.
> The use of mild laxatives, if necessary, to avoid straining.[46]

Bruenn also called for a battery of medical tests, including—significantly—a prostate exam. There is no record of the results, and Bruenn, either in his notes or in his 1970 paper on FDR's illness, never mentioned anything about his prostate. Another test he called for was an examination of Roosevelt's eye grounds—the retinal blood vessels—for signs of hypertension. McIntire, as an eye, ear, nose, and throat specialist, would have performed this. Again, there is no record of his findings, but in his 1951 interview, McIntire claimed that "the retinal vessels never showed any change. They looked perfectly normal, even the last time I looked at them."[47]* On March 31, 1944, yet another group consultation took place at the White House, this time with the addition of two eminent physicians who were honorary Navy consultants: James A. Paullin of Atlanta, a former president of the American Medical Association, and

*Interestingly, Bruenn's notes mention a suggested radiologic evaluation of the left frontal and ethmoid sinus, the area behind the pigmented lesion, as well as McIntire's "thick secretions" from the latter, but no mention of them appears in his 1970 paper.

Frank Lahey, founder of Boston's Lahey Clinic and arguably the most famous surgeon in America, followed by a second conference the following morning.* According to Bruenn's notes, there was "lots of discussion" and "beating around the bush" on the part of the noted doctors, as well as "much skepticism despite the overwhelming evidence."[48] Significantly, Lahey "was particularly interested in the gastrointestinal tract"—a curious request, given that the original complaint had been bronchial, the issue at hand was cardiac failure, and Bruenn had offered no gastrointestinal diagnosis—"but admitted that no surgical procedure was indicated." Still, he said, Lahey believed "the situation was serious enough to warrant acquainting the President with the full facts."[49] As for Paullin, he agreed with Bruenn's diagnosis but did not believe the heart failure was serious enough to require digitalization—whose possible side effects included lethargy, heart palpitations, hallucinations, and blurry eyesight—and instead "advocated no specific therapy at this time."[50] But Bruenn said he held his ground: "Despite everything else, the need for digitalization, I thought was over-riding. Said so to Admiral McIntire. Told him I literally didn't want to have anything to do with the situation unless."[51] So Lahey and Paullin "went to see the President the next morning and examined him. When they came back, they agreed that I could go ahead with the digitalization."[52] As for the other recommendations, a compromise list was decided on that limited Roosevelt's smoking to six cigarettes a day, his drinking to a cocktail before dinner, and his food intake to 1,800 calories, and placed sharp restrictions on his work schedule, including setting aside two hours each afternoon for relaxation.[53]

If Lahey's insistence that the president be informed of his situation was followed, then FDR seems to have been less than candid with Daisy. "He said they took X-rays & all sorts of tests, found nothing drastically wrong, but one sinus clogged up," she recorded. "But they are going to put him on a strict diet, a good beginning."[54] A week later, though, when she learned that Lahey and Paullin were scheduled to examine him, Daisy

*In 1943, when Roosevelt appointed Joseph Davies to be ambassador to the Soviet Union, the president instructed him to first undergo a thorough physical examination. But instead of sending him to the celebrated Mayo Clinic, where his son James and top aide, Harry Hopkins, had both been operated on, Roosevelt instead told Davies to go to the Lahey Clinic. (Keith Eubank, *Summit at Teheran*, p. 71)

found herself skeptical of FDR's rosy reassurances. "I'm worried," she wrote, "for there must be something definitely wrong."[55]

If Roosevelt was less than candid with Daisy, McIntire was downright disingenuous with the entire country. As with the leak of information from Bethesda on the wen operation, rumors were spreading in Washington that the president was seriously ill. So McIntire appeared in Steve Early's office on April 4 to deliver what a front-page *New York Times* article labeled "an unprecedented report to the press" to discuss Roosevelt's physical checkup. "When we got through," McIntire declared, "we decided that for a man of 62-plus, we had very little to argue about" and that his health was "satisfactory"—this, less than a week after the president of the United States had been found to be in severe, life-threatening congestive heart failure. Questions from the reporters about the examination, which McIntire claimed was nothing more than an annual physical, revolved around FDR's diet, weight, and bronchitis. All the president needed, he said, was a little sunshine and "then I wouldn't complain."[56] *Time* wrote that Roosevelt, at his own press conference, "pooh-poohed his illness," which the magazine described as "a mild case of bronchitis, going into its third week," but added ominously that the president "continued to cough softly but persistently."[57]

Meanwhile, the regimen of digitalis had done the trick. After ten days of medication, Bruenn noted, "the results were spectacular. His lungs, which initially had been congested with a small amount of fluid, were now clear. His heart, which was enlarged, had diminished in size. His coughing had stopped and he was sleeping soundly at night."[58] When this was presented to Lahey and Paullin at another meeting, Bruenn wrote in his notes, "these results were admitted (grudgingly!! Paullin!!!)" and accompanied by "McIntire's wink at me!"[59]

The hypertension had in no way been curbed, of course—in fact, it continued to escalate to frighteningly high levels—but never again was Roosevelt reported to be in frank, congestive heart failure. And, from that point, Bruenn joined McIntire in serving as the president's primary physician, seeing him on a daily basis and accompanying him on trips. Yet "at no time," Bruenn later wrote, "did the President ever comment on the frequency of these visits or question the reason for the electrocardiograms and the other laboratory tests that were performed from time to time."[60] Indeed, he told Jan Herman in 1990, throughout the time he was treating FDR, "he never asked me a question about the medications I was giving him, what his blood pressure was, nothing. He was not interested. He had a job to do and the hell with everything else."[61] That, at least, was the accepted story for thirty years, until the discovery of Daisy Suckley's diary disclosed that Roosevelt was far more concerned with the state of his health than Bruenn always claimed.

Despite the president's improvement, wrote Bruenn, "it was decided that it would be wise to provide a period of rest and relaxation away from Washington." But the original plan to visit Guantanamo Bay in Cuba had to be changed, he wrote, "because of the War, the state of his health and other considerations."[62] However, material on file at Hyde Park tells a very different story—one that, yet again, suggests McIntire knew that Roosevelt was seriously ill even before Bruenn's reported first visit.

In fact, Roosevelt had planned to hold another summit conference with Winston Churchill on April 5 in Bermuda to finalize plans for Operation Overlord, the Allied invasion of Europe, scheduled for D-Day two months later. Yet on March 20, a week *before* his exam at Bethesda—the exam that supposedly prompted the urgent need for a vacation—FDR wrote to Churchill canceling the trip for health reasons in favor of a lengthy getaway for rest and relaxation (and rewriting his cable from a formal demurral in favor of a more folksy message):

> *Washington (via U.S. Navy)*
> *March 20, 1944, 6:30 p.m.*
> *Personal and Secret. From the President for the Former Naval Person. [Churchill had previously served as First Lord of the Admiralty]*
>
> ~~*Replying to your 624 and in reference to your suggestion that we have a staff meeting on the Teheran scale in Bermuda about the fifth of April, it is not now possible for me to meet that date.*~~
>
> ~~*Not having had any opportunity for relaxation since my recent attack of grippe which has not been more completely eliminated leaves me from time to time with a temperature.*~~
>
> ~~*My doctor considers it*~~ *I am very angry with myself. The old attack of grippe having hung on and on, leaving me with an intermittent temperature, Ross decided about a week ago that it is necessary for me to take a*

> *complete rest of about two to three weeks in a suitable climate which I am definitely planning to do at the end of the month. I see no way out and I am furious.*[63]

Churchill cabled back the following day regretting the cancellation but hoping that "you are still planning your visit here for the great event after you are fully recovered," meaning that Roosevelt originally planned to be in England for D-Day, though he never made the trip. But as FDR's cable demonstrates, McIntire had decided by March 13—two weeks before the comprehensive examination at Bethesda—that the president needed to get away for a lengthy "rest only" trip. At a May 6 press conference, Roosevelt confirmed that he'd planned to stay at Guantanamo, but claimed "off the record" that the reason for the change in plans was that "Cuba is absolutely lousy with anarchists, murderers, et cetera, and a lot of prevaricators."[64]

Yet Bruenn's diagnosis of acute heart failure must have made McIntire realize that even such a short trip via airplane—the schedule laid out by Mike Reilly, head of Roosevelt's Secret Service detail, called for two three-hour flights, one from Washington to West Palm Beach, Florida, and another, leaving several hours later, to Cuba—might endanger the president's life. And so a call was made to Bernard Baruch, the venerable financier and longtime government adviser, who had long sought to host FDR for an extended stay at his 23,000-acre South Carolina estate, Hobcaw Barony, to which the president could easily travel the 500-mile distance entirely by train. That he needed rest was obvious: Daisy Suckley recorded that FDR was barely functioning as president: "He gets up about noon, goes to his desk in his study for lunch, works with GGT [Grace Tully], goes back to bed at 6"[65]—meaning that Roosevelt, just weeks before the Allied invasion of Europe, was working no more than four hours a day. Two days later she added that the president's curtailed schedule also included a ninety-minute afternoon nap.[66]

Roosevelt arrived at Hobcaw on April 9 and, by his own admission, devoted himself to little else but rest on what Merriman Smith of the United Press later noted was "the longest actual vacation he had had since becoming president."[67] Certainly he followed a pure vacation schedule, rising at 11:30 a.m., followed by lunch at 1, a two-hour nap, dinner, and a 9 p.m. bedtime; the president, in other words, was sleeping more than sixteen hours each day.[68] Which, to be honest, is all he really wanted to do: "Sleep and sleep," he replied when asked what he wanted to do at Hobcaw, "twelve hours a night and let the world hang."[69] In a letter he wrote to Daisy upon his arrival but never sent, FDR said, "I am really feeling 'no good'—don't want to do anything & want to sleep all the time."[70]

Back in Washington, Anna's husband, John Boettiger, had gotten what he believed was a thorough briefing from McIntire about his father-in-law's health. "Had a long talk with Ross about OM [Old Man]," he wrote his wife. "I think he is OK, but I want to tell you how I feel about the long pull."[71] Yet, if McIntire was willing to discuss the president's health with his son-in-law, he wasn't prepared to extend the same courtesy to FDR's wife. Quite the opposite: Eleanor actually had to prevail on Steve Early to send McIntire a telegram at Hobcaw saying that the First Lady "would be most grateful for some word . . . about the President. She ha(s) heard nothing and [is] anxious for information."[72] It's not clear whether McIntire ever responded.

Down at Hobcaw, Roosevelt was getting the quiet and solitude he said he so desired—even as the timetable to the great Allied invasion of the European mainland was ticking away. "In a word, I have rested," FDR told a press conference upon his departure a month later. "I have had a very quiet time. Been out in the sun as much as possible. Done some fishing."[73]* The three wire service reporters who constituted the White House press pool were kept far away with orders from the Secret Service "to 'stay out of the old man's way.' He wanted seclusion, and lots of it," recalled Merriman Smith.[74] But the veteran journalist also noted that "it was Mr. Roosevelt's intense desire for seclusion that made the reporters wonder why. He did not take to fishing as he had a few years before, and was content to catch catfish off a dock, when Roosevelt, the deep-sea angler, would have scorned such a humble pastime in his better

*Roosevelt also told the reporters he'd come to Hobcaw because none of the other locations he wanted—including Sugar Loaf Mountain, the Blue Ridge Mountains and Gettysburg—had been given security clearance. (FDR press conference, May 6, 1944)

physical days." And, Smith added, FDR "sunned himself behind a special glass windbreak on the bayside terrace of Baruch's handsome old colonial home."[75]

The insistence on privacy was so strict, according to Smith, that when he published a lengthy story on Roosevelt's stay, full of inside information, that ran on the day of FDR's return to Washington, the president was "incensed" and ordered the FBI to find out whom the correspondent had bribed to learn the details of his fishing expeditions. The astonished Smith explained to Steve Early that Roosevelt's "fishing guide dropped by the hotel virtually every night and volunteered to the whole lobby the details of the day. Also, Baruch invited quite a few people . . . to meet the President at Hobcaw and they always let us know about it." That cut short the FBI probe, but it left Smith wondering: "Why was Mr. Roosevelt so suddenly touchy about publicity?"[76]

The prolonged rest at Hobcaw certainly did Roosevelt some good: Bruenn's notes record the disappearance of his cough, an increase in his appetite, a lessening of the rales in his lungs, and an "absence of cardiac [failure] symptoms."[77] But the cardiologist also noted a continuing escalation of FDR's blood pressure—though, in a reversal of the normal pattern, his pressure was higher in the morning than at night.* For example, on April 19 he woke with a pressure of 230/126–128; an hour later, after breakfast, it was 210/106. For unexplained reasons, Bruenn took another reading just five minutes later and found it had risen to 218/112. But in the evening, Roosevelt's pressure was at its lowest level of the day, a still alarming 190/90.[78] Similar readings were taken throughout the president's monthlong stay at Hobcaw; on April 23, doctors McIntire, Bruenn, John Harper, and Paul Dickens agreed in a phone conference to increase Roosevelt's dosage of digitalis.[79]

Five days later Roosevelt faced an unexpected crisis: On March 28 Bruenn had noted "occasional abdominal distress and distention and

*Further evidence that Roosevelt was kept fully informed of the specific details of his condition appears in Daisy's diary: "He says the blood pressure is acting queerly & against the rules; up in the morning, after a good night, instead of down, as one would expect." This is precisely the observation that appears in Bruenn's notes. (Daisy Suckley diary, June 22, 1944; Howard Bruenn notes, April 19–20, 1944)

sudden spells of profuse perspiration," discomfort that lasted for two weeks.[80] Now, late on the afternoon of April 28, FDR began "to complain of abdominal pain and tenderness associated with slight nausea."* Despite treatment with injections of codeine, the pain persisted for three days, disappeared, then returned the following day. Daisy, who—at FDR's request—had come down to Hobcaw on May 4, noted in her diary that he "feels good-for-nothing" and that "they don't know what is the matter with him," adding suspiciously: "I wonder if perhaps they don't want to tell him."[81] Three weeks after his return to Washington, according to Bruenn, an X-ray showed the president had cholesterol gallstones; the only treatment noted was that he was placed on "a low-fat diet" of 1,800 calories, which was also intended to induce weight loss.[82] Interestingly, there is no indication that the abdominal attack was treated or examined by anyone other than the four doctors at Hobcaw, even though James Paullin—a specialist in internal medicine—was in Atlanta, just 130 miles away. Bruenn later insisted that the nature of the attack was such that he felt comfortable treating it himself, without outside consultations. But Dr. David Preston Boyd, a noted Lahey Clinic surgeon, wrote in his official history of the famed Boston facility that it was "beyond the outposts of reason for Lahey not to almost certainly have been consulted when Roosevelt suffered an acute abdomen."[83]**

Roosevelt himself was not quite as dismissive of the problem, though, telling Harold Ickes upon his return that he'd "had some trouble with his colon, which at first he thought was a growth. Then it suddenly moved to his left side under his heart. It was very painful. Then, without notice, it moved over to his right side, where it again caused him pain. At

*There is a gap in Bruenn's contemporary notes between April 23 and April 28. That's because he was in Washington at the bedside of Navy Secretary Frank Knox, who'd been stricken with a heart attack on the 23rd while attending the funeral in New Hampshire of his longtime publishing partner, John A. Muehling. Knox suffered a series of attacks over the next few days and died on the 28th at his home. Also in attendance was Paul Dudley White; though Bruenn never acknowledged the connection, it's not unlikely that he discussed Roosevelt's case with the famed heart specialist. (*New York Times*, April 29, 1944; Frank Knox medical records, Ross McIntire papers, FDRL-HP)

**Boyd did not complete the manuscript before his death and it was never published. But he did show his chapter on Lahey's connection to FDR to Dr. Harry Goldsmith.

any rate, this had the effect of persuading him that it could not be a growth. Then suddenly it disappeared and he had no pain."[84] Either Roosevelt was being disingenuous with Ickes, or he was unaware that his melanoma may have metastasized to his abdomen.

Daisy's presence at Hobcaw also puts the lie to Bruenn's repeated assertion that Roosevelt showed not the slightest interest in, or awareness of, his condition, or even who the cardiologist was and why he was examining him every day. FDR gave her fragments of two letters he had started but never finished. In one of them, the president wrote, "I forgot to tell you that Dr. Bruin [*sic*] came down, too—He is one of the best heart men—Tho' my own [heart] is definitely better—does queer things still."[85] The following day, she noted, Roosevelt told her that "the trouble is evidently with his heart—the diastole & systole are not working properly in unison—but there is definite improvement." Later that day, after Bruenn had flown on ahead to Washington, Daisy "had a good talk with the P. about himself—He said he discovered that the doctors had not agreed together about what to tell him, so that he found out that they were not telling *him* the *whole* truth & that he was evidently more sick than they said!" Added Daisy scornfully: "It is foolish of them to attempt to put anything over on *him!*"[86]

Meanwhile, McIntire publicly pronounced himself "perfectly satisfied" with Roosevelt's health, which he called "excellent in all respects" and better than average for a man his age. "We have gained everything we hoped to gain in these four weeks' rest," he told the White House press corps.[87] Others, like Merriman Smith, were not so sure. At his May 5 press conference, called to explain why he did not attend Frank Knox's funeral (Ross McIntire's orders, he said), Roosevelt "did not look particularly healthy," the reporter observed. "He was fairly well tanned, but his color was muddy."[88] And, on his return to the White House, the president instructed General Edwin "Pa" Watson, his appointments secretary, to keep visitors to an absolute minimum. Under his new reduced workload of four hours or less a day, he would see visitors only between 11 a.m. and 1 p.m., have no business lunches, and then sign papers for no more than two hours in the afternoon, after a ninety-minute nap, with the weekends entirely free of work.[89] Harold Ickes, taking note of this in his diary, suggested that "he must have been in much worse shape than I had realized [before going to Hobcaw], but everyone insists that he is much better now. Bernie Baruch, who lunched with me yesterday, said that if FDR would take care of himself, he could go through the coming campaign and be elected, but only in that event."[90]

Life magazine, in an effort to ascertain the facts, assigned reporter Jeanne Perkins to write a profile of Ross McIntire. The project was temporarily shelved after D-Day (it ran in the July 31 issue), but not before she posed a series of questions to the surgeon general in writing and received a wholly misleading response from his secretary:

> *Here are the answers to your several questions in regard to the President:*
>
> *1. No mention may be made of the number of cigarettes the President smokes in a day.*
>
> *2. The sick days during the past twelve (12) years have been very few in number. There have been only two occasions when he has been in bed over a period of ten days during that time. If he had been operating on a Civil Service basis, he would have a great backlog of sick leave.*
>
> *3. The annual physical examination for the senior naval officers takes from two to four hours. The President's annual physical examination is the same as that of the senior officers.*
>
> *4. The final checkup on his last physical examination is extremely satisfactory.*
>
> *5. Specific figures in regard to blood pressure, eyes, ears, etc. are never given. Such matters are considered a patient's personal affair.*
>
> *6. He wears glasses when he wishes to see long distances and when he is going to read for a long period of time.*
>
> *7. Considering the difference in age, his past physical examination is equally as good as the one made on him twelve years ago.*[91]

Life's sister publication, *Time*, reported that newsmen who were seeing Roosevelt for the first time in a month after his return from Hobcaw "were struck by the realization that Franklin Roosevelt at 62 is an old man." Still, the magazine reassured its readers, "His health, it appeared, was going to be all right now—provided he does not overwork."[92]

Still the rumors continued: Merriman Smith's editors at United Press presented him with "two files of reports and tips from Rochester

[Minnesota, site of the Mayo Clinic] and Boston [site of the Lahey Clinic]" claiming "the president had been 'hospitalized' at both places while we were in the South."[93] He later wrote that Steve Early actually thanked him for filing that article to which FDR had so strenuously objected because "it showed where he was every minute. It gave a perfect answer to the stories about his being in the hospital."[94]

But some of the stories came a lot closer to the truth. At a June 8 press conference (which was largely ignored because it took place two days after D-Day), McIntire was asked directly about "a rumor that there was quite a bit of trouble with [FDR's] heart, maybe." The doctor gave a firm, total, and completely false denial: "No," he said. "I have been very factual with you. I have given the exact—" At which point Steve Early quickly interrupted: "I don't think it is a good thing to start denying rumors." Whereupon the assembled reporters simply dropped the matter.[95]

Nor did the journalists press McIntire on his assertion that, at 180 pounds, Roosevelt was lighter than at any time since entering the White House. "The President says it's a fine weight and he's going to stay there," the doctor said. To the growing horror of those around him, that was a vow Franklin Roosevelt would prove unable to keep. But the president had a more pressing domestic concern: He was about to seek another four years in the White House. It was a campaign that some of those close to him—including a top doctor and a trusted aide—tried to convince him not to undertake.

Not Planning for the Succession

CHAPTER 9

By the middle of 1944, Franklin Roosevelt was a president with seriously compromised health, whose condition was only worsening. Few Americans understood this; not even the disclosure of his heavily abridged working schedule—Harold Ickes wrote in his diary that FDR was scheduling too few appointments "to transact any meaningful business"—persuaded them that Roosevelt was not fully functioning as president. Most people doubtless were set at ease by the public reassurances of *New York Times* columnist Anne O'Hare McCormick, who wrote that "according to the reporters who have seen him, the President comes back to Washington bronzed, rested and fit," and noted that "only a man of extraordinary and temperamental resilience could have weathered as buoyantly as he has done the continual and ever-accelerating crisis he has presided over."[1]

That Roosevelt, having already served longer than any other president in history, was preparing to seek a fourth term was universally acknowledged, especially after the Allied invasion on June 6 and the successful push eastward across Nazi-occupied Europe. Secretary of Labor Frances Perkins wrote in her memoir that no one in the cabinet feared that the president's health would keep him from running again.[2] Any trepidation those around him felt was unrelated to his health. Ickes and James Forrestal, who had succeeded Knox as secretary of the Navy, agreed that Roosevelt would probably not serve a full fourth term. "I don't necessarily mean that the president will die in office or become so incapacitated that he might not be capable of carrying on," Ickes wrote in his diary. "He might very well resign. I believe that he is sick of domestic affairs and after the war would like to devote himself exclusively to the world situation."[3] (Roosevelt himself would tell Daisy just days before his death that he was prepared "to retire next year," once the United Nations was established,[4] and reportedly said the same thing to the Democratic national chairman, Robert Hannegan.)[5]

Although, unlike four years earlier, no Democrat stepped forward as a prospective candidate in the expectation that FDR might not run, there were those who thought he was no longer fit to serve another term. Aubrey Williams, Harry Hopkins's former deputy and the founding director of the National Youth Administration, after dining with FDR at the White House in late March, publicly declared that the president "looked so tired and worn that I was shocked," and added that he'd gotten "the distinct impression that [Roosevelt] wouldn't run again, although he didn't say so directly."[6] The president, as usual, played it coy—even with Daisy, with whom he normally was much more candid. When she asked him in May whether he'd decided on a running mate, he replied, "I haven't even decided if I will run myself." Daisy, taking him at his word, then asked what the deciding factor would be. "What will decide me," he told her, "will be the way I feel in a couple of months. If I know I am not going to be able to carry on for another four years, it wouldn't be fair to the American people to run for another term."[7]*

*In that same conversation, Roosevelt proposed as a possible successor Henry J. Kaiser, the West Coast industrialist who today is considered the father of U.S. shipbuilding and who had impressed FDR with his ability to quickly turn out so-called Liberty ships—cargo vessels that took his shipyard just forty-five days to produce. Roosevelt told Daisy he felt sure he could "persuade the country to elect" Kaiser. He changed his mind after Sam Rosenman informed him that Kaiser had publicly proposed a national 10 percent sales tax, which FDR's union supporters bitterly opposed. (Geoffrey Ward, *Closest Companion*, p. 302)

His wife, however, knew better: "I knew without asking," recalled Eleanor, "that as long as the war was on, it was a foregone conclusion that Franklin, if he was well enough, would run again."[8] And as FDR himself would tell his eldest son, James: "The people elected me their leader and I can't quit in the middle of the war."[9] Yet a touch of fatalism had begun to creep into Roosevelt's thoughts and would grow more frequent over the coming months. Barely a week after returning from Hobcaw, the supposedly reinvigorated FDR said to Jonathan Daniels, one of his press aides, during a discussion about presidential power: "Here is something you ought to write if I should pop off."[10]

Still, the president's determination to run didn't stop some of those closest to him from trying to somehow persuade or pressure him not to make the race. Ed Flynn, the longtime Bronx political boss and FDR confidant who had just stepped down as chairman of the Democratic National Committee, met with Roosevelt after his return from Hobcaw and was so shocked by his appearance, as well as a most atypical sense of apathy, that he begged Eleanor to convince him not to run.[11] Flynn's assessment concurred with that of Merriman Smith, who wrote of Roosevelt's news conferences during this period: "He became listless and poor of voice. He reached the point where he lost enthusiasm for denouncing certain irritant correspondents as liars.* He, however, became increasingly quarrelsome about petty things. Reporters in the back of his office began to have difficulty hearing his once rich and powerful voice."[12] Even "Pa" Watson, his trusted personal aide, complained privately that the president "just doesn't seem to give a damn."[13]

Only one top adviser, however, decided to confront Roosevelt directly over his plans for a fourth term. Benjamin V. Cohen was widely acclaimed as one of the architects of the New Deal and the "top brain" of FDR's Brains Trust; in 1944 he was serving as general counsel to James F. Byrnes in the Office of Economic Stabilization. Cohen sent Roosevelt

*Two years earlier, in a famous incident at one of his press conferences, Roosevelt had shocked even the assembled correspondents when he displayed a Nazi Iron Cross decoration and said it should be presented to John O'Donnell, the fiercely anti-FDR columnist of the *New York Daily News*. (Betty Houchin Winfield, *FDR and the News Media*, p. 68)

a personal memorandum arguing "soberly, and possibly too gloomily" against a fourth term—not out of any concern for the president's health, which he did not raise, but because he felt another term "would be an anticlimax," in which "political conditions" would make it impossible for FDR's postwar ideas to be "accepted or even fairly understood." Cohen proposed that Roosevelt broker a bipartisan deal in which the two presidential nominees would agree to continue his war policies and work to establish the United Nations, thus avoiding the kind of crippling battle that Woodrow Wilson had faced over the League of Nations. To cap it off, Cohen argued, "both parties [would] pledge themselves and their nominees to the support of the suggestion that President Roosevelt accept an invitation to become the Chief Executive Officer of the new international organization to maintain the peace."[14]

The idea of heading up the UN was one to which Roosevelt, as noted above, was attracted. But as for leaving office at the end of his third term, the president shot that one down in two brief sentences:

> *Dear Ben:*
>
> *That is a tremendously interesting analysis—and I think a very just one.*
>
> *You have only left out one matter—and that is the matter of my own feelings!*[15]

The question of running for reelection, in other words, was one that Roosevelt would decide for himself—and, in fact, had long ago decided. (Though Daisy, as late as June 20, still believed that "the P. doesn't know if he will run or not.")[16] And he was not interested in any input or suggestions from anyone else, no matter how close a friend or trusted an adviser.

That included doctors, as well. In an interview with Dr. Hugh E. Evans in 1993, Howard Bruenn said "thank God" no one asked his opinion on whether Roosevelt should make the race,[17] adding in a separate interview that had he been asked, he frankly would have advised against it.[18]* *Life* magazine asked McIntire directly whether Roosevelt could "survive a

---

*Bruenn, it should be noted, also insisted the president "was loathe to run" and had to be talked into it by those around him—a claim that simply is not backed up by the historical facts. (Hugh E. Evans, *The Hidden Campaign*, pp. 61, 63)

fourth term"; surprisingly, the magazine reported, "on this question Dr. McIntire will not commit himself," though he did maintain that "the President's health is excellent. I can say that unqualifiedly."[19] After FDR's death, however, McIntire would claim that, in private discussions with the president, he did not hold back on "stating my fears" about the prospect of four more years in office. However, he insisted he told Roosevelt that "with proper care and strict adherence to rules, I gave it as my best judgment that his chances of winning through to 1948 were *good*" (emphasis in original).[20] But in a blatant postdated exercise in covering himself, McIntire added that he had also told the president that "unless he slowed down, I would not be answerable for the consequences."[21]

In a letter to the *New York Times* in 1974, Anna's current husband, Dr. James Halsted, conceded that "from a *purely medical standpoint* . . . it is fair to say that he should not have run in 1944" (emphasis in original).[22] And James Roosevelt, in his memoir, declared: "I never have been reconciled to the fact that Father's doctors did not flatly forbid him to run"[23]—a most surprising statement, given that he more than anyone should have understood that no one could flatly forbid Franklin Roosevelt to do anything, let alone run for reelection.

Still, one of FDR's doctors *did* try to send a strong message that he should not run: Frank Lahey. And he recorded that message in a private memorandum whose contents remained a closely guarded secret for more than four decades.* Written July 10, 1944, it read:

> I wish to record the following information regarding my opinions in relation to President Roosevelt's condition and to have them on record in

*Lahey entrusted this memorandum to his business manager and executor, Linda Strand, who had formally witnessed it, with instructions that it be published only if he should ever come under public criticism for his medical treatment of FDR. In 1983 Dr. Harry Goldsmith persuaded her that the document should be made public, but her law firm, to which she had given the memorandum, refused to turn it over. With Goldsmith's backing, Strand filed suit to recover the memorandum in a case that went all the way to the Massachusetts Supreme Court; in 1986 that court ruled unanimously that the condition set by Lahey for disclosure had been satisfied and that the document should be returned to her. Although Strand subsequently gave the memorandum to Goldsmith, it remained unpublished until 2005, when *Newsweek* ran a story containing lengthy excerpts. ("History: A Roosevelt Mystery," *Newsweek*, April 11, 2005)

the event there comes any criticism of me at a later date. I want to do this after having seen him in consultation as a private record.

On Saturday July 8, I talked with Admiral McIntire in my capacity as one of the group of three, Admiral McIntire, Dr. James Paullin of Atlanta, Georgia, and myself, who saw President Roosevelt in consultation and who have been over his physical examination, x-rays, and laboratory findings concerning his physical condition. I have reviewed all of his x-rays and findings over the past years and compared them with all the present findings and am recording my opinion concerning Mr. Roosevelt's condition and capacities now. I am recording these opinions in the light of having informed Admiral McIntire Saturday afternoon July 8, 1944 that I did not believe that, if Mr. Roosevelt was elected President again, he had the physical capacity to complete a term. I told him that, as a result of activities in his trip to Russia* he had been in a state which was, if not in heart failure, at least on the verge of it, that this was the result of high blood pressure he has had now for a long time, plus a question of a coronary damage. With this in mind it was my opinion that over the four years of another term with its burdens, he would again have heart failure and be unable to complete it. Admiral McIntire was in agreement with this.

In addition to that I stated that it was not my duty to advise concerning whether or not such a term was undertaken, but to inform Admiral McIntire, as his family Physician[,] my opinion concerning his capacity to do it and that it was my opinion that it was Admiral McIntire's duty to inform him concerning his capacity.

In addition to the above I have told Admiral McIntire that I feel strongly that if he does accept another term, he had a very serious responsibility concerning who is the Vice President. Admiral McIntire agreed with this and has, he states, so informed Mr. Roosevelt.

I am putting this on record, I am asking that it be witnessed, sealed and placed in safekeeping. It is to be opened and utilized only in the event that there might be criticism of me should this later eventuate and the criticisms be directed toward me for not having made this public. As I see my duty as a physician, I cannot violate my professional position nor

*The only trip Roosevelt ever made to Russia was the summit meeting at Yalta, which took place six months after this memo was written. Lahey probably meant the Teheran conference, which took place the previous November.

possible professional confidence, but I do wish to be on record concerning possible later criticism.

The memo is strikingly definitive: the president's personal doctor and one of the country's leading specialists concur that he probably would not survive a fourth term. The memo, written knowingly for posterity, is silent on the subject of cancer. Why doesn't Lahey mention it? Skeptics can point to this as an indication that there was no known malignancy. Problem is, apart from the medical evidence already cited, this also flies in the face of repeated credible firsthand reports from reputable physicians, several of them closely associated with Lahey, who all quote him as definitely reporting that the president had cancer.

Moreover, even Lahey's mention that he had just advised McIntire that the president was "if not in heart failure, at least on the verge of it," makes no sense, either. After all, as is well documented, Lahey had been apprised of Bruenn's definitive diagnosis more than two months earlier and had then personally examined Roosevelt in order to confirm it.

Most likely, Ross McIntire and Frank Lahey—two of the most famous doctors in America—came to a meeting of minds. The two men worked together, not only on the president, but in administrative matters regarding Navy medicine; there was mutual respect and accommodation.* But Lahey was a man who worried about his reputation and always felt the need to "cover" himself. A few months later, when a newspaper reporter approached him to ask whether he had seen the president professionally,

*The depth of Lahey's feelings about McIntire are evident in a letter Lahey sent to an Albert Maisel in January 1945. "Of all the group [of surgeons general]," he wrote, "the most satisfactory man to work with is Admiral McIntire. He has a breadth of vision that is refreshing. . . . I have never known a more completely unselfish individual in such a high and influential position. He wants nothing for himself. . . . His modesty is amazing. His understanding is complete and at no time have I ever known him to trade upon the fact that he is the President's physician. . . . All feel as I do that the Navy and the Country is blessed with such a Surgeon General. If you think these are unduly laudatory remarks, as you well may, you could easily find out that I am quite a hard-boiled person." Lahey then sent an FYI copy of the letter to McIntire's secretary, Claire Murphy, with instructions that she "destroy it and not show it to Admiral McIntire." It's unlikely that this is what he actually meant for her to do; indeed, she kept the letter and deposited it in McIntire's papers. (Ross McIntire papers, FDRL-HP)

A December 1942 photo of Ross McIntire (top right) with one of several panels of distinguished medical consultants on whom he called throughout World War II, all of which were chaired by Frank Lahey (front row, center). Widely considered the world's most famous surgeon, Lahey in July 1944 wrote a secret "for the record" memorandum warning that Roosevelt would not survive a fourth term. The memo only came to light a half-century later after a fierce legal battle. (U.S. Navy photo)

he refused to answer and fired off an official "for the record" letter to McIntire giving his account of the incident. McIntire may well have agreed to let Lahey put his judgment on a fourth term in writing, on the condition that it be kept secret unless needed to counter public criticism much later on. The president's heart trouble was already becoming widely known; Roosevelt's family and top aides knew of it, and some reporters had already begun questioning McIntire and Steve Early about it directly, albeit tentatively. Cancer, on the other hand, remained FDR's deadly secret, not even to be hinted at and certainly never be acknowledged in writing. Even in 1944, with the war reaching its critical phase, the idea that Roosevelt had cancer might have been enough to derail his reelection. The lengths to which the White House would go to squelch even the slightest rumor of cancer will be seen in the next chapter.

That Lahey would take part in such an arrangement might seem like the stuff of "conspiracy theory" thinking. But consider that Dr. David Boyd, a trustee of the Lahey Clinic and former president of the American Society of Thoracic Surgery, would write, in his unpublished history of the Lahey Clinic, of his surprise that "a man as resolute as Frank H. Lahey . . . would go along with this outright deception"—by which he meant that the oath of secrecy taken by Roosevelt's doctors, including Lahey, transcended their professional responsibility.[24] Moreover, he wrote:

> To contemplate Frank H. Lahey as a partner to a cover-up is almost beyond the capability of those who knew him best and are still here to testify; but all can see that the circumstances were unique. That Lahey would certify as fit and well a man . . . in whom he found a terminal malignancy is to pull the snout of reason. But he may have done it.[25]

At any rate, just one day after Lahey wrote his memorandum advising the president not to run again, Roosevelt sent a letter to Bob Hannegan informing him that "reluctantly, but as a good soldier . . . I will accept and serve in the office, if I am so ordered by the Commander in Chief of us all—the sovereign people of the United States."* That set off one of the great battles in American political history, which ended in the selection of Senator Harry S. Truman as FDR's running mate.

Despite Lahey's warning that, in the event he chose to run, Roosevelt consider very carefully his choice for vice president, by all accounts FDR's first inclination was to keep Henry Wallace on the ticket. It was a decision even more fervently shared by Eleanor, who planned to devote one of her "My Day" syndicated newspaper columns to praising Wallace—but her husband, perhaps sensing trouble ahead, told her to "hold it till after the convention."[26] Sure enough, there was widespread opposition

---

*In a signal of the theme of the coming campaign, the Republican ticket of Thomas E. Dewey and John W. Bricker charged that Roosevelt was using his status as commander in chief "as a pretext to perpetuate himself in political office." (*New York Times*, July 13, 1944)

within the party to Wallace, dating back to Roosevelt's decision to select him four years earlier; despite his loyalty to FDR, the general feeling among most party leaders was that Wallace "was not a fit man to be president of the United States," as party treasurer Edwin Pauley put it.[27]

Unlike in 1940, FDR was not in a strong enough position politically simply to impose his will on the convention without facing a challenge; moreover, some of those closest to Roosevelt actively joined the "Stop Wallace" movement—people like Pauley, Ed Flynn, and even "Pa" Watson. Though few said it openly, most believed, or at least suspected, that Roosevelt "would not survive another term," said Flynn.[28] For his part, Pauley would later insist that "I could make no greater individual contribution to the Nation's good than to do everything in my power to protect it from Wallace during the war and postwar period. My pre-convention slogan was, 'You are not nominating a Vice President of the United States, but a President.'"[29]

He wasn't alone in expressing that sentiment, though few gave voice to it openly, and certainly no one publicly speculated that Roosevelt was too ill to serve a fourth term. *Time* magazine skirted the line in its coverage, reporting that "almost all of the most powerful New Dealers were involved" in the struggle over the ticket's number-two spot, "because they think the next Vice President may very possibly become President"—though the magazine explained that this was because "Franklin Roosevelt will make his fourth-term try as the oldest nominee of either major party since 1856."[30]

While Roosevelt wanted to keep Wallace, he wasn't about to divide the Democratic Party to do so. It was a fight he simply wasn't up to waging. "I am just not going to go through a convention like 1940 again," he told Sam Rosenman. "It will split the party wide open, and it is already split enough between North and South; it may kill our chances for election this fall, and if it does, it will prolong the war and knock into a cocked hat all the plans we've been making for the future."[31] Though Rosenman and Harold Ickes told the vice president he had become a political liability, Wallace refused to quit the ticket; in fact, he made clear he was going to fight for his job and tried to persuade FDR personally that he could not only be nominated, but that only he could keep the black vote in the Democratic column, given his outspokenness on civil rights and the disappointment of African-American leaders with FDR's refusal to fully integrate the armed forces. Roosevelt, he later said, reassured him that "I hope it's the same team again, Henry."[32]

Roosevelt, however, was not one for direct confrontation; nor, in such matters, would he make a deliberate decision when evasion and political gamesmanship would serve him better. As Wallace once said of him: "He certainly is a water man. He looks one direction and rows the other with utmost skill."[33] Publicly, Roosevelt was noncommittal, though he seemed to indicate privately that his choice to succeed Wallace was Jimmy Byrnes, a former U.S. senator and Supreme Court justice, and then head of the Office of War Mobilization, whom Harry Hopkins had quietly sounded out for the job the previous fall. Certainly Byrnes came away believing he had the president's fervent backing. But it quickly became obvious that his political problems were as difficult as Wallace's: Labor leaders considered him too conservative (even Roosevelt did not believe he was a genuine New Dealer); blacks refused to accept a Southerner; while big-city bosses worried about the effect on the Catholic vote, since Byrnes had converted out of the Church. Still, he went into the convention convinced the president was behind him. Others, however, were seeking the job, including House Majority Leader Sam Rayburn and Senator Alben Barkley. Some party leaders were talking up Supreme Court Justice William O. Douglas for the post. And then there was a possible compromise candidate, Senator Harry Truman of Missouri, who insisted to anyone who asked that he was not a candidate and wasn't even interested in the job.

According to his daughter, Margaret, Truman's reluctance to join the ticket went far beyond his loyalty to Byrnes. It was his very knowledge that Roosevelt was sick—and he did not want to succeed him as president. "Yes, they are plotting against your Dad," he wrote Margaret ten days before the start of the convention. "Every columnist prognosticator is trying to make him VP against his will. It is funny how some people would give a fortune to be as close to it as I am, and I don't want it. Hope I can dodge it. 1600 Pennsylvania is a nice address, but I'd rather not move in through the back door—or any other door at 60."[34]

According to Margaret, her father noted that throughout American history, so-called accidental presidents "were ridiculed in office, had their hearts broken, lost any vestige of respect they had before. I don't want that to happen to me."[35]

On July 11, just before the convention began, Roosevelt met with his top aides and party leaders, ostensibly to resolve the issue. Unhelpfully, the president had just sent a note to the convention, stating that "I personally would vote for [Wallace's] renomination if I were a delegate"—though, he added, "I do not wish to appear in any way to be dictating to the convention." And Truman, who was actively being promoted by fellow Missourian Hannegan, had agreed to place Byrnes's name in nomination. After hours of discussion in the classic smoke-filled room, a weary Roosevelt said that Douglas and Truman seemed to be the consensus choices and that either was acceptable to him. Hannegan asked the president to put it in writing, and he agreed, scrawling a note—which he said could be made public only "if necessary"—reading:

> *Dear Bob:*
>
> *You have written me about Harry Truman and Bill Douglas. I should, of course, be very glad to run with either of them and believe that either of them would bring real strength to the ticket.*[36]

Yet Roosevelt was still telling Byrnes that "I am not favoring anybody." Asked about the note to Hannegan, which Byrnes had learned about, FDR replied, according to Byrnes's stenographic notes, "That is not what I told them. . . . They asked me if I would object to Truman and Douglas and I said no. That is different from using the word 'prefer.'"[37]

The machinations and political back-and-forth continued for several days, until it became clear to Roosevelt—who had been renominated overwhelmingly, with just a smattering of Southern votes for Senator Harry Byrd of Virginia—that those around him supported Truman, though he was still supporting Byrnes, who remained a determined candidate until he was told point-blank by labor leaders Sidney Hillman and Phillip Murray that they could not back him.* So it was arranged that the president

*This came about after Roosevelt, still clinging to his tacit support of Byrnes, instructed Hannegan and Flynn to "clear it with Sidney," who was chairman of the powerful Political Action Committee of the CIO labor federation. The phrase leaked out when it was disclosed by Arthur Krock of the *New York Times*, and it became a Republican rallying cry during the fall campaign, designed to demonstrate that FDR was in the pocket of the unions.

would phone Hannegan, Ed Flynn, and Postmaster General Frank Walker at Chicago's Blackstone Hotel while Truman was in the room.

"Have you got that fellow lined up yet?" Roosevelt asked, referring to Truman.

"Not yet," replied Hannegan.

"Well," said the president, "tell the senator that if he wants to break up the Democratic Party by staying out, he can. But he knows as well as I what that might mean at this dangerous time in the world."

That was enough for Truman: The once-reluctant candidate now accepted the call from his party's leader and agreed to join the ticket. Bob Hannegan would later tell a newspaper reporter: "When I die, I would like to have one thing on my headstone—that I was the man who kept Henry Wallace from becoming president of the United States."[38]

But it was hardly a done deal as far as the delegates were concerned. Unlike today's campaigns, when running mates are revealed in huge media events, there was no formal announcement that Truman had been selected. In fact, there was no announcement at all. So the delegates, who had seen several contradictory letters emanating from the White House, still weren't sure exactly whom the president was supporting. Which is why Wallace actually led at the end of the first ballot, with 429 ½ votes to 319 ½ for Truman, the remaining 400 votes scattered among a number of other hopefuls and favorite sons. On the second ballot, some of the big states, which had remained neutral the first time around, began switching to Truman, and the stampede was on; he was nominated easily.

Just what was at stake in the vice presidential selection was underscored by Senator Bennett Champ Clark in his nominating speech for Truman: "In this year of destiny, it is more than ever necessary to select a vice president possessing all the qualities and all the qualifications desirable and necessary for a president of the United States." His meaning must have been clear to those listening in the hall and on the radio. It certainly was clear to Harry Truman: In September he took his old World War I buddy Edward McKim to a White House reception. "You're going to be living in that house before long," McKim joked.

Truman grew somber. "Eddie," he said, "I'm afraid I am. And it scares the hell out of me."[39]

That fear was only heightened when he and Roosevelt met after the convention. As Margaret Truman later recalled: "[FDR] asked Dad how he planned to campaign, and Dad said that he was thinking of using an airplane. The president vetoed that idea. 'One of us has to stay alive,' he said."[40]

But the choice of Truman had not been made by a president who'd carefully considered from among the nation's political leaders who was best suited to take over from him at a moment's notice. It had been a purely political decision, based mostly on preserving the fragile unity of the Democratic Party. Few Americans, if asked to name a worthy successor to FDR, would have picked Truman, who remained largely an unknown quantity outside of Missouri. Even knowing just how compromised his health was at this point, Franklin Roosevelt had been unable to contemplate his own mortality and plan accordingly, in the nation's best interests. He had gotten Truman—but he had not chosen him.

The Republicans knew they were underdogs against the still-popular president. But they also knew they had an issue—one they hammered home by campaigning against the "tired old men" in Washington. Their presidential candidate may have spoken in the plural, but everyone understood that he really was referring to a single "tired old man." And the stories about that man's failing health continued to spread.

In the past, the White House had countered those whispers with a loud torrent of public rebuttals. This time, however, Steve Early decided to silence the gossipers, using the most powerful weapon available: the investigative force of J. Edgar Hoover's Federal Bureau of Investigation.

An Avalanche of Rumors

CHAPTER 10

Unlike the three previous elections, Franklin Roosevelt did not accept the 1944 Democratic nomination by appearing at the national convention. Instead he delivered his acceptance speech via radio from Camp Pendleton in San Diego; he'd spent the past six days onboard the presidential train on what one reporter called "a cross-country trip that was shrouded in secrecy." He was preparing for a trip to Hawaii to inspect the Pacific Fleet.

In the speech, Roosevelt disclosed that he would not be engaging in the kind of vigorous electioneering to which the voters had become accustomed, citing his responsibilities as commander in chief. "I shall not campaign, in the usual sense, for the office," he said. "In these days of tragic sorrow, I do not consider it fitting. And besides, in these days of global warfare, I shall not be able to find the time. I shall, however, feel free to report to the people the facts about matters that concern them and especially to correct any misrepresentation."[1] He also made clear how he and the Democrats planned to depict the election: as a choice between turning the presidency over "to inexperienced or immature hands"—GOP nominee Thomas E. Dewey was forty-two years old and had been governor of New York for less than two years—or leaving it "to those who saw the danger from abroad, who met it head-on and who now have seized the offensive and carried the war to its present stages of success."[2]

That Roosevelt was not going to spend the fall on the hustings made perfect sense politically. But concerns for the president's health played a part in that decision, too—like recurring bouts of excruciating pain caused by the cancer that had metastasized to his bowel. One instance occurred aboard his train. He joked about it in a letter to Eleanor, telling her, "I had a grand view of the landing operation at Camp Pendleton and then I got the collywobbles and stayed in the train in the p.m. Better today."[3] FDR never explained what he meant by "collywobbles," but his son Jimmy did, years later.

"Suddenly, he began to groan," Jimmy wrote. "His face took on an expression of pain and suffering, and all the color seemed to drain from it. He said, 'Jimmy, I don't know if I can make it. I have horrible pains.'" The young man helped his father to the floor, gripped his hand, and offered to call a doctor. But the president refused, insisting that the abdominal pains that now gripped him were merely a case of indigestion. "Father lay on the floor of his railroad car, his eyes closed, his face drawn, his powerful torso occasionally convulsed as the waves of pain stabbed him. Never in all my life had I felt so alone with him—and so helpless," he wrote.[4] Jimmy could only watch as his father writhed in agony; he felt terribly conflicted about what he should do, he wrote: After all, "he was not only my father, he was the commander in chief." After several minutes, FDR opened his eyes, the color returned to his face, and he began to breathe normally. "Help me up now, Jimmy," he said, and proceeded to review the troops—yet another example of FDR's amazing ability to fend off pain. By mutual agreement, or so Jimmy believed, neither Roosevelt mentioned the incident to anyone else—including either Ross McIntire or Howard Bruenn, who was onboard the train.[5]*

From San Diego, Roosevelt sailed aboard the cruiser USS *Baltimore* for Pearl Harbor, where he would confer with General Douglas MacArthur

*Following publication of this story, Anna Roosevelt said she did not believe it actually took place, doubting her brother's ability to lift their father by himself. But if it did, she added, then Jimmy had been "horribly irresponsible" in not immediately notifying Bruenn.

and Admiral Chester Nimitz over the war plan against Japan, and then on for an inspection tour of the Pacific Fleet. FDR's naval planning group had proposed, through Nimitz, a westward assault, culminating with an invasion of the island of Formosa as the quickest and most direct path to directly attacking Japan. But MacArthur, who had famously vowed "I shall return" when forced to withdraw from the Philippines, insisted instead on leading an attack against Luzon, where 7,000 American POWs were imprisoned, and then moving on to Manila. "You cannot abandon seventeen million loyal Filipino Christians to the Japanese in favor of first liberating Formosa and returning it to China," he berated Roosevelt. "American public opinion will condemn you, and it would be justified." After two hours of discussion, FDR ruled in favor of MacArthur. Some historians have cited the president's health as a factor in this decision, saying he either was not able to fully concentrate or just simply grew tired of MacArthur's insistent tirade. Harold Ickes reported hearing from New Deal power broker Thomas "Tommy the Cork" Corcoran the "disturbing news" that "FDR's health is not good and he had had to break some engagements in Honolulu."[6] But a key argument in MacArthur's favor is that the chief of staff, George Marshall, agreed with him. Still, MacArthur later wrote in his memoir that Roosevelt's failing health was obvious: "I had not seen him for a number of years, and physically he was just a shell of the man I had known. It was clearly evident that his days were numbered."[7] He added that he later told his staff that the president would be dead within a year.

Roosevelt arrived back in the United States, via the Aleutian Islands, on August 12 at Bremerton Naval Yard in Washington, where he spoke to the assembled naval workers from the deck of the destroyer USS *Cummings*, and delivered a nationally broadcast address. It was a speech he'd written himself, dictating it to Lieutenant William Rigdon, a naval stenographer, without the aid of any of his speechwriters, and it was a notably lackluster effort. "The Boss . . . knew it was not one of his best efforts," Grace Tully wrote, "and he explained almost apologetically that he intended it to be simply 'a homey report' on his trip." It turned out, she said, to be "one of the poorest speeches he made, both in form and in delivery."[8] Harold Ickes noted in his diary that "people would be inclined to reason from this speech that the President is not a well man and that would not spell votes."[9] Assistant Secretary of War John J. McCloy, a pro-FDR Republican, told Ickes that "his Republican friends might hesitate to vote for Roosevelt if his health was as bad as this speech might seem to indicate." And, Ickes added, "one or two others" he asked for their reaction "thought that the President's delivery indicated that he might have had an extra cocktail too much."[10]

Sam Rosenman, listening over the radio, had "a sinking sensation"—the president sounded "hesitant, halting and indecisive. . . . It was a dismal failure."[11] Roosevelt himself later wrote his aide, acknowledging that it was "a very bad performance."[12] Daisy Suckley was listening at home, too, and though she noted that "his voice sounded strong," she picked up on something that most others missed: "It seemed to be as though he was tired and that he once or twice got mixed up on his words."[13] He had indeed—with good reason. For one thing, the president was unsteady on his feet. It was the first time he'd stood in his braces in months, but they no longer fit him because he'd already lost at least fifteen pounds since the end of March (two and a half pounds on the Pacific trip alone, Daisy noted)[14]—even though he had long ago abandoned the 1,800-calorie low-fat diet on which he'd been placed the previous spring. More significant, though, in the middle of the speech he'd been stricken with severe chest pain, described by Bruenn as substernal oppression. "He kept on with the speech," the cardiologist recalled years later, then "came below and said, 'I had a helluva pain!' We stripped him down in the cabin of the ship, took a cardiogram, some blood and so forth, and fortunately it was a transient episode, a so-called angina [pain caused by a lack of blood supply to the heart, without residual damage], not a myocardial infarction [a heart attack with overt damage to the heart muscle]. But that was really a very disturbing situation. That was the first time under my observation that he had something like this. He had denied any pain before."[15]

Ross McIntire, forever denying all, wrote that the incident "gave me the worst scare of the trip," but for an entirely different reason: "A stiff wind was blowing," he claimed, "and there was quite a slant to the deck, two things that called for bracing on his part, and as a result he finished up with considerable pain." Concluded McIntire: "Purely muscular, it turned out," adding that on FDR's return to the White House, "he was in better shape than when we left."[16]

In fact, the angina attack, which lasted about fifteen minutes, was a further testament to Roosevelt's amazing resilience and force of will. The authors have obtained an unedited private film of the entire speech; it is impossible to tell at what point he was stricken. There is no physical indication, and even his voice, despite his lackluster delivery, shows no evidence of the "helluva pain" he was in. In that respect alone, it actually was one of FDR's most remarkable public performances.

But, as Rosenman noted, the president's poor delivery "started tongues wagging—friendly and unfriendly tongues—all through the United States."[17] But they had already begun wagging when Roosevelt delivered his acceptance speech: A photograph taken by *Life* magazine's George Skadding caught him glassy eyed, with his mouth agape, making him appear as if he'd suffered some sort of stroke—Harold Ickes said it made him look "like a sitting ghost."[18] Robert G. Nixon, White House correspondent of the International News Service, received an urgent call from his editor in New York: "My god, that photograph," the editor said. "Is Roosevelt dying?"[19] Steve Early was furious: "I was terrifically disappointed, let down to a new low, when I saw the photograph of the President delivering his speech of acceptance," he wrote Grace Tully. "I can't imagine what was wrong with Skadding, or his camera, or his subject. But something decidedly was wrong. . . . The rumor factory is working overtime—making all it can out of rumors and lies about the President's health. That is why some of the photographs I have seen caused me much concern at this time."[20]

Skadding, called on the carpet by the president's press secretary, tried to explain that he'd hurriedly turned his negatives over to the various wire photo agencies; hard on deadline, "they grabbed the first shot they looked at and before I knew it they had this particular bad shot on the wires."[21] As for the "terrible picture of the Boss" that his own magazine published in its July 31 issue—with FDR, his face gaunt, his mouth agape, and a strange expression on his face, the extra-wide pants legs, designed to hide his own withered limbs, clearly visible—"I feel like apologizing—but the dam [*sic*] picture's been used. . . . I have already gripped [*sic*] like hell to my office—That kind of a shot does not do me any good." And, in a telling example of the close cooperation that still existed between the press and the White House, the photographer promised

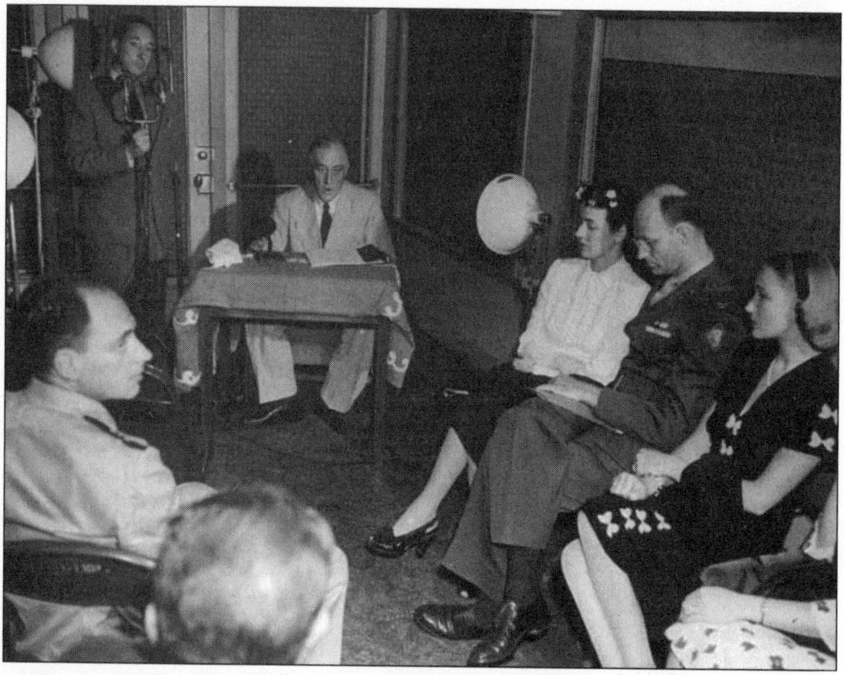

The controversial *Life* magazine photo that unmasked FDR's treatment by a heart specialist; it shows Roosevelt accepting his nomination via radio to the 1944 Democratic convention. Seated on the couch is his son James (second from right). Many were alarmed by the sight of the gaunt-faced president with his mouth agape. Walter Trohan of the *Chicago Tribune* discovered that the officer on the left, who was not identified by the magazine, was Howard Bruenn, a Navy cardiologist, and that he was part of Roosevelt's regular entourage. (Getty Images)

that "to try and make up for this I'm going to personally supervise the next ones made and show the boss as he really is."[22]

The *Life* photo showed the president reading his speech surrounded by his son Jimmy and two of his daughters-in-law, none of whom seemed to be paying close attention. In the bottom of the photo can be seen Admiral William Leahy, FDR's chief of staff—or at least the back of his head. But there was one more person sitting in the tiny audience; his expressionless face was clearly visible, though he wasn't identified or ever referred to in the photo caption. It was Howard Bruenn.

The ever-alert Walter Trohan of the *Chicago Tribune* had seen one of the wire service versions of Skadding's photos, in which Bruenn's face had been cropped out. But Trohan noticed "the hand and lower sleeve of

-4-

The second purpose was to continue to build the foundation for an international accord which would bring order and security after the chaos of war, and which would give some assurance of lasting peace among the nations of the world.

misses "toward" on the left margin which causes multiple repetitions, trying to say something logical until he finds his place → too -- in that goal -- toward that goal

~~Toward~~ that goal^~~also,~~ a tremendous stride was made.

a little

At Teheran, over a year ago, there were long-range military plans laid by the Chiefs of Staff of the three most powerful nations. Among the civilian leaders at Teheran,

at that time

however,^there were only exchanges of views and expressions

reads "*agree*ments" as *arrange*ments" → arrangements

of opinion. No political^~~agreements~~ were made -- and none was attempted.

At the Crimean Conference, however, the time had come for getting down to specific cases in the political field.

There was on all sides at this Conference an

an

enthusiastic effort to reach^agreement. Since the time of

misses "the" on the left margin, then eliminates "conference" to be logical →

a year ago

~~the~~ Teheran^~~Conference,~~ there had developed among all of us

what should I call it-- a

that

can't find the left margin → a^greater facility in negotiating with each other,^~~which~~ augurs well for the future peace of the world.

A page from the original reading copy that Roosevelt used while delivering his Yalta report to Congress on March 1, 1945. The page is annotated to show FDR's many mistakes, brought about by left hemianopia, a visual deficit caused by a metastatic brain tumor. As part of the neurological examination to test for this problem, patients are asked to read a word such as "northwestern." Affected patients ignore the left side of the word and read "western" or "stern." The hour-long speech contained over a dozen instances of this type of word substitution, along with many other digressions due to his visual problem. (Franklin D. Roosevelt Library [FDRL])

Circa 1928

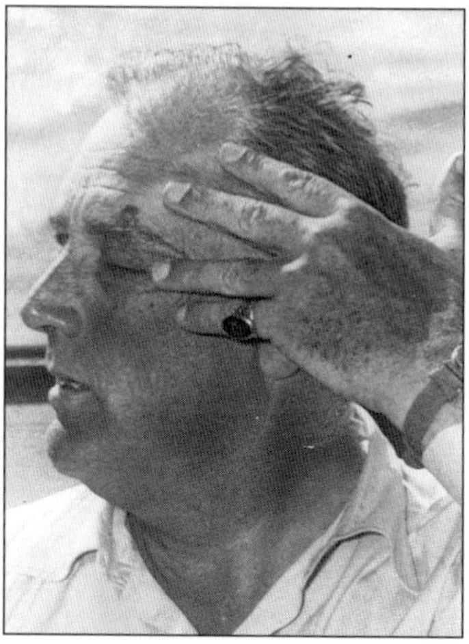

1937

1938

January 1940

April 1940

The lesion over Roosevelt's left eye, which resembled a tiny sunspot in the early 1920s, gradually grew over the years until it had spread through the eyebrow and assumed the characteristics consistent with melanoma as utilized by present-day dermatologists. It reached its peak growth by the beginning of 1940, but then began to undergo radical changes. By December of that year, it had lightened considerably; by the time of Pearl Harbor, a year later, it was no more than a faint shadow. (FDRL)

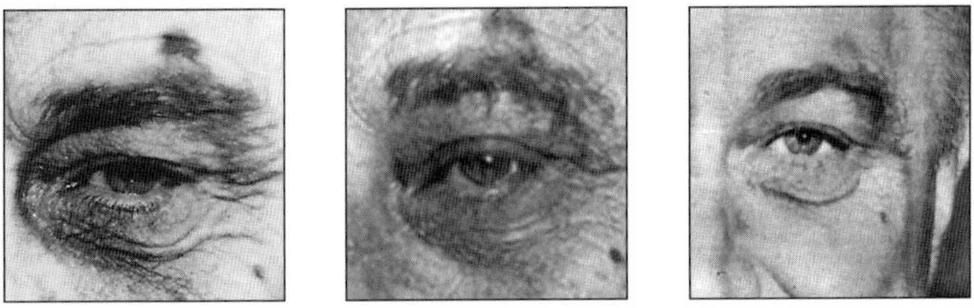

Beginning in mid-1940, the expanding lesion over Roosevelt's eye slowly began to disappear as a result of surgery, though his doctors made no mention of any procedures ever being performed on his face. (From left to right) January 1939: The lesion is seen at its greatest extent. (FDRL) August 1940: A fresh surgical scar is visible across the base of the eyebrow, with hairs combed across it. In addition, the small pigmented lesion just above the eyebrow has been replaced by a small diagonal surgical scar, and one of the two small pigmented lesions below the eye has been removed. (FDRL) 1942: Only a faint residual scar remains above the eye. (*Yank* magazine, April 27, 1945)

FDR conducts a press conference during a July 4, 1939, picnic at Val-Kill, Eleanor's cottage down the road from his own family home at Hyde Park. Taking notes to his right, in the dark jacket, is the president's journalistic bête noire, Walter Trohan of the *Chicago Tribune.* Next to him is Merriman Smith of United Press. Sitting behind the president is William Hassett, his confidential secretary, while FDR's mother, Sara Delano Roosevelt, is immediately behind Trohan. The woman in the white patterned dress is Grace Tully, the president's personal secretary; next to her in sunglasses is Marguerite "Missy" LeHand, who is widely believed to have had a long-standing romantic relationship with the president. (AP Worldwide)

WOL

The dramatic scene in Congress as President Roosevelt makes his final appearance there to deliver his post-Yalta report to the nation. For the first and only time, FDR publicly acknowledged his physical disability, apologizing for the "unusual posture of sitting down" because he wasn't wearing "about ten pounds of steel around my legs." (Bettmann/CORBIS)

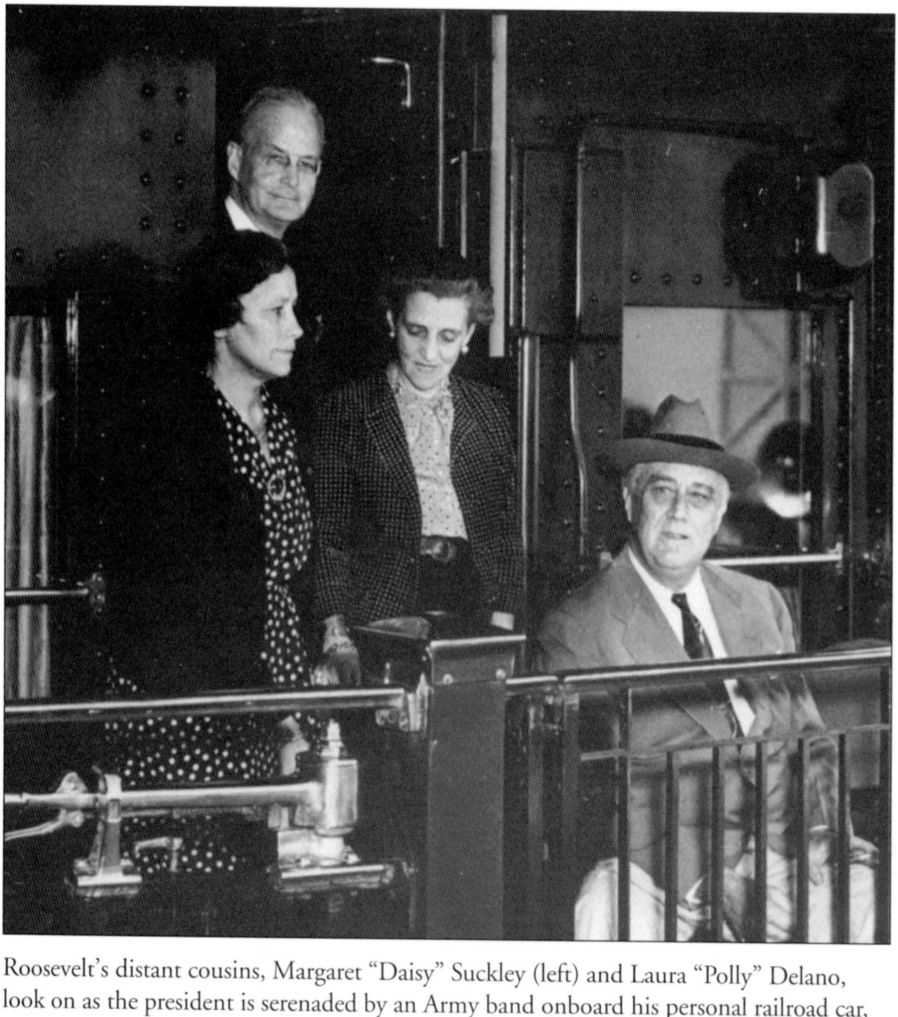

Roosevelt's distant cousins, Margaret "Daisy" Suckley (left) and Laura "Polly" Delano, look on as the president is serenaded by an Army band onboard his personal railroad car, the *Ferdinand Magellan*, during a 1943 tour of military installations. Standing behind them is Harry Hooker, FDR's former law partner and Daisy's frequent escort at social occasions. Daisy's diary, discovered only after her death in 1991, sheds dramatic new light on Roosevelt's true feelings as ill health overtook him. (FDRL)

Louis Howe, Roosevelt's political guru, who masterminded his political recovery from polio and his rise to the presidency; Press Secretary Stephen T. Early, who fiercely controlled how FDR was portrayed in the press; and Marvin McIntyre, who served at various times as the president's appointments, traveling, and correspondence secretary, shortly after the first inauguration in 1933. (Bettmann/CORBIS)

Dr. James Paullin, the Atlanta internist McIntire called in to confirm Howard Bruenn's diagnosis that the president was suffering congestive heart failure, and who would arrive at FDR's bedside at Warm Springs just moments before his death. (Courtesy Dr. Hal Raper)

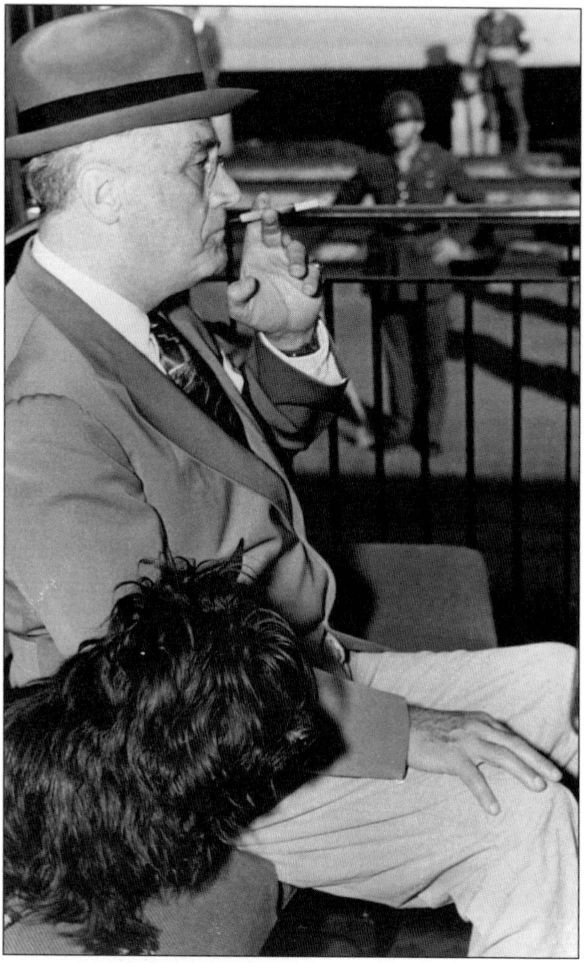

These photos, taken less than two years apart, document Roosevelt's shocking and rapid physical deterioration. The president poses in late 1943 with his famous Scottish terrier, Fala (right). Barely a year later, a haggard and exhausted FDR (below), some thirty-five pounds below his normal weight, visits Newburgh, New York, on the last day of his final campaign in 1944. (Bettmann/Corbis, FDRL)

a naval commander. I couldn't imagine how so low-ranking an officer could be the only armed services guest at such a historic address." So Trohan "asked for an uncropped copy of the original photograph. Then I took the photo to the Navy Department for identification. I was told he was Commander Howard Bruenn. Further inquiry revealed that he was a . . . heart specialist."[23]

Trohan immediately went public with the story, which ran on Page 3 of the *Tribune* on August 6 under the headline "Disclose Heart Specialist Is With Roosevelt." The article reported that "President Roosevelt's health and stamina again became a major topic of capital conversation today with the disclosure that a heart specialist is a member of his official party" and then proceeded to identify Bruenn, adding that "it was reported in capital circles [that] Bruenn has been commissioned to look after Mr. Roosevelt."* There was no comment from Bruenn, McIntire, or anyone else at the White House, nor was there any indication that Trohan had sought one. It was an indication of just how poorly the rest of the national press thought of the fiercely anti-FDR *Tribune*—and of Trohan, in particular—that no other paper or wire service picked up on his story, or even ran an account noting the Chicago paper's reporting.

But others did notice. There had long been gossip at Bethesda about Bruenn's frequent absences, which always seemed to coincide with Roosevelt's leaving town. Then someone at the hospital received a clipping of Trohan's story and the gossip revived even more furiously than before; one physician estimated that "at least half the doctors" at the naval facility were involved in heated discussions about the president's health. Eventually Breckinridge Long, an assistant secretary of state, got wind of the rumors and began investigating them on his own. He traced the source to Colonel Byrl R. Kirklin of the Army Medical Corps, who in civilian life was the highly regarded radiology specialist at the Mayo Clinic and a founder of the American Board of Radiology. From time to time, Kirklin was allowed to take leave from his military duties to return to Mayo.

---

*Though his story correctly identified Bruenn as being from New York, Trohan's memoir wrongly says he was a "Boston heart specialist." The claim, repeated in his memoir, that Bruenn was "inducted into the Navy for the specific purpose of looking after the President's heart" was incorrect, but not far from the truth, since the evidence suggests strongly that Bruenn was transferred to Bethesda for precisely that purpose.

Long discovered that Kirklin, speaking to a group of doctors at the clinic, had been asked about the president's condition and informed his audience that Roosevelt had heart disease: "His answer, as quoted to me, was that 'It is common knowledge at Bethesda and in the Surgeon General's office in Washington, etc.' He then said, 'I have this direct from Bethesda.' To this statement was also appended the remark that 'in spite of his illness, he is going ahead anyhow and doing his regular job.'"[24]

Long immediately notified Steve Early of his findings. The press secretary's immediate instinct was to nip this in the bud—so he forwarded Long's letter to J. Edgar Hoover, with instructions that the FBI director put his agents on the case.

This wasn't the first time Early had recruited the FBI to stamp out rumors regarding Roosevelt's health. Back in March 1940, a persistent young office-seeker named Joseph Leib had begun harassing Ross McIntire and other administration officials after reading a story in the *Nashville Tennessean* reporting that Walter Davenport, the chief political writer for *Collier's*, had told a local audience that Roosevelt might not run for a third term because his doctor had told him "his health may not stand the strain of another term."[25] Leib, an early Roosevelt supporter who had turned against FDR after being disappointed with the low level of jobs he was offered, began bombarding McIntire with letters demanding an explanation, which the surgeon general ignored. He also sent out scores of missives to prominent Roosevelt backers, calling their attention to the article; many of the concerned recipients, in turn, anxiously wrote McIntire asking if there was any basis to the story. To these, McIntire responded with a private reassurance that the president "is fine" and complained that "this troublesome individual is apparently conducting some sort of a malicious campaign, about which I am not clear."[26] Then he suggested that Early find some way of putting an end to Leib's mischief.

Armed with Davenport's fervent denial of having "never said to anybody, privately, publicly or 'off the record,' what the *Tennessean* is alleged to have reputed to me,"* Early sent Leib's file to Hoover, with the sug-

---

*John Thompson, the author of the article, told Early that "I would never have published such quotations in the newspaper unless they were completely factual." Most likely, Davenport—whose speech promoted Secretary of State Cordell Hull as FDR's successor—got carried away in his remarks and quickly tried to cover his tracks.

gestion that the bureau send "an operator" to ask Leib "whether he is functioning for the deliberate purpose of creating fear that the President is failing physically and cannot be entrusted to carry on." Such behavior, Early told Hoover, "is subversive in character and closely akin to the fifth column and Trojan horse tactics."[27] Within a few days, Leib had been questioned by an FBI agent; obviously chastened, he promised immediately to stop.

Recalling the FBI's success in halting Leib, a persistent but relatively harmless crackpot,* Early enlisted the agency once again, this time against a far more widespread and potentially dangerous political threat, based on Breckinridge Long's letter. For unknown reasons, Early's request was passed to Hoover's deputy, Edward A. Tamm, who thought the inquiry smacked too much of politics and suggested that the military investigate.[28] A reluctant Early was about to enlist the Secret Service when Long, undeterred, approached Hoover directly, who responded as quickly and eagerly as he had in 1940.[29]

Within three days, a squad of agents had interviewed Kirklin and several other doctors and filed their report to Hoover:

> Colonel Kirklin stated that on October 21, 1944, he was at luncheon at the Kahler Hotel in Rochester, Minnesota, with a number of persons from the Mayo Clinic [including] . . . Dr. A.R. Barnes, head of the Diagnostic Section. Dr. Barnes had but recently returned from Bethesda, Maryland, where he had attended a meeting of heart specialists. During the luncheon, Dr. Barnes stated that the President had a serious heart ailment. Colonel Kirklin heard Dr. Barnes make this comment . . .
>
> Later on October 21st, according to Colonel Kirklin, he participated in a poker game at Rochester, Minnesota [with, among others, four doctors]. During the course of the poker game, Colonel Kirklin quoted Dr. Barnes' previous statement made at the luncheon that the President had a serious heart ailment. . . .

*Leib did not vanish from the scene altogether. In 1984, at age seventy-three, he wrote an article for *Hustler* in which he claimed that Cordell Hull had given him advance word of the attack on Pearl Harbor. The piece, which can still be found on the Internet, has become a staple of conspiracy theorists, who contend it proves FDR deliberately provoked the Japanese attack in order to bring the United States into the war.

Collaterally, Colonel Kirklin stated that he had previously heard some discussion of the President's health on the occasion of a meeting of the Board of Examiners of Radiology, held in the Palmer House, Chicago, about September 23, 1944. . . . Dr. Ross Golden, a radiologist assigned to the Presbyterian Hospital in New York City, referred to a photograph of the President giving his acceptance speech in San Diego, and stated—"Did you notice the unidentified profile in the picture to the right of the President? That man is Dr.———, a radiologist at the Presbyterian Hospital." . . . Colonel Kirklin said he did not remember the name of the man referred to by Dr. Golden. . . .

Dr. A.R. Barnes, a civilian, head of the Diagnostic Section at the Mayo Clinic, admitted making the statement attributed to him by Colonel Kirklin. . . . When questioned about the source of his information, Dr. Barnes stated that he visited with Dr. Howard Odel, a Navy Lieutenant at the Naval Hospital in Bethesda, at 11:00 a.m. Thursday, October 19th. Dr. Odel is a close personal friend of Dr. Barnes and a former protégé of his at the Mayo Clinic. . . . They began discussing Minnesota politics, at which time Dr. Odel made the statement—"The President is a very sick man. Heart disease." Dr. Barnes stated that he asked no questions, but that Dr. Odel made this statement as a fact and with no reference to the source of his information. . . .

It was ascertained that Dr. Howard Odel is a Lieutenant in the Navy assigned to the Bethesda Naval Medical Center. . . . Dr. Odel denied making any statements of this kind, but stated that the President's health had been the subject of a general discussion at a luncheon recently held at the Naval Hospital. When asked to name specifically the persons who had attended this luncheon, Dr. Odel declined to do so. . . . Dr. Odel stated that the reason the President's health had been discussed at the hospital was because members of the hospital staff recognized the picture of one of the Navy Hospital doctors, H.G. Bruenn, on the President's train. . . . Dr. Odel was obviously disturbed and uneasy during this interview. . . .

He was confronted with the fact that Dr. Barnes specifically attributed the statement heretofore set out to Dr. Odel. . . . Dr. Odel stated that . . . he had been showing Dr. Barnes through the Bethesda Naval Center and upon reaching the seventeenth "deck" of the hospital, he,

> Dr. Odel, explained that this floor was reserved for high-ranking Government officials. Dr. Barnes asked whether this was where the President stayed and Dr. Odel stated that the President had not stayed there but had been at the hospital on two or three occasions for examination. Dr. Odel stated to Dr. Barnes that there had been rumors circulating about the President's health and he, Dr. Odel, wondered if the President had heart disease or hypertension . . . [and that] he may have added something to the effect that "I suspect there may be something to it."[30]

Hoover sent the report to Early, along with a letter dismissing the entire story as idle gossip, all "predicated upon the supposition that the President was suffering from some sort of heart ailment by reason of the fact that Doctor Bruenn's picture appeared in the group with the President."[31] Though the letter seems to accept that the rumors are untrue, it's far more likely that Hoover—who even then was the keeper of Washington's political secrets—knew otherwise. Certainly the FBI report was a loud warning siren to Steve Early, who knew the truth: Credible information about the president's dire heart condition was seeping out into the medical community and beyond, though the agency's involvement—or perhaps threats of military courts-martial—appears to have stanched the gossipers' casual talk.

Still, there had been no leak of any information about Roosevelt's cancer or any related ailments. But a few weeks later, Hoover notified Early that he'd received a tip of "another avalanche of rumors in and around Washington" and had ordered a second investigation.[32] The material the bureau's agents picked up this time went far beyond the president's heart problems:

> Recurrent rumors concerning the President's health are surging and echoing through Washington. The present "inside" story currently being discussed by most people, but mostly newspaper men, is alleged to emanate from "informed White House circles." The story is as follows:
>
> Dr. William Calhoun "Pete" Sterling [*sic*] has established a good reputation for surgery specializing in prostate, kidney and similar ailments. The story states that "Pete" Sterling was recently called for an extensive examination of the President and although an operation was necessary,

> Dr. Sterling refused to operate because of the very bad condition of the President's health. "Pete" Sterling is alleged to have declined to operate on the grounds that the President's condition was so bad he would probably die from the operation and Dr. Sterling did not want to jeopardize his entire future in the medical practice by being known as the man who had killed the President. Accordingly, the "White House" called into the case Dr. Frank Lahey of Boston. Dr. Lahey allegedly concluded that an operation was absolutely necessary and "the White House" decided that the operation would be performed after the Presidential election. . . .
>
> The rumor then outlines that Dr. Lahey was insistent that the President build up his physical condition, as a result of which the President went to Warm Springs, Georgia, for a stay of ten days, which has been lengthened to 20 days, in order to build up all possible resistance.* Dr. Lahey allegedly has demanded that the operation be performed at the Lahey Clinic in Boston, because it is alleged that the advertising value of his operating upon the President in Boston will be worth "millions of dollars" to the Lahey Clinic. Dr. Lahey is supposed to reason that even [if] the operation is unsuccessful and the President dies, most people would concede that Dr. Lahey and his clinic must be pre-eminent if the President went there for an operation. Accordingly, it is alleged that the rumor has spread throughout New England that the President is to be operated upon in Boston, the operation to take place about the first of the year, or possibly even sooner.
>
> The rumor states that Dr. Lahey performs many of his operations at the Baptist Hospital in Boston, and that on or about December 8th, a United States Secret Service man from Washington, whose name is Barker, was in Boston, checking up on the facilities. . . . Congressional discussion has emphasized the fact that Dr. Lahey has recently been in Washington reviewing medical charts with Admiral McIntyre [*sic*].[33]

This report, in many ways, was even more alarming than the first. It raised the names of two doctors who knew about Roosevelt's cancer and who had not been publicly identified as having treated the president. It also suggested, no doubt correctly, that Stirling and Lahey themselves

*This refers to the post-election trip the president did indeed make to Warm Springs.

were the sources of information and that the stories had spread to the press—where Walter Trohan would later acknowledge that Stirling had been one of his sources—and to the halls of Congress.

Despite its almost fanciful allegations, the second memorandum has a ring of truth about it, based on other information. Stirling, as we know, did say precisely these things to Trohan, and possibly other journalists; the information was confirmed for us by his daughter, Margheritta Stirling Allardice, who had worked in his office as a medical assistant.[34] Lahey also, according to numerous credible accounts, was forthcoming about his treatment of the president, including the fact that a malignancy was involved (see Chapter 15). That Lahey preferred to have prominent patients treated at his clinic also is well established: In 1953 Lahey's deputy, Dr. Richard Cattell, repaired British Foreign Secretary Anthony Eden's bile duct after surgeons in London botched the initial operation; at Lahey's urging, the surgery took place at his clinic, despite the heated insistence of Prime Minister Winston Churchill that Eden not leave England.[35]

As for Roosevelt, Lahey's business manager, intimate confidante, and executor, Linda Strand, told Dr. Harry Goldsmith, with whose help she reacquired the Lahey memorandum, that "she had met FDR at the New England Baptist Hospital, where he had been a patient listed under a different name."[36]* And Stanley P. Lovell, the longtime director of research and development for the Office of Strategic Services, forerunner of the CIA, wrote in his memoir that, at about the time of the 1944 Democratic convention, "we in OSS . . . had seen a report from the Lahey Clinic in Boston whose doctors, after examining the President, stated that he would not survive another term."[37]

While all this was going on, Roosevelt still had to contend with his reelection campaign. The Democrats still led in the polls, but the margin

---

*Another report of Roosevelt's having been in a Boston hospital comes from Dr. Rutledge W. Howard, who was a resident surgeon in the city during World War II and contacted Dr. Harry Goldsmith after publication of his 1979 paper on FDR's health. During the winter of 1944, Howard said, he saw from his apartment window overlooking the Lahey Clinic–affiliated Deaconess Hospital "a man in a wheelchair with a fedora and a cigarette holder in his mouth" who "looked like FDR or his double" being spirited into the hospital late one night. The next day, he said, several of the house staff said they had seen him, too. (Harry Goldsmith, *A Conspiracy of Silence*, pp. 65–66)

was not as comfortable as in FDR's previous campaigns; the GOP's "tired old men" jibe clearly was having an effect. But despite his perilous condition, Roosevelt summoned his inner strength and managed to turn things around and cement his victory, thanks to two key events.

The first took place on September 23 before a dinner of the International Brotherhood of Teamsters at the Washington Statler Hotel. The decidedly pro-Roosevelt audience presented the president with a much-needed opportunity to demonstrate that his performance at Bremerton had been an aberration. It was an opportunity of which some of those closest to him initially feared he would not be able to take full political advantage. After Bremerton, Anna "had secretly expressed to me her apprehension about whether her father would still have enough of his old campaign fire to meet the young and forceful Dewey," Sam Rosenman recalled.[38]

It was agreed that from this point out, Roosevelt would no longer deliver any speeches while standing. And the president's staff, including Rosenman and Labor Secretary Frances Perkins, worked for days to craft a union-oriented speech that would underscore FDR's long-standing commitment to organized labor. But several days before Roosevelt was scheduled to speak, Dewey delivered his own labor speech that, said Perkins, essentially endorsed the Democrats' record. So she worked furiously to craft some fresh material, only to be told by Roosevelt not to worry. "I'm not going to use any of the stuff you sent me," he told her. "I've got my mind on something else, and I'm going to have a good time."[39]

That he certainly did. The speech he gave touched only briefly on labor matters; instead he used the occasion to eloquently defend his record, needle Dewey's speech as "the Old Guard trying to pass itself off as the New Deal," and lambaste the Republicans and their ongoing campaign of falsehoods. It was a rousing speech, one of the best he'd given in some time. But toward the end he delivered the remarks that made it one of the most memorable campaign speeches in American history:

> These Republican leaders have not been content with attacks on me, or my wife, or on my sons. No, not content with that, they now include my little dog, Fala. Well, of course, I don't resent attacks, and my family doesn't resent attacks, but Fala does resent them. You know, Fala is

> Scotch, and being a Scottie, as soon as he learned that the Republican fiction writers in Congress and out had concocted a story that I had left him behind on the Aleutian Islands and had sent a destroyer back to find him—at a cost to the taxpayers of two or three, or eight or twenty million dollars—his Scotch soul was furious. He has not been the same dog since. I am accustomed to hearing malicious falsehoods about myself, such as that old, worm-eaten chestnut that I have represented myself as indispensable. But I think I have a right to resent, to object, to libelous statements about my dog.[40]

The audience roared with laughter; so did the millions listening via radio. "No one could have delivered this short passage more effectively," Rosenman wrote. "His mock-serious face and his sad tone of voice set the audience shouting with glee, but he continued through the statement with the same serious note of righteous indignation, never cracking a smile until the end."[41] It was Roosevelt at his "vigorous best," he added, and left everyone with the same thought: "The old maestro is back again—the champ is now out on the road. The old boy has the same old fighting stuff and he cannot be licked."[42]

But if FDR had proved that he could rally his strength when he needed it most—Daisy Suckley wrote that he must have delivered the speech "through sheer will power & determination"[43]—the fact remained that he was still a very sick man, and it showed. A week before his Fala speech, he traveled to Quebec to meet with Churchill and Canadian Prime Minister Mackenzie King; the latter wrote in his diary that "it seemed to me . . . that he had failed very much since I last saw him. He is very much thinner in body and also is much thinner in his face. He looks distinctly older and worn. I confess I was just a little shocked at his appearance."[44] Concerned, he asked Admiral Wilson Brown, FDR's naval aide, about Roosevelt's health; the latter conceded that Ross McIntire was "really concerned about him." King was also greatly concerned with Roosevelt's judgment, recording in his diary that "he certainly has not the grasp today that he had a year ago." During the three-day conference, he noted, the president delivered a long, rambling, and inappropriate dinner toast. Following Roosevelt's departure, King noticed the absence of the American flag outside the assembly building and felt it was "an ill omen, as if the President might be the first to be taken of the three of us."[45]

There was another worrisome incident during the Quebec conference. The attendees were given a screening of the motion picture *Wilson*, starring Alexander Knox in his Oscar-nominated performance as FDR's mentor. The film focused on the WWI president's unsuccessful postwar battle for American entry into the League of Nations, which broke Wilson physically. It was as he watched the movie that Bruenn heard Roosevelt mutter quietly, "By God, that's not going to happen to me!" Even more significant, the doctor measured FDR's blood pressure shortly afterward at an alarming 240/130.[46]

Back home, Daisy Suckley remained deathly afraid of the president's growing physical weakness. "It is hard to talk about & harder to write about," she confided to her diary, "but I am really frightened at his condition. He seems to me to be slowly failing." But, ever loyal to her Franklin, she decided that "it would be best for him to win this election, as his heart is so completely in the desire to create a better world—even if he cannot get through four more years."[47]

Roosevelt himself was asked directly about his health only once during the fall campaign. At a press conference on October 17, a reporter jokingly asked, "Mr. President, you read the ominous reports about your health, printed by some of the more rugged correspondents?" FDR joined in the general laughter that accompanied the question, and replied: "More what correspondents? Look—don't—don't get me commenting on the word 'rugged,' because I might say things that I would be sorry for. On some of them, I think I know more about their health than they know about mine.* I think it's pretty good health."[48]

Most of the nation's columnists and editorial pages refrained from commenting directly on the president's health. Notable exceptions were the longtime leaders of the anti-Roosevelt press, the *New York Daily News* and its sister paper, the *Chicago Tribune*. And neither paper beat

*As William Hassett noted in his diary, FDR's bitterest journalistic foe, John O'Donnell of the *New York Daily News*, "is himself a sick man. Ironically, too, his malady is a diseased spleen." (William Hassett, *Off the Record With FDR*, p. 279; diary entry from October 21, 1944)

around the bush. The *Tribune*, in particular, published two editorials in a twelve-day period that frankly predicted Roosevelt's death in office. "Evidence increases that Mr. Roosevelt is not in fit physical condition to meet those demands," the paper wrote, adding that "if he dies or becomes incapacitated, [those around him] figure they can do business with Truman."[49] With barely a week to go before the election, the paper dropped any pretenses whatsoever: "In view of Mr. Roosevelt's age and brittle health, a vote for Mr. Roosevelt is very likely to be a vote for Truman for President."[50]

Meanwhile, the *Syracuse Post-Standard* reported that "for many months, photographers have revealed deepening lines of age and weariness in the president's face. Now, orders have been given that there must be no more pictures taken in the telltale glare of flash bulbs and unflattering floodlights. Walter Wanger sent expert electricians from Hollywood to supervise lighting of future Roosevelt pictures,* the first of which, taken two nights ago, made the president look much younger and healthier. Such precautions are an indication of the anxiety felt in White House circles over the president's health."[51]

Such sentiments were few and far between, of course. But if the Fala speech had reassured the public about Roosevelt's mental acuity, something else was needed to reassure them about his physical stamina. Although the White House had declared that the president would give no more public speeches during the campaign, Bob Hannegan persuaded FDR's aides that he needed to demonstrate conclusively that he was physically up for the job. So it was decided to undertake a four-hour campaign swing through New York City on October 21, including a speech at Ebbets Field, home of the Brooklyn Dodgers. "After the people have seen him," predicted Hannegan, "they can make up their own

*Rumors flooded Washington in late October that Wanger, a Democratic activist and the Academy Award–winning producer of such films as *Stagecoach* and *Foreign Correspondent*, had provided makeup artists to work on Roosevelt's face before his public appearances. Early insisted this was untrue, saying the real story was that Hal Rosson, head cameraman for MGM, had volunteered to improve the lighting in the White House. At Rosson's suggestion, a makeshift movie studio was set up in the White House with incandescent lights shipped from Hollywood and installed. (Peter Edson, *Dunkirk* [New York] *Evening Observer*, November 7, 1944)

minds about his vigor and health."[52] The campaign couldn't have picked a worse day; "it had never rained more incessantly and gloomily than now," wrote *Time*,[53] and what had been a steady, lashing rain in Brooklyn turned into a virtual torrent in Manhattan. Through fifty-one miles, a hatless Roosevelt braved the elements in the backseat of his open Packard; photos the next morning showed his trademark pince-nez glasses completely spattered with rain, the water rolling down his cheeks and dripping from his chin. Moreover, it was cold; people along the motorcade route—police estimated the crowd at between 1.5 million and 3 million—stood for hours, "their legs chilled by the wind" and "their teeth chattering," the *New York Times* wrote.[54]

What the public and press did not know was that at several points along the route

> the President's car was turned out of the parade into the warmth of a heated [garage]. Secret Service agents quickly lifted the President from the car and stretched him out full length on blankets laid on the floor. They removed his clothes down to the skin. He was toweled dry and given a rubdown. He was redressed in dry clothes, brandy was poured down his throat and he was lifted back into the car. The pit stop was quickly done, and the President was soon back in the cavalcade.[55]

Moreover, during a stopover at Eleanor's house on Washington Square, Ross McIntire "immediately prescribed some medicinal bourbon," according to Grace Tully, adding that after a couple of what she called "good hookers, the Boss had a nap and then had another late afternoon bourbon 'treatment.'"[56]

Despite the degree of stage management required, it was a bravura performance, one that would have sorely tested even a fully healthy man. Roosevelt felt so invigorated by the public reception he received—and the overwhelmingly powerful response in the press, which declared that he had put the health issue to rest—that he scheduled repeat performances in Philadelphia and Chicago, as well as Boston, his only acknowledged visit there in 1944. "Now fired with the old fire-horse enthusiasm," wrote *Time*, "Candidate Roosevelt would give it all he had."[57]

On November 7, Franklin Roosevelt was returned to office for an unprecedented fourth term. His popular-vote margin was comfortable—53 percent to 46 percent—but by no means overwhelming. In the Electoral College, however, he scored his customary landslide, besting Dewey, 432–99, and carrying thirty-six states. Yet fourteen of those states had been decided by a margin of 5 percent or less.

Roosevelt now looked ahead to what promised to be the closing months of the war and his hoped-for adoption of a world peacekeeping body. But though the public now by and large seemed convinced that he was, as Ross McIntire had insisted once more just before the election, "in excellent health," Roosevelt was exhibiting some strange behavior that remained unknown to the American people—though scores of people who'd seen him privately had become increasingly alarmed by it.

The president was having repeated seizures.

"He'll Come Out of It. He Always Does"

CHAPTER 11

The end of the physical strain of campaigning brought no relief to Franklin Roosevelt. He was continually exhausted and feeling ill. Moreover, his abdominal pains continued, probably caused by a cancerous bowel obstruction; certainly this was not the colicky pain that typically accompanies gallstones.* Moreover, it contradicts Bruenn's assertion that after FDR's return from the Pacific, "there were no complaints at this time, or subsequently, of abdominal discomfort."[1]

In an effort to marshal his strength, Daisy Suckley wrote, FDR planned to go to Walter Reed Army Hospital "for some 6 weeks' complete rest"[2]—more likely, to undergo the operation Stirling had refused to undertake because of the president's condition, though it's difficult to see how hospitalizing the president for such an extended period could have been accomplished without arousing concern and setting tongues

*Daisy Suckley on November 22 recorded that "[he] doesn't feel awfully well, with odd aches & pains around the region of his belt, and no appetite."

wagging once more. Instead it was announced that he would go to Warm Springs at the end of November for three weeks, his first long vacation there since Pearl Harbor.

But there was another alarming problem—one that has never directly been addressed by most historians, even though it was observed by over a dozen reliable witnesses. Nor was it ever even alluded to by Howard Bruenn, although he must have witnessed it.

Budget Director Harold Smith noticed it in January 1944 when he went to the White House bedroom to review the president's annual budget message to Congress with him. "I have never seen him so listless," he wrote in his contemporary notes of the meeting. "At one stage, when he was about two-thirds of the way through the message . . . I saw his head nod. I could not see his eyes, but it seemed as though they were completely shut."[3]

A much more vivid example occurred three months later in front of Turner Catledge, a reporter in the Washington bureau of the *New York Times* (and later the paper's top editor). Having just returned from Europe and the Near East, he was called to the White House and told that FDR wanted to speak to him about his travels and observations. "When I entered the president's office," he wrote, "I had my first glimpse of him in several months. I was shocked and horrified—so much so that my impulse was to turn around and leave. I felt I was seeing something I shouldn't see. He had lost a great deal of weight. His shirt collar hung so loose around his neck that you could have put your hand inside it."

But it was when Catledge began talking with the president that he truly was horrified: "He was sitting there with a vague, glassy-eyed expression on his face and his mouth hanging open. . . . He would start talking about something, then in mid-sentence he would stop and his mouth would drop open and he'd sit staring at me in silence." Over the course of the hour-long visit, "repeatedly, he would lose his train of thought, stop and stare blankly at me. It was an agonizing experience. . . . Finally, a waiter brought his lunch and I was able to make my escape."[4]

It was a legitimate and powerful news story—visible firsthand evidence of Roosevelt's ill health, rumors of which already were sweeping Washington. But Catledge chose not to write it, nor did he tell any of his editors what he had witnessed. Not until he wrote his memoir, more than a quarter-century after Roosevelt's death, did he tell the story.

John Flynn, author of the harshly anti-FDR book *The Roosevelt Myth*, told of an incident during the president's postconvention Hawaii trip, which he said was related to him by an unnamed high-ranking naval officer who witnessed it from a few yards away. During dinner one night, according to Flynn's source, Roosevelt was delivering some prepared remarks when, at one point, "he faltered and paused, his eyes became glassy, consciousness drifted from him. The man at his side nudged him, shook him a little, pointed to the place in his manuscript at which he broke off and said, 'Here, Mr. President, is your place.' With an effort, he resumed. As he was wheeled from his quarters, officers noticed his head drooping forward, his jaw hanging loosely."[5]

It would be easy to dismiss this story as maliciously partisan, secondhand gossip. But not only does it match the description of similar incidents given by others, it actually predates nearly every other published account, having been written in 1948.

Over the next few months, others outside the White House circle would speak of having witnessed similar frightening episodes, in which the president seemed to lose all sense of where he was. Senator Frank Maloney of Connecticut went to the White House a few months later for a presidential chat; on his way in, he met one of his colleagues, Senator Joseph O'Mahoney of Wyoming, who'd just finished chatting with Roosevelt. "He was absolutely terrific," O'Mahoney reassured his colleague. "He was funny, he was charming; it was just like old times." Thus encouraged, Maloney hurried into the Oval Office and sat down in front of the president's desk. FDR looked up but said nothing; his eyes were fixed in a glassy stare. It soon became obvious, Maloney related, that Roosevelt had no idea who he was, or even that anyone was there. Convinced the president had suffered a stroke right before his eyes, the senator crossed himself and rushed from the room in search of "Pa" Watson—who calmly told him: "Don't worry. He'll come out of it. He always does." And indeed, by the time Maloney had returned to the Oval Office, Roosevelt had made a miraculous recovery and behaved as if nothing had happened.[6]

Watson's dismissive reaction—"He'll come out of it. He always does"—makes clear that he not only wasn't surprised by this incident, which had so startled the visiting legislator, he regarded it as nothing out of the ordinary, an everyday occurrence. His reaction also demonstrates that these episodes were short-lived and that FDR was able to "snap out of it" without any lasting effect. And, in fact, that's precisely what those who witnessed them would always report.

Alonzo Fields, the White House butler, recalled that "you could see him just fade away. He would come to the table sometimes and he would be bright and cheerful, but if any agitation happened in the conversation, he would again sag and he'd sort of droop and drop his head, or he would drop his jaw."[7]

Aside from the reported public incident in Hawaii, Roosevelt apparently had one of his attacks in full view of the assembled Washington press corps, at the White House Correspondents Dinner not long before his death. Allen Drury, then the congressional correspondent of the *New York Times*, wrote in his diary that as FDR was wheeled in to the dinner, the president uncharacteristically "paid no attention to us at all as we stood and applauded. . . . [He] was staring straight out at us and did [not] acknowledge the reception in any way. We might not have been there at all, and for a moment it gave one the uneasy feeling that, perhaps preoccupied, beyond all such social graces, he didn't know we were."[8]* Later on during the dinner, Drury added, the audience could see him "sitting there listening with an intent, vague expression, letting his jaw drop and his mouth fall open."[9]

Labor Secretary Frances Perkins, who had known Roosevelt for forty years, described how the president could change, in the space of just a couple of hours, from looking "like a ghost" to reverting to his usual "fine" demeanor, "his eyes bright." Her description of the more acute phenomenon, the most graphic of all, appears in an oral history interview—although, pointedly, she did not write about it in her own earlier memoir:

---

*Walter Trohan claimed in his memoir that he and John O'Donnell of the *New York Daily News* "smuggled" an unnamed doctor from Johns Hopkins University into the dinner and seated him directly beneath Roosevelt's place on the dais. "After the long evening," he wrote, "the doctor reported FDR was failing rapidly and could not last out a year. The physician made much of the fact that the nape of Roosevelt's neck had as much sag as the front." (Trohan, *Political Animals*, p. 101)

> The change in appearance had to do with the oncoming of a kind of glassy eye, and an extremely drawn look around the jaw and cheeks, and even a sort of dropping of the muscles of control of the jaw and mouth, as though they weren't working exactly. I think they were, but there was a great weakness in those muscles. Also, if you saw him close to, you would see that his hands were weak. When he fainted, as he did occasionally . . . that was all accentuated. It would be momentary. It would be very brief, and he'd be back again.[10]

The medically naive Perkins's mention of fainting recalls the way Grace Tully wrote about him repeatedly "nodding off" while going through his mail, and Anna recalling times when her father seemed "very quiet, almost introspective." (Perkins also said the attacks went on "for several years," meaning that they must have predated Turner Catledge's encounter.) However, there is evidence that Roosevelt did indeed have actual fainting spells: Milton Lipson, a Secret Service agent, recalled "several occasions when [FDR] had the misfortune to fall out of his chair, and you'd have to come in and there was the president of the United States helpless on the floor. And you [had to] gently pick him up, say nothing about it, put him back on the chair and that was it. But your heart would break."[11] Grace Tully also recalled "a fainting spell" that Roosevelt suffered at Hyde Park back in 1938—and how he "recovered so quickly that he was present with the dinner gathering in the library in fifteen minutes without any sign of indisposition."[12] A well-documented incident of sudden unconsciousness occurred in February 1940 when FDR "collapsed" while dining with his secretary, Missy LeHand, and Ambassador William Bullitt. McIntire later told the guests that the president had suffered "a very slight heart attack," although he most likely meant a general cardiac problem.[13]

From the sheer volume of the reports, as well as their strikingly similar accounts, the overwhelming probability is that these events were seizures—momentary neurological dysfunctions provoked by abnormal electrical activity in the brain. Contrary to popular belief, not all seizures are convulsive; the ones FDR suffered, with a temporary impairment of consciousness, are best categorized in present-day neurological parlance as "partial complex," highly suggestive of an abnormality of the temporal lobe of the brain. It is tempting to suggest that these episodes were the first indications that Roosevelt's melanoma had metastasized to his brain, given that brain hemorrhages from metastases are the second most common cause of death in melanoma patients. But though this most probably did occur later on, the time element involved—Catledge witnessed it a year before his death—makes it most unlikely that these incidents were caused by a metastatic brain tumor, which generally causes death within a matter of weeks or months.

The most probable cause of Roosevelt's seizures was an otherwise asymptomatic stroke, attributable to his severe cardiovascular disease. Unlike hypertension, for which there was no effective treatment in 1944, seizures had been treated with bromine since the late nineteenth century and with phenobarbital since 1912. Roosevelt had been taking phenobarbital, between 90 and 180 milligrams per day, since April 1944, ostensibly as a sedative—though it is curious why a powerful "downer" would be given to someone who was sleeping sixteen hours a day. More likely, it was given as a treatment for his seizures.* Roosevelt may not have been aware of its side effects when he complained to Daisy that he had "a sleeping sickness of some sort."[14]

Bert Edward Park, a neurosurgeon who has written on the impact of illness on various historical figures, blamed Roosevelt's lethargy and jaw-drop episodes on encephalopathy, or generalized brain dysfunction, from a reduced supply of oxygen to the brain. No doubt, Roosevelt had many reasons to be suffering from encephalopathy, among them his weakened heart and soaring blood pressure, as well as reduced performance of his lungs and kidneys. This might explain his difficulty in focusing and concentrating, but not partial-complex seizures. Interestingly, patients with low-grade encephalopathy often perform better in situations involving high activity and stimulation, which may explain why Roosevelt performed so well in public—and, particularly, why he did so well on his whirlwind campaign tour of New York in the midst of a driving rainstorm.

*By this time, these events had to have been cause for medical concern, Watson's dismissal notwithstanding, although the exact date cannot be pinpointed. Still, phenobarbital was in wide use at the time as the only effective anti-seizure medication.

There is other evidence that FDR's doctors suspected he had a neurological problem: Historian Robert Ferrell disclosed that Winchell Craig—who'd positioned the president's head during the wen operation at Bethesda—told a Mayo Clinic colleague, David Voris, that at some point—the date was not identified—he'd performed a pneumoencephalogram on the president to check for an intracranial mass.[15] This intensely invasive and uncomfortable procedure, thankfully obsolete due to advances in brain imaging, involved replacing the spinal fluid with gas in order to enhance X-ray contrast and would have been performed only if doctors had strongly believed he had a space-occupying brain lesion. Ferrell and Voris (who first disclosed Craig's connection to Roosevelt) were unable to locate any papers that would confirm the report. Craig's nephew, Dr. Joseph Craig, confirmed to us that his uncle had treated Roosevelt but couldn't provide further details.[16] Neither McIntire nor Bruenn ever mentioned Roosevelt's seizures in their accounts of FDR's health. It was politically no more possible to suggest that the president's brain was imperfect than it was possible to say he had cancer. Both notions were unspeakable in public.

However, another problem could not be disguised simply by not talking about it: It was too visibly obvious to those who were with the president every day, and especially to those who saw him only on occasion. Roosevelt was continuing to lose weight at a dramatic clip, and his doctors were growing concerned. It went far beyond any desired weight loss: The president declared he had no appetite, no interest in his food—which he couldn't taste anyway.*

From his baseline weight of 188 in March 1944, the restricted-calorie diet imposed by Bruenn had lowered his weight to 174 ¾ two months later. Roosevelt was delighted with his thinner stomach, Daisy noted:

---

*There is an outside possibility that Roosevelt may have been one of the first persons to be treated by the groundbreaking antibiotic streptomycin, which was discovered in 1943; the first human trials of the drug took place at the Mayo Clinic in November 1944. It was about this time that FDR began complaining of the inability to taste food; moreover, reporters and others noted that he was having increasing difficulty with his hearing. Both of these are rather immediate side effects of streptomycin, although this was not recognized until after Roosevelt's death. That the president and his doctors would have access to an experimental drug is entirely logical.

"He wants to go up a lb. or two, to not be less than 175 and not more than 180. He feels better thin, however, and walked much more easily in the water than a month ago."[17] The ability to stand during speeches and "walk" were always among Roosevelt's top priorities; with the anticipated rigors of the upcoming campaign, he perceived this weight range as ideal. But Roosevelt did not, could not, gain weight. Directly contrary to Daisy's diary entry of the previous month, Bruenn insisted that in August, "despite the best efforts of the cook, liberalization of calories and much persuasion, he obstinately kept himself on his restricted diet" and was "insistent on a further loss to around 170 lb."[18] However, this does not make sense, because by that time he was already down to about 165 pounds. Bruenn was beginning the effort to disguise the problem by attributing it to a president who had decided unnecessarily to keep to a frugal diet.

In mid-October 1944, about three weeks before the election, Ross McIntire addressed the president's all-too-noticeable weight loss at a press conference and attributed it to Roosevelt's ego. FDR, he joked, "is proud of his flat—repeat, f-l-a-t—tummy." According to McIntire, the entire weight loss had come "in the spring. He was getting a little too heavy, and we had him reduce by cutting down on the quantity of food, and by swimming and other exercises in the White House pool." But now, though free of any dietary restrictions and able to eat anything he wished, said the doctor, Roosevelt had become so consumed with keeping his youthful figure that he was willing to "take" the public seeing him with a gaunt face. McIntire claimed that FDR had dropped to 175 pounds, put several pounds back on, and was now "eight or nine pounds below his ideal weight." Reminded by a reporter that the president still looked thin, McIntire agreed: "I know it. But did you ever hear of a man who recovered his flat tummy and got proud of it? . . . The President doesn't want to get that bulge back." Though maintaining that "I wish he would put on a few pounds," McIntire nonetheless said that "we've not made any special attempt to pick up on his weight."[19] It was a smoke screen.

Privately, McIntire claimed in his memoir, he told the president: "You may feel fine, but you don't look it. Your neck is scrawny and your face is gullied by lines that have added ten years to your age. And while we're on the subject, for heaven's sake, get some new clothes.

That old shirt is sizes too big, and the coat hangs on your shoulders like a bag." The president, he wrote, "threw back his head and laughed, but he gave no promises."[20]

FDR's true weight was far below the figure McIntire cited at his press conference. Once Roosevelt started losing weight, he hadn't regained any of it, even when his appetite temporarily improved. Before long, the president's doctors *would* start making a concerted effort to pack on some weight, even lowering his dosage of digitalis, in the hope that the medication had been causing his poor appetite. The low-fat diet enforced for his reported gallbladder disease had long been abandoned: At the very same time in which Bruenn maintained that Roosevelt "obstinately kept himself on his restricted diet," Daisy wrote he was being given eggnog at 11 a.m. and a large glass of orange juice at 4 p.m., in addition to his regular meals.

Arriving in Warm Springs just after Thanksgiving, Daisy "found myself looking at the Pres. at least half the time. He looked so pale & thin & tired. I try so hard to make myself think he looks well, but he gets very grey when tired, and it shows so much. . . . He looks ten years older than last year." And, she added significantly, "he knows it himself."[21] Bruenn noted that "he continued to have difficulty eating," complaining, "can't eat—cannot taste food," and, as a result, "had lost a little more weight. He was urged to eat, and its importance was stressed."[22]

The weight loss, almost certainly related to his abdominal cancer, continued inexorably until Roosevelt's death, when he probably weighed no more than 150 pounds and possibly less.*

As the new year arrived, Roosevelt prepared for his fourth inauguration. But there was something different about his mood: For the first time, Eleanor noted, "perhaps having a premonition that he would not be with us very long, Franklin insisted that every grandchild come to the White House" for the inauguration and then stay "for a few days."[23] A

---

*A viable alternative explanation offered by Dr. Bert Park is a poorly understood condition of unexplained weight loss associated with severe congestive heart failure, known as cardiac cachexia. In Roosevelt's case, however, the presence of continued abdominal pain, which is not a feature of the heart-related condition, strongly supports malignancy as the cause. Numerous cardiologists confirmed to us that this extensive weight loss in anything other than a "cardiac cripple," which Roosevelt was not, is most atypical.

few days before the January 20 ceremony, as he was working on his speech with Sam Rosenman and Robert Sherwood, Roosevelt suddenly turned to Grace Tully and her assistant, Dorothy Brady. "Grace," he asked, "what in this room reminds you most of me?" She indicated a naval portrait of an old man-of-war. Brady, asked the same question—FDR addressed her by his usual nickname for her, "Child"—selected a painting of the eighteenth-century U.S. naval commander John Paul Jones, to whom she was distantly related. The president then dictated two memos, stating that "in the event of my death," the two women should receive the portraits they'd selected; the notes, at Rosenman's suggestion, were placed in the White House safe.[24]

The inauguration itself was a modest affair, as such ceremonies go: Roosevelt scaled back the usual budget by 90 percent, citing wartime economies, and ordered it held at the White House portico instead of its customary location outside the U.S. Capitol. His inaugural address had been whittled down to a mere five hundred words, the shortest in history; it was the first time he'd been on his feet, save for brief periods during the campaign, since Bremerton five months earlier. The weather was raw, and Roosevelt insisted on delivering the speech without an overcoat. When it was finished, the president made his way back inside the White House, where he collapsed into his wheelchair and urgently asked his son, Jimmy, to take him to the Green Room: "The same type of pain, somewhat less acute, that had bothered him in San Diego was stabbing him again," his son recalled. "Jimmy," he said, "I can't stand this unless you get me a stiff drink." And, he added, "you'd better make it straight." The younger Roosevelt filled a tumbler with bourbon and watched his father gulp it down. "In all my years, I had never seen Father take a drink in that manner," he wrote.[25]* In yet another sign of the president's growing preoccupation with death, according to Jimmy, the president later discussed with him the details of his will, and also told him of his intention to give him the family ring.[26]

Secretary of State Edward Stettinius first grew concerned as he watched the president deliver his inaugural address: "He had seemed to

---

*Writing of the same incident sixteen years later, Jimmy Roosevelt gave a far less dramatic version of his father's drinking. (James Roosevelt, *My Parents*, pp. 283–284)

tremble all over. It was not just that his hands shook, but his whole body, as well. . . . It seemed to me that some kind of deterioration in the President's health had taken place between the middle of December and the inauguration."[27]

Among the White House luncheon guests that day was Edith Bolling Wilson, the widow of Woodrow Wilson, who had orchestrated the cover-up of her own husband's failing health as president. "He looks exactly as my husband did when he went into his decline," the shocked former First Lady told Frances Perkins. "Don't say that to another soul," responded the secretary of labor—who, just the day before, had confided to her secretary her own fears about the president's health: "He has a great and terrible job to do, and he's got to do it, even if it kills him."[28]

Indeed he did. Within days Roosevelt would set out on the most arduous trip of his life, for the final meeting of the wartime Big Three—a summit that remains one of the most controversial such gatherings in history, and which many still believe was directly affected by the president's increasingly fragile health.

Franklin Roosevelt was headed for Yalta.

Yalta

CHAPTER 12

No single episode of Roosevelt's presidency became as controversial—and remains so today—as his participation in the week-long Yalta summit in the Crimea. At this second meeting between FDR, Churchill, and Stalin, several critical issues pertaining to the war and its immediate aftermath were negotiated, including the date of Moscow's entry into the war in Japan, the partition of postwar Europe, the political status of Poland, and the terms of Soviet participation in the United Nations.

Almost from its conclusion, and particularly following the communist takeover of China in 1949, conservatives charged that Roosevelt, "the sick old man of Yalta," who had long been naive about the true nature of the USSR and entirely too trusting of its dictatorial leader, had "sold out" Eastern Europe to the duplicitous Stalin. That case was put forward by President George W. Bush in a speech commemorating the sixtieth anniversary of V-E Day:

> The agreement at Yalta followed in the unjust tradition of Munich and the Molotov-Ribbentrop Pact. Once again, when powerful governments negotiated, the freedom of small nations was somehow expendable. Yet

> this attempt to sacrifice freedom for the sake of stability left a continent divided and unstable. The captivity of millions in Central and Eastern Europe will be remembered as one of the greatest wrongs of history.[1]

That Roosevelt was a sick man, older than his years, at Yalta, is undeniable. Sir Alexander Cadogan, of the British foreign office, "got the impression that most of the time he hardly knew what it was all about."[2] But whether he was so sick as to be unfit to participate in Yalta, or whether his astonishing resilience and recuperative powers allowed him to marshal the mental acuity necessary to conduct such critical negotiations is another question entirely. Charles Bohlen, FDR's interpreter and a senior U.S. diplomat and Soviet expert, maintained in 1973 that "our leader was ill at Yalta, but he was effective. . . . I so believed at the time and still so believe."[3]

Roosevelt had wanted the conference to take place along the Mediterranean. But Stalin, citing—ironically—the advice of his own doctors, who'd ordered him not to undertake a long trip, insisted on a site closer to home for him. The three leaders ultimately settled on Yalta, a resort on the Black Sea. But Churchill, who arrived there first, sent word to Roosevelt that the Soviet leader had picked the most remote and inconvenient—not to mention inhospitable—location possible. "If we had spent ten years on research, we could not have picked a worse place in the world than Yalta," he told Harry Hopkins, who relayed the message to FDR. "It is good for typhus and deadly lice, which thrive in these parts."[4] Moreover, recalled Howard Bruenn, this was followed by another dire message from Churchill:

> The drive from the airfield at Saki to Yalta [was] 6 hr instead of 2 hr as originally reported by Mr. [Averell] Harriman [the U.S. ambassador to Moscow]; that one of his people had reported the mountain part of the drive as frightening and at times impassable; and the health conditions as wholly unsanitary, as the Germans had left the building infested with vermin. It was, therefore, a great relief upon landing at Malta to learn from Mr. Harriman and our advance party that, although we would face a difficult drive after landing at the airport at Saki, it would not be too tiring if completed during daylight and if we had clear weather; also, that

the medical officers of the USS *Catoctin*, anchored at Sevastopol, had accomplished a very effective job of debugging.[5]

The trip took nearly two weeks: eight days' travel to Malta aboard the heavy cruiser USS *Quincy*, a 1,200-mile flight to the remote Crimean airfield of Saki—at a low altitude, Bruenn noted, between 6,000 and 8,000 feet, which Roosevelt weathered well—and then the eighty-mile trip to Yalta, which did indeed take six hours.

Even before his arrival at the summit, some of those around the president had grown concerned. At a White House movie screening a few days before his departure, Roosevelt announced to the guests that they were going to see a film about Yalta. "No, Father," whispered Anna, "not Yalta"—the location of the upcoming conference was top secret—"but Casablanca."[6] Upon his arrival in Malta, Fleet Admiral Ernest J. King, commander in chief of the U.S. fleet and chief of naval operations, and others in FDR's military entourage were troubled by Roosevelt's attitude during his briefings: He listened but did not talk. In fact, King recalled, the president seemed to want to get rid of them, so they quickly left without a word.[7]

Jimmy Byrnes, who took copious notes of the conference, complained that "so far as I could see, the President had made little preparation. . . . Not until the day before we landed at Malta did I learn that we had on board a very complete file of studies and recommendations prepared by the State Department. . . . I am sure that the failure to study them while en route was due to the President's illness."[8]

Things did not improve once FDR reached Yalta. William Rigdon, the president's deputy naval aide, recalled that "some of us noticed, but without concern, that his lower jaw often hung down." Writing in 1962, seventeen years after the events, Rigdon admitted that "it is incredible that many of us who were with Roosevelt daily did not see that he was declining."[9] During the first three nights, the president developed a paroxysmal cough that would rouse him from his sleep; it disappeared, Bruenn disclosed, "with the use of terpin hydrate and codeine."[10]

The summit began on February 4 and followed the same daily schedule: preparation sessions in the mornings, then formal meetings convened at 4 p.m. at the Livadia Palace; these lasted three to four hours and were followed by dinner and, in the evenings, social gatherings. During the first day, Anna, who'd accompanied her father, wrote to her husband, John Boettiger:

> Just between you and me, we are having to watch OM very carefully from the physical standpoints. He gets all wound up, seems to thoroughly enjoy it all, but wants too many people around, and then won't go to bed early enough. The result is that he doesn't sleep well. Ross and Bruenn are both worried because of the old "ticker" trouble—which, of course, no one knows about but those two and me. I am working closely with Ross and Bruenn, and am using all the ingenuity and tact that I can muster to try and separate the wheat from the chaff—to keep unnecessary people out of OM's room and to steer the necessary ones in at the best times. This is actually taking place at the Conf so that I will know who should and who should not see OM. I have found out through Bruenn (who won't let me tell Ross that I know) that this "ticker" situation is far more serious than I ever knew. And, the biggest difficulty in handling the situation here is that we can, of course, tell no one of the "ticker" trouble. It's truly worrisome—and there's not a helluva lot anyone can do about it. (Better tear off and destroy this paragraph.)[11]

Unbeknownst to Anna, however, she and the doctors were not the only ones at Yalta who were aware of Roosevelt's "ticker trouble." Charles McMoran Wilson, Lord Moran, who was Winston Churchill's personal physician, confided to his diary that the day before he and the prime minister left England for the conference, he'd received a confidential letter from his longtime close friend, Dr. Roger I. Lee of Boston. It said:

> Roosevelt had heart failure eight months ago. There are, of course, degrees of congestive failure, but Roosevelt had enlargement of his liver and was puffy. A post-mortem would have shown congestion of his organs. He was irascible, and became very irritable if he had to concentrate his mind for long. If anything was brought up that wanted thinking out, he would change the subject. He was, too, sleeping badly.[12]

The final summit of the Big Three: Winston Churchill, FDR, and Joseph Stalin, two months before FDR's death. "I didn't say it was good," Roosevelt told Assistant Secretary of State Adolf Berle of the still hotly debated agreements on postwar Europe that were negotiated at the parley by the "sick man" of Yalta. "I said it was the best I could do." (Franklin D. Roosevelt Library)

Though off in some details—FDR's heart failure actually had been diagnosed eleven months earlier—it was a remarkably accurate assessment of the March 1944 examination at Bethesda and the state of Roosevelt's health at the time. His source, Roger Lee, was a prominent physician, a founder of the Harvard School of Public Health who had played a pioneering role in overcoming the clinical impediments to blood transfusion in the early part of the century.[13] His own 1956 memoir does not mention FDR, although he does confirm that he and Lord Moran were close friends. So where did Lee obtain his obviously accurate information? We can't be sure, but it's significant that two of his immediate predecessors as president of the American Medical Association in the 1940s were Frank Lahey and James Paullin—the two "honorary consultants" Ross McIntire had brought in to examine Roosevelt at Bethesda the previous March and confirm Bruenn's dire diagnosis.[14]

Armed with this advance knowledge, it's hardly surprising that Lord Moran's assessment of FDR, confided to his diary, appears so prescient. "To a doctor's eye," he wrote, "the President appears a sick man. He has all the symptoms of hardening of the arteries of the brain in an advanced stage, so that I give him only a few months to live. But men shut their eyes when they do not want to see, and the Americans here cannot bring themselves to believe that he is finished. His daughter thinks he is not really ill, and his doctor backs her up."[15] (Obviously, Anna's letter to her husband reveals that she knew FDR was ill, though it's likely that she was told of the cardiac illness in order to conceal from her the other threats to the president: seizures and cancer.)

But Lord Moran also was a skilled physician, and his eyes confirmed what Roger Lee had told him earlier—and what so many others had seen over the past several months. "The President looked old and thin and drawn," he wrote of his first observation of FDR at Yalta. "He had a cape or shawl over his shoulders and appeared shrunken; he sat looking straight ahead with his mouth open, as if he were not taking things in. Everyone was shocked by his appearance and gabbled about it afterwards."[16]

But "it was not only [Roosevelt's] physical deterioration that had caught their attention," he wrote several days later. "He intervened very little in the discussions, sitting with his mouth open."[17] Yet, Moran added, "if he has sometimes been short of facts about the subject under discussion, his shrewdness has covered this up. Now, they say, the shrewdness has gone, and there is nothing left. I doubt, from what I have seen, whether he is fit for his job here."[18]

Whether Churchill privately shared his physician's assessment isn't known, but clearly he was "puzzled and distressed," Moran recorded. "The President no longer seems to take an intelligent interest in the war," he said Churchill told him. "Often he does not seem even to read the papers the p.m. gives him. Sometimes he appears as if he has no thought-out recipe for anything beyond his troubles with Congress."[19] In his own memoir, Churchill would write only that "at Yalta, I noticed that the President was ailing. His captivating smile, his gay and charming manner, had not deserted him, but his face had a transparency, an air of purification, and often there was a faraway look in his eyes."[20] Churchill was poetically suggesting that Roosevelt, a man he admired greatly and whose dignity he would never wish to impugn, looked as if he was dying.

Lord Moran's description of his British colleagues' astonishment at Roosevelt's appearance and demeanor is confirmed by the contemporary recollections of Sir Alexander Cadogan, Churchill's permanent under-secretary for foreign affairs, who noted: "Whenever he was called on to preside over any meeting, he failed to make any attempt to grip it or guide it, and sat generally speechless, or, if he made any intervention, it was generally completely irrelevant."[21]

On the night of February 8, after a grueling debate over the issue of Poland—Roosevelt and Churchill insisted on free elections; Stalin demanded more control, citing the fact that "throughout history, Poland has been the corridor through which [Germany] has passed into Russia"—Roosevelt suffered an attack of *pulsus alternans*, in which strong and weak heartbeats alternate. "That's a very bad sign," Bruenn explained years later. "It indicated he didn't have much reserve." Once the president's activity was cut back, the alternating pulse "disappeared, thank goodness, after three or four days."[22] In the end, Stalin promised free elections, though it soon became clear that he had no intention of following through.

Other issues were equally difficult: Stalin agreed to join the United Nations but demanded a formula in which a set of permanent members, including the USSR, would enjoy veto powers; he also wanted three extra votes for the Soviet Union. And his agreement on entering the war against Japan following the defeat of Nazi Germany was made contingent on U.S. recognition of Manchurian independence from China.

All these, along with other agreements that ensured Soviet control over the rest of Eastern Europe, have been cited over the years by FDR's critics as proof that the decisions taken at Yalta were seriously flawed and heavily tilted in Stalin's favor, making the Cold War inevitable. There is a fascinating exchange of letters to the editor in the *New York Times*, published in 1954, in which a young Robert F. Kennedy, who had been an aide to Senator Joseph R. McCarthy, pilloried the Yalta agreements, saying they had "caused some of the heartbreak and problems of post-war Europe." FDR, he charged, "made the agreement with Russia with inadequate knowledge and without consulting any of the personages, military or political, who would ordinarily have had the most complete knowledge of the problems involved."[23] He was answered by the historian Arthur Schlesinger Jr., whose reply blasted Kennedy's "astonishing mixture of distortion and error."[24]

Certainly Roosevelt has been faulted for being too trusting of Stalin, and not just by his political enemies. Charles Bohlen wrote that FDR "felt that Stalin viewed the world in somewhat the same light as he did. . . . What he did not understand was that Stalin's enmity was based on profound ideological convictions. The existence of a gap between the Soviet Union and the United States, a gap that could not be bridged, was never fully perceived by Franklin Roosevelt."[25] Harry Hopkins confirmed this, saying that "in our hearts, we really believed a new day had dawned. . . . The Russians had proved that they could be reasonable and far-sighted and neither the President nor any one of us had the slightest doubt that we could live with them and get on peaceably with them far into the future."[26] But the point at Yalta was that Roosevelt was in possession of the information—he just lacked the mental focus to use it, except minimally. He had little stamina, and only sporadic attention to detail. He was, in short, not a forceful negotiator, and if he believed that the shortfalls of Yalta could be sorted out later on, he was deluding himself equally about the character of his opponent and how much time was available to him.

(It is hardly reassuring that Ross McIntire would cite Alger Hiss, Secretary of State Edward Stettinius's deputy—later exposed as having been a Soviet agent—as having been "most emphatic" that "he had never seen the President conduct himself in any better fashion than he did [at Yalta].")[27]

But could Roosevelt and Churchill really have done any better at Yalta? Britain's military commander, Field Marshal Sir Bernard Law Montgomery, would claim that Stalin "had no difficulty fooling Roosevelt," charging that he and Churchill "behaved to the communist dictators at Yalta much as their despised predecessors had to the Nazi dictator at Munich."[28]

Yet Jimmy Byrnes would write that "it was not a question of what we would let the Russians do, but what we could get the Russians to do." Poland, after all, already was occupied by Stalin—along with most of the rest of what eventually would become the Soviet bloc. "Theoretically,

Churchill and Roosevelt could have refused to cut any deal with Stalin at Yalta," Jacob Heilbrunn has written. "But that could have started the Cold War on the spot. . . . FDR's approach was not particularly different from that of Churchill, who had declared that he would 'sup with the devil' to win the war, which is what he and Roosevelt, in effect, did."[29]

For his part, FDR probably gave the most honest assessment of his week at Yalta. "I didn't say it was good," he told Assistant Secretary of State Adolf Berle, "I said it was the best I could do."[30] Before long, Roosevelt realized that the agreements he'd reached at Yalta essentially were worthless. "Averell [Harriman] is right," he confided to Anna Rosenberg of the War Manpower Commission. "We can't do business with Stalin. He has broken every one of the promises he made at Yalta."[31]

Yalta proved to be a worthless journey. Promises were made and not kept, lasting enmities were not set aside, and for Roosevelt it was too arduous a voyage for a man so near the end of his days.

"Did You See This Thing Coming?"

CHAPTER 13

Daisy Suckley was growing increasingly concerned as she waited impatiently at home for word about—and, more important, from—her beloved Franklin. She'd been closely inspecting the photos from Yalta that the newspapers had published and she didn't like what she saw. "In all the pictures that have come out," she recorded, "he looks really sick, even when he was at Malta." Worse still, "even the papers say 'his aides are worried about his health.'"[1] As the days stretched on, her anxiety increased, fearing that the president was ailing but taking hope in the fact that "Churchill has just returned to London" and "I don't *think* he would, if FDR were critically ill."[2]

Even a note from the president, dated a week earlier, reassuring her that "I'm *really all right*" (emphasis in FDR's original) and that the Yalta conference, of which he was then in "the last stretch," was "I think a real success"[3] didn't completely convince her. After all, she noted, "it doesn't cover the eight days since then." Only when she heard a radio report that Roosevelt and Churchill had been to several Middle East cities to meet with local political leaders did her anxiety relax: "so my fears are groundless!—and I am much relieved!"[4]

Little did she know, but the growing concern for Roosevelt's health was felt by more than just his aides. Anna, bolstered by the alarming—and, she believed, completely candid—briefing she'd been given by Howard Bruenn at Yalta, wrote her husband from the return voyage: "My fear . . . is that he will have a terrific letdown when he gets home and possibly crack under it, as he did last year.* But all we can do is hold our fingers crossed."

With Roosevelt's return to Washington, Daisy was ecstatic: "F looks so much better than anyone can suspect—his colour is good & his blood pressure is pretty good."[5] (Bruenn's notes, while giving no precise figures, indicate that the president's blood pressure readings during this period were "somewhat" lower, though hardly "pretty good.") Even though Roosevelt told Daisy that "he thinks he has lost more weight" and remained "so very tired," she was encouraged by his appearance and demeanor.[6]

Interestingly, her diary contains no comment at all with respect to Roosevelt's disastrous Yalta speech to Congress (described in Chapter 1), which is most uncharacteristic for someone who subjected all of the president's public remarks to the most minute parsing, as she'd done with the Bremerton speech the previous summer, for the slightest sign of any problem. Given the rambling nature of the speech, the frequent and irrelevant ad libs, and—particularly—the president's first public reference to his disability, one would have expected a lengthy and emotional entry in Daisy's diary. But nothing at all appears, not even a simple mention that FDR would be speaking to the nation. All of which reinforces the notion that Daisy subjected her diary to heavy self-censorship before leaving it to be discovered after her death.

Daisy's relief at FDR's improved appearance was decidedly short-lived. On March 25, Franklin and Eleanor paid a visit to her home, Wilderstein, not far from Hyde Park; to her horror, she wrote, "The President looks terribly badly—so tired that every word seems to be an effort. . . . He just can't stand this strain indefinitely."[7]

---

*It's unclear to what Anna was referring. If she meant the lengthy illness her father suffered after returning from Teheran in December 1943, then writing that he'd "crack(ed)" is a curious, and significant, choice of words.

Others close to FDR felt the same way: Supreme Court Justice Robert Jackson (who previously had been FDR's attorney general) and his wife, Irene, were among four couples who helped celebrate the Roosevelts' fortieth wedding anniversary on St. Patrick's Day. On the way home from the White House, Mrs. Jackson suddenly remarked, "We're not going to have Mr. Roosevelt with us very long." The justice was so startled that he stopped the car and demanded an explanation. "Why, didn't you see how he looked and how he dropped his head down after he would say a few words?" she replied.[8]

The president was having other problems besides his continuing seizures. Canadian Prime Minister Mackenzie King visited the White House shortly after Roosevelt's return from Yalta and noted in his diary that FDR kept repeating himself. One night over dinner, he told King a story about Jimmy Byrnes having left the Catholic Church to marry "a Presbyterian girl," then repeated it the next afternoon. He did the same thing with a long anecdote about Churchill going for a swim in the ocean in Miami, telling the story two nights in succession, completely oblivious to the fact that he had related both stories previously.[9]

At about this time, Jonathan Daniels and speechwriter Archibald MacLeish saw Roosevelt about a statement they'd prepared for him regarding Stalin's demand for extra votes at the United Nations. The president, Daniels later recalled, made a change in the document; only after they'd left the Oval Office did they realize that FDR's editing had actually reversed the statement's entire meaning. "It was a matter of such importance," said Daniels, "that, despite his distressing condition, we felt we had to go back and say, 'Mr. President, look.' And that was a damn tough walk back when you realized how—in such a bad state the President was at that moment." MacLeish, he said, noted somberly that there was "a look of death" in Roosevelt's eyes.[10]

Daisy Suckley was unaware of these incidents, but one thought gave her some comfort: "Thank Heavens he gets to WS [Warm Springs] Thursday night."[11] Like the president, she had an almost religious faith in the recuperative powers of the environs of the small Georgia cottage that the nation knew as the Little White House. She would be going with him. The exhausted chief executive needed the rest and relaxation that Warm Springs always provided, she wrote. "He looks really ill—thin &

worn," she confided while aboard Roosevelt's train, the *Ferdinand Magellan*, for the ride south.[12]

He would be heading there on March 29—for the last time.

The presidential entourage arrived in Warm Springs the following afternoon. Joining Daisy in making the trip was another FDR spinster cousin, the more eccentric and less circumspect Laura "Polly" Delano. The usual contingent of aides—correspondence secretary Bill Hassett, Grace Tully, Dorothy Brady, switchboard operator Louise "Hacky" Hackmeister, Secret Service agent Mike Reilly—came along, as did Basil O'Connor, the president's onetime law partner and now chairman of the Warm Springs Foundation, as well as Leighton McCarthy, the Canadian ambassador to Washington, who owned a cottage there. Each of the three news wire services—Associated Press, United Press, and International News Service—had sent their White House reporters. As he had been for at least a year, Howard Bruenn was the physician in charge, aided by pharmacist/masseur George A. Fox; Ross McIntire, scheduled to testify before a congressional committee, remained behind. Anna also stayed in Washington, tending to her sick child; Eleanor, who did not enjoy the atmosphere of Warm Springs, was involved in her normal hectic schedule of activities in the capital.

As usual, Roosevelt's train was greeted by a large crowd of well-wishers as it pulled into the station. But Mabel Irwin, whose husband, Ed, was the foundation's medical director and chief surgeon, was stunned when she saw the president wheeled out onto a platform. "My heart sank at the sight of him," she recalled. "President Roosevelt looked so thin, so old—and he looked deathly tired."[13] She also noticed something unusual: "I had the impression that the President was holding very firmly to his wheelchair. He was in a small portable wheelchair without side arms and he was holding very tensely to the seat of the chair."[14] Mike Reilly was equally distressed, noting that whereas Roosevelt normally used his own strength to help as he was lifted into his car, on this day he was "heavy" and "dead weight." He passed the word to Bruenn and to the other agents.[15]

Perhaps seeing an opening in McIntire's absence, Hassett approached Bruenn that first night in Warm Springs and told him somberly, "He is slipping away from us and no earthly power can keep him here." When the cardiologist, abandoning his rigid vow of silence, expressed some skepticism, Hassett told Bruenn how he "understood his position—his obligation to save life, not to admit defeat." Reminding him that he'd given the same warning the previous December, Hassett added: "I know you don't want to make the admission, and I have talked to no one else save one. To all the staff, to the family and with the Boss himself I have maintained the bluff; but I am convinced that there is no help for him."[16]

Bruenn grew somber and emotional, admitting that "the Boss is in a precarious position, but he could be saved if measures were adopted to rescue him from certain mental strains and emotional influences."[17] Hassett, ever the realist, told him that those "conditions could not be met" and later wrote that the conversation had "confirmed my suspicions that the Boss is leaving us."[18]

The following day was Daisy's turn to question the doctor. They had a long talk, which left her "a little happier about it, for he confessed to a feeling of frustration in trying to help." Bruenn, as he'd told Hassett, tried to reinforce the need to limit the president's strain and emotional upsets. But Daisy, offering a plan of action formulated from her unique and intimate knowledge of Roosevelt's concerns, pleaded for help to "put it very plainly to FDR himself: FDR's one really great wish is to get this international organization for peace started. Nothing else counts next to that. That is the means by which they must make him take care of himself: 'You want to carry out the United Nations plan. Without your health, you will not be able to do it. Therefore—take care of yourself.'"[19]

For a time, Warm Springs seemed to be working its magic. In a desperate bid to put some weight on him, it was agreed that Roosevelt would be fed small helpings of gruel—oatmeal cooked and recooked a total of six times—between meals; to Daisy's delight, he seemed "to like it."[20] In fact, she noted, the president said to her, "Wouldn't it be strange if this gruel should be the one thing that put weight on me!"[21]* Regardless, his appetite appeared to be improving; no longer did he turn away his dinner plate and complain that he couldn't taste the food. On April 5, Daisy

*Daisy, ever the amateur nutritionist, tried to get Bruenn to add dextrin, a light carbohydrate, to his gruel. The doctor demurred, saying it "has little in it that sugar has not from a fattening point of view." Nonsense, Daisy confided to her diary: "I know that 'baby foods' are what run-down people need." (Daisy Suckley diary, April 11, 1945)

recorded that he'd had "an excellent dinner: a very rich mushroom soup, scrambled eggs & bacon, peas, stewed peaches & cream."[22] Work was kept to a bare minimum—mostly mail sent down in a daily pouch from Washington, along with some editing of his Jefferson Day radio broadcast, scheduled for the 13th—and, though he slept badly and continued to be racked by coughing, he seemed to be getting some rest. Still, the fatalism of the past few months was never far from his mind: He'd brought with him a large wooden crate filled with books; for the first time anyone could recall, he kept referring to the box as a "coffin." Several times he asked Arthur Prettyman, his valet, to "move the coffin closer to the chair."[23]

Roosevelt attended Easter Sunday services in the chapel at Warm Springs. To Mabel Irwin's eyes, "his face looked almost as gray as his suit. During the service, he dropped his glasses and prayer book. As he came out of the chapel, he looked neither right nor to the left. He kept his eyes straight and did not speak to anyone. I had never seen him do that before."[24] By this time, the president's weight, which had been 188 just a year earlier, was probably below 150 pounds.

On the last night of Roosevelt's life, April 11, Treasury Secretary Henry Morgenthau came to dinner. The president's hands shook so badly during his beloved ritual of pouring cocktails that he knocked over glasses when he poured, and he kept confusing names.[25]*

---

*While the tremor, which had grown uncontrollable by June 1943, varied in intensity, it progressed throughout 1944 and increasingly had a marked effect on his handwriting. Many reliable observers expressed concern; the most dramatic description was given by the White House director of public relations, David Noyes, who noted shortly before FDR's final trip to Warm Springs that "the president was trying to light a cigarette and put the cigarette in his holder to light it in the usual way. Unable to connect the match, his hand shaking badly, he opened the desk drawer, placed his bent elbow inside, partly closed the drawer and got a firm hold on his hand."

There is no evidence that Roosevelt developed Parkinson's disease, which is defined by a specific tremor at rest and many other associated neurological symptoms, none of which FDR had. The fact that the shaking occurred with movement (defined by neurologists as an intention tremor), the improvement with alcohol observed by Morgenthau, and the knowledge that Roosevelt's mother and two of his children had similar tremors all mean it most probably was a hereditary, or "essential" tremor. Its marked worsening as FDR's health deteriorated suggests strongly that his multiple medical problems—most pertinently, encephalopathy from heart, lung, and kidney disease—made it considerably worse.

April 12 was a typically hot Georgia spring day. Bruenn examined the president in the morning, noting a complaint of some neck pain, which was relieved by the doctor's light massage. Bruenn called Ross McIntire to make his routine daily report: blood pressure 180/110–120 and no change in FDR's cardiac action, which he would later describe as "an enlarged heart limping along with a murmur." Still, he noted, the president was in unusually good spirits and seemed to be less fatigued than usual.

After signing some correspondence, Roosevelt donned his red Harvard tie and naval cape to continue posing for a portrait by Elizabeth Shoumatoff, a friend of Lucy Mercer Rutherfurd, who had arrived with the artist on March 9 from her estate at nearby Aiken, South Carolina. Shoumatoff had painted Roosevelt in 1943 for Lucy's only child, Barbara, FDR's surreptitious godchild. Later that afternoon, Roosevelt was scheduled to attend a local minstrel show and picnic, where, as a surprise, he was to be served one of his favorite dishes, Brunswick stew.

At about 1:10 p.m., Daisy was crocheting on the sofa of the Little White House's living room when she glanced up and noticed that the president "seemed to be looking for something; his head forward, his hands fumbling."

"Have you dropped your cigarette?" she asked. As she later recorded, "He looked at me with his forehead furrowed in pain and tried to smile. He put his left hand up to the back of his head & said: 'I have a terrific pain in the back of my head.'* He said it distinctly, but so low that I don't think anyone else heard it—My head was not a foot from his."[26]

As FDR slumped forward, Polly Delano and Lucy tried to hold him up while Daisy grabbed for the phone and told the switchboard operator to find Bruenn and tell him to come at once. Louise Hackmeister located the doctor by the swimming pool and urgently told him there was an emergency with the president. Back at the cottage, Arthur Prettyman, Daisy, Polly, and Ireneo "Joe" Esperancilla, a Filipino houseboy, carried Roosevelt to the bedroom.** Meanwhile, Lucy, Madame Shoumatoff,

*Newspapers the next day recorded FDR's final words as, "I have a terrific headache." Daisy, however, was probably the only one who actually heard him. The president's actual last words were "be careful," heard by Polly as he was carried into the bedroom.

**In later interviews, Bruenn would claim that he was also involved in moving the president, but everyone else who was present agreed that Roosevelt was already in the bedroom when Bruenn arrived.

and her aide, Nicholas Robbins, hurried from the cottage and started driving back to South Carolina; Lucy instinctively understood that there would be a huge scandal if Eleanor learned that she had been there.*

Bruenn arrived about fifteen minutes after the president was stricken, and found him "pale, cold and sweating profusely."** Within minutes, his right pupil became "widely dilated," a clear indication of a severe hemorrhage originating in the right side of Roosevelt's brain. FDR's blood pressure was literally off the charts—300/190—and there was incontinence of urine.[27] Bruenn administered papaverine, Amyl nitrate, and nitroglycerine, all potent vasodilators, in an effort to reduce the skyrocketing blood pressure.

He immediately realized that the president had suffered a massive cerebral hemorrhage—and that the outlook was grave. He would admit much later, "When I was aware of the amount of damage that his brain had received from this episode, it would have been a tragedy if he had survived."[28] Despite all his heroic efforts to treat the catastrophic stroke, all that was left to do was wait for the inevitable.

Bruenn called Washington and spoke to McIntire; the surgeon general had just gotten off the phone with James Paullin, who along with Frank Lahey had examined Roosevelt the previous year, and asked the Atlanta internist to join him in Warm Springs later that week. Bruenn informed McIntire that FDR had fainted and was unconscious, promising to call back in five minutes. He did so, giving his diagnosis; McIntire would also insist in his memoir that the cardiologist "held out hope, for the heart rate was excellent."[29] As usual, McIntire was writing a version of the story for posterity

*In fact, Eleanor did learn of Lucy's presence that night from Polly, who also told her that Anna had even helped arrange White House dinners for the president and his longtime mistress in her absence. Not until 1966, with the publication of Jonathan Daniels's book *The Time Between the Wars*, did it become publicly known that Lucy had been at Warm Springs and that she and FDR had carried on a long romance.

**James Paullin later wrote McIntire to say that, according to Bruenn's notes, which he'd reviewed, the president was "still conscious with his hand on the back of his neck, complaining of intense pain." But the contemporary notes which Bruenn said he kept convincingly demonstrate that the president already was unconscious when he arrived. This discrepancy has never been explained. (James A. Paullin to Ross McIntire, June 24, 1946, RTM papers, FDRL-HP)

and not for accuracy. What Bruenn actually told McIntire was to prepare "for a long siege."[30] And what he was saying to himself was, "Oh God, this poor man has really had it."[31] McIntire, however, got Paullin back on the phone and told him to rush to Warm Springs as quickly as possible.

Yet, even with the president in extremis, Bruenn made no effort to seek help from the local medical community. (Paullin was 130 miles away, normally a three-hour drive.) Certainly there was plenty of help—not to mention adequate emergency facilities—not half a mile away: H. Stewart Raper, an internist, orthopedist Edwin Irwin, and physiatrist Robert Bennett were all at Warm Springs, which had a fully functioning operating room, in which major orthopedic surgery, including spinal fusion, was routinely performed.[32]* Even at the final moment of dire emergency, McIntire and Bruenn maintained the need to keep Roosevelt's treatment "within the family," for fear of outsiders learning the deadly secret of his true ailment.

After finishing with Paullin, McIntire phoned Anna: "I wanted to tell you that your father has had some sort of seizure," he told her. "What kind of seizure?" she asked cautiously. "Howard Bruenn has been calling from Warm Springs," the surgeon general replied. "Whatever it is, we don't think it will affect his brain." It was a phrase, she later said, that she would remember for the rest of her days.[33] And it was vintage McIntire, right to the end—completely untrue.

Before long, McIntire got a call from the First Lady; Polly Delano, her voice somehow under control, had phoned from Warm Springs and told Eleanor that her husband had fainted and was being attended by Dr. Bruenn. Now Mrs. Roosevelt wanted more information, but McIntire had none to give. However, she later recalled, he did not sound particularly alarmed—surprising, in view of Bruenn's dire prognosis.[34]

Meanwhile, Bruenn waited and monitored the unconscious president's breathing, which was "irregular and stentorous, but not deep." Waiting anxiously in the living room, as she listened to Roosevelt's "*very* heavy and labored" breathing and watched the flurry of activity by the

---

*Raper's wife reported that Paullin called Homer Swanson, a local neurosurgeon, and told him to "bring your instruments," but the president died while he was still en route. (Evans, *The Dying President,* p. 101). Her son, Hal, a dentist who still practices in the Warm Springs area, confirmed that his parents knew Swanson. (Interview with the authors, 2008)

doctor and Arthur Prettyman, Daisy "had a distinct feeling that this was the beginning of the end."[35]

At 3:30, Paullin arrived, having sped through the back roads of the Georgia countryside. He went straight to Roosevelt's bedroom while Bruenn fielded another phone call from McIntire. As he bent over the patient, Paullin noted that FDR's "pulse was barely perceptible"; suddenly, just a couple of minutes later, "his heart sounds disappeared completely." Bruenn, alerted by a shout from the other room, dropped the phone and hurried to the bedside as Paullin administered a shot of adrenaline to FDR's heart. But it was no use; after three or four heartbeats following the injection, all signs of life disappeared. At 3:35 p.m., the two doctors went out to the living room and informed Polly and Daisy that their cousin, the president of the United States, was dead.

Paullin and Bruenn were in immediate agreement: "There is only one [diagnosis] that I know of which would fit this picture," Paullin wrote McIntire. "He had . . . a massive intracerebral hemorrhage which ruptured into the subarachnoid space, giving him his intense pain and stiff neck."[36] They also agreed that no autopsy would be performed, though no one could ever agree on why: Paullin insisted, correctly, that "there were no facilities whatever [at Warm Springs] for performing an autopsy."[37] Bruenn and Steve Early would maintain that Eleanor opposed an autopsy, though there is no record of her having said so. And Ross McIntire, in what would become a regular refrain after FDR's death, argued that "there was no useful purpose to be served by it"[38]—an astonishing excuse, given that the precise cause of the president's death, though strongly suspected, remained unknown.

Bruenn and Paullin—with McIntire's agreement—maintained they were certain of their diagnosis. But they were also aware that an autopsy could only raise more questions than anyone, most notably Roosevelt himself, would have wanted answered.

The three wire service reporters were called to the cottage and informed of FDR's death; Steve Early made a simultaneous announcement over the phone from the White House. For the first time, those who did not read Walter Trohan and the *Chicago Tribune* learned the name of Howard Bruenn; he was identified in news stories simply as "a Navy physician" who had been at FDR's bedside when the end came, with no mention that he was a cardiologist.

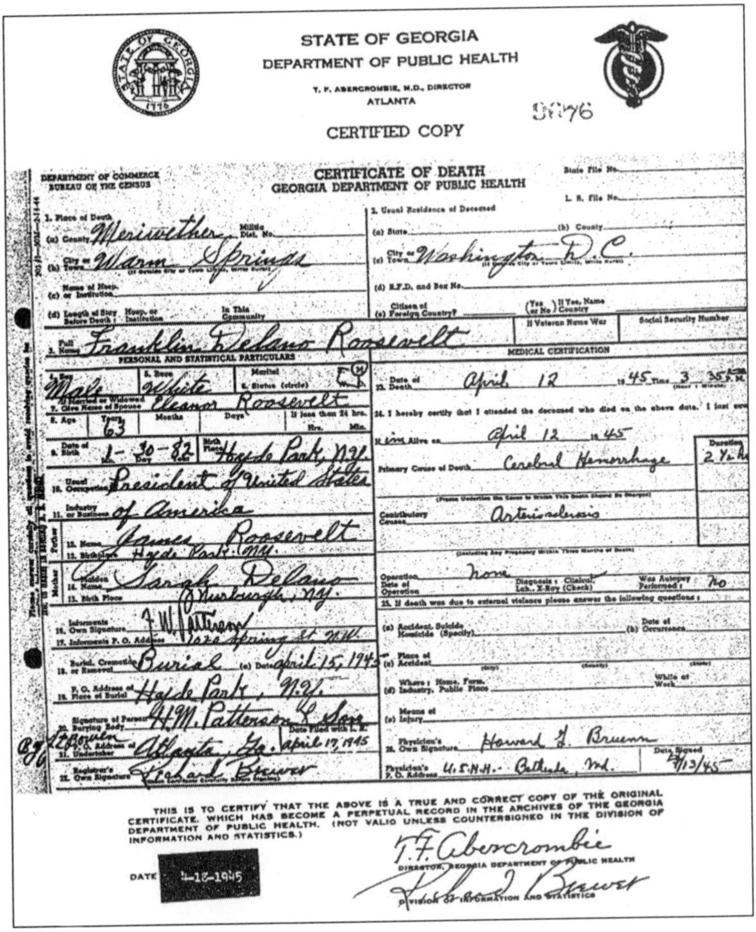

STATE OF GEORGIA
DEPARTMENT OF PUBLIC HEALTH
T. F. ABERCROMBIE, M.D., DIRECTOR
ATLANTA

9676

CERTIFIED COPY

DEPARTMENT OF COMMERCE
BUREAU OF THE CENSUS

CERTIFICATE OF DEATH
GEORGIA DEPARTMENT OF PUBLIC HEALTH

State File No.
L. R. File No.

1. Place of Death
(a) County Meriwether Militia Dist. No.
(b) City or Town Warm Springs
(c) Name of Hosp. or Institution
(d) Length of Stay Before Death: Hosp. or Institution In This Community

2. Usual Residence of Deceased
(a) State (b) County
(c) City or Town Washington D.C.
(d) R.F.D. and Box No.
(e) Citizen of Foreign Country? (Yes or No) If Yes, Name Country

3. Full Name Franklin Delano Roosevelt

If Veteran Name War | Social Security Number

PERSONAL AND STATISTICAL PARTICULARS
4. Sex Male
5. Race White
6. Marital Status (circle) M
7. If Married or Widowed Give Name of Spouse Eleanor Roosevelt
8. Age Years 63 Months Days If less than 24 hrs. Hrs. Min.
9. Date of Birth 1-30-82 Birth Place Hyde Park, N.Y.
10. Usual Occupation President of United States
11. Industry or Business of America
Father 12. Name James Roosevelt
13. Birthplace Hyde Park. N.Y.
Mother 14. Maiden Name Sarah Delano
15. Birth Place Newburgh, N.Y.
16. Informants Own Signature F. W. Patterson
17. Informants P. O. Address 1020 Spring St. N.W.
18. Burial, Cremation or Removal Burial (a) Date April 15, 1945
19. P. O. Address of Place of Burial Hyde Park, N.Y.
20. Signature of Person Burying Body H. M. Patterson & Son
21. P. O. Address of Undertaker Atlanta, Ga. Date Filed with L. R. April 17, 1945
22. Registrar's Own Signature Richard Brewer

MEDICAL CERTIFICATION
23. Date of Death April 12 19 45 Time 3 35 P.M.
24. I hereby certify that I attended the deceased who died on the above date. I last saw him Alive on April 12 19 45
Primary Cause of Death Cerebral Hemorrhage Duration 2 ½ hr
Contributory Causes Arteriosclerosis
Operation none Diagnosis: Clinical, Lab., X-Ray (Check) Was Autopsy Performed: no
25. If death was due to external violence please answer the following questions:
(a) Accident, Suicide Homicide (Specify) (b) Date of Occurrence
(c) Place of Accident (City) (County) (State)
(d) Where: Home, Farm, Industry, Public Place While at Work
(e) Means of Injury
26. Physician's Own Signature Howard G. Bruenn
Physician's P. O. Address U.S.N.H. - Bethesda, Md. Date Signed 4/13/45

THIS IS TO CERTIFY THAT THE ABOVE IS A TRUE AND CORRECT COPY OF THE ORIGINAL CERTIFICATE, WHICH HAS BECOME A PERPETUAL RECORD IN THE ARCHIVES OF THE GEORGIA DEPARTMENT OF PUBLIC HEALTH. (NOT VALID UNLESS COUNTERSIGNED IN THE DIVISION OF INFORMATION AND STATISTICS.)

DATE 4-18-1945

T. F. Abercrombie
DIRECTOR, GEORGIA DEPARTMENT OF PUBLIC HEALTH
Richard Brewer
DIVISION OF INFORMATION AND STATISTICS

Franklin Roosevelt's death certificate, completed and signed by Howard Bruenn. The cause of death is given as cerebral hemorrhage, with arteriosclerosis as the only contributing cause.

Still reeling from the shock, Bruenn gave an impromptu medical briefing to the reporters in the moments following the president's death—but made certain not to give any hint that Roosevelt had in any way been ill before the end came. "It was just like a bolt of lightning or getting hit by a train," he said. "One minute he was alive and laughing. The next minute—wham!"

"Howard," UP's Merriman Smith asked, "did you see this thing coming?"

Bruenn equivocated: "This wasn't the sort of thing you could forecast. Doctors can't just say 'this man is going to have a cerebral.' It doesn't happen that way. He'd been feeling fine. He was awfully tired when we first came down here. You saw him the other day—wasn't he in fine spirits?"

Added Smith in his memoir: "Yes, the president was in fine spirits that day. But he looked unhealthy."[39]

What Bruenn had said was true enough, of course—doctors can't flatly predict that a patient is going to have a cerebral hemorrhage. But with his intimate knowledge of Roosevelt's ongoing medical condition, he could hardly have been surprised.

It certainly was no surprise to those around FDR. Bill Hassett wrote in his diary that when Basil O'Connor, who'd returned to New York, called and was told the news, Roosevelt's longtime friend and associate said simply, "You and I knew it was coming."[40]

McIntire instructed Hassett and Bruenn to contact a local undertaker and select a coffin, but that nothing further should be done until he and Steve Early arrived in Warm Springs later that night with Eleanor. The two men enlisted the services of H. Patterson & Co., one of Atlanta's oldest and most respected firms. Although Paullin later wrote that Polly Delano distinctly told him that FDR "did not wish to be embalmed," that service was arranged for. The actual embalmer, F. Haden Snoderly, later wrote out his memories of that long night, in a letter that is published here for the first time:

> At 7:35 that evening, Mr. Patterson phoned me at home to get George Marchman to go to Warm Springs to prepare the President's remains.
>
> After considerable telephoning and discussing as to the type of casket to be used, and getting the necessary equipment needed to take with us, we—Mr. Patterson, Marchman and Snoderly—left Spring Hill at 9:02. The paramount thought in my mind while en route was: Would we be able to get proper preservation, restoration and sanitation on this case, since so much time had elapsed from time of death until time when we would begin to prepare the remains.
>
> At 10:40 p.m. we arrived at the entrance to Warm Springs Foundation. There was no crowd or commotion, only the Marine guard and Secret Serv-

ice man. After stating our mission, and this being checked, we were escorted to the Little White House by Secret Service men. On the way there from the main entrance, we were stopped twice and our escort gave proper password that permitted us to pass. I might explain here that the Foundation was well guarded. The outside and all entrances are guarded by Marines and the inner grounds and the White House are guarded by Secret Service men.

We arrived at the Little White House at 10:50 p.m. and parked our car directly in front of the house, Mr. Patterson entered to see in what manner we were to proceed. He shortly returned with information that we were to await the arrival of the First Lady, Mrs. Roosevelt, before proceeding with the embalming. Our car was moved to clear the entrance. I would like at this point to give you a description of the Little White House. I asked Benjamin Lesesne to do this for me, since he and Mr. Patterson spent the night there waiting for us to embalm the President.

The Little White House is a small, unpretentious white clapboard house, sitting on the side of a hill. It is reached by a winding road leading about a mile and a half back into the woods from the main road. It is encircled by a fence and at the gate is a guardhouse with a Marine constantly on duty while the President is there. All around through the woods, completely surrounding the house, is a system of such small guardhouses, a Marine in each one on guard. The house itself is similar to any other summer vacation house in that it is not a fine house, but well built, very comfortable and decorated with rough furniture. As you approach the house, you see four medium-size white columns supporting the roof over the small front porch. On each column, a brilliant red rose bush is in full bloom.

As you enter the house, you come into a small anteroom about 12 feet square. The door to the right leads into a small kitchen. A door opening off the left leads into a bedroom about 15 feet square. A large double door directly opposite the entrance leads into a large room about 20 or 25 feet, serving as a combination living room and dining room. A door opening off the left of this room leads directly into the President's room.

At 11:30, Mrs. Roosevelt arrived, and in her quiet, dignified manner greeted the officials there and embraced the President's cousin. She then entered the house to go to the President's room.

At 12:15 a.m., we were admitted to prepare the remains. Upon entering the room, which was very small, we found the President on his bed with a sheet drawn over his face. When the sheet was removed, we found tied underneath his chin and over his head a strip of ½-inch gauze, which had been fixed to close his mouth. This, of course, caused indentation under the chin and on each cheek, also very bad discoloration, both of which were difficult to remove.

Rigor mortis had set in, since nine hours had elapsed since time of death. Discoloration was very evident about the face and hands. Numerous skin blisters all over the body. Apparently, he had lost considerable weight. There was heavy puffing under the eyes. Naturally, his limbs were not normal. His abdomen was noticeably distended.

We replaced the remains on our embalming table and cooling table, removed all the shades from the lights and had large floor lamps brought in to give us plenty of light to work with. One of the Marine guards and Arthur Prettyman, the President's valet, stayed in the room while we bathed the face and shaved him and fixed his features. When we were ready to continue, they asked permission to leave the room.

We raised the right carotid artery and jugular vein and started injecting down with very weak solution and very slowly, so as not to cause any swelling. For commercial reasons, we will not mention the name of the fluid used. After observing the slow reaction of the fluid, we stepped up the strength greater than we normally would. The fluid would block off in given spaces and cause swelling. We massaged all during the injection. Taking all into consideration, we had fair drainage. Seeing that we would have to raise the femoral arteries and radial arteries, we stopped injections down. The arteries were sclerotic. Injected up and very little pressure, but again blocked off and caused swelling of neck. We immediately discontinued this, and put straight cavity fluid pack on right side of face and over right eye and under lid. This was all that could be done.

We aspirated and made trocar injections of arterial and cavity fluids, let them stay in until we had injected the femoral arteries and up and down radial arteries, and sutured all incisions. Then aspirated the thoracic and abdominal cavities and injected cavity fluid.

We used four bottles of arterial fluid and two bottles of cavity fluid [in] five hours of hard work. From what has been said about the condition of the remains, the time elements and the cause of death, which was cerebral hemorrhage, you readily understand and realize what a difficult case we had to prepare. True, this was a very important case, but it was one of the most difficult cases in every case that either of us had ever had to embalm.

After we had finished suturing all incisions, our next precaution was to prevent any leakage. We wrapped with rubber bandage the arms and limbs to cover the blistered area. Put a pair of rubber coveralls on, and made bib out of oilcloth to cover the carotid injection.

We then trimmed the hair around the temples, removed the hair from nostrils and cleaned fingernails, then proceeded to dress the remains, using a dark gray business suit, white shirt and black tie with white stripes and white pocket handkerchief. We, of course, had to use heavy cosmetics to cover the discolored area. We had Arthur Prettyman, the President's valet, come in and comb [his] hair.

At Mr. Patterson's suggestion, we placed the remains back on his bed. We were undecided as to what type of spread to use. Mr. Patterson suggested the President's Navy cape, which we used. This proved to be a good suggestion, as it was appreciated by Mrs. Roosevelt. It was 5:45 Friday morning when this was completed. Mr. Patterson then notified Mrs. Roosevelt that the President was ready to be seen. After viewing the remains, Mrs. Roosevelt was very well pleased and complimentary.

Mr. Lesesne, Shrader and Cannon Young brought a mahogany copper-lined casket and a copper deposit bronze casket down. The copper bronze casket was selected and used.

Immediately after Mrs. Roosevelt had returned to her room, we placed the President in the casket. The first to view the remains in the casket [were] one of the Marines and the Secret Service man. It was quite a relief to hear them say that the President had the fullness back in his face and neck like he normally was.

After we had completed our work, the Government took charge as to final arrangements. At 9:15, the casket was placed in the hearse to begin this last journey back to Hyde Park, his final resting place. The Color Guard, band and about 3,000 soldiers preceded the casket on the way to the depot. They marched by the Foundation, where the crippled children and servicemen in wheelchairs could pay tribute to their Commander in Chief and to the man they loved and who had done so much for them.

> Behind the hearse [were] high military and naval officers. Behind them, the car with Mrs. Roosevelt and party, and then other cars followed. As the procession left the grounds and moved on to the station, paratroopers lined the streets on both sides.
>
> At 10:01 a.m. the procession reached the station. The Navy, Army and Marine personnel acting as pallbearers lifted the casket from the hearse, with the assistance of Mr. Marchman, Mr. Lesesne and Mr. Schrader, carried it up a specially constructed ramp and placed the casket in the observation car, though a window onto a special [word missing] built in the case.
>
> At 10:15 a.m., the train moved slowly, heading for the final resting place of our President.
>
> Trusting on our humble way, we have given you a picture of what we did and witnessed while doing our work. We considered it indeed a very high honor to be asked to perform this task.[41]

The embalmer's letter adds some interesting new information, the most significant of which is the reference to the "noticeably distended" abdomen—a condition that clearly preceded death and strongly suggests a bowel obstruction consistent with metastatic abdominal cancer. The presence of skin blisters is cryptic: Roosevelt had informed former Secretary of State Cordell Hull in March that he had a "penicillin reaction," yet the exact diagnosis cannot be determined. And the "sclerotic" arteries, which caused so much difficulty for the embalmers, confirm the seriousness of FDR's arteriosclerosis, which McIntire would later insist was just "moderate."

Roosevelt's body was carried by train to Washington; after a full procession drawing 400,000 onlookers to the streets of Washington, and a funeral service in the East Room of the White House—during which the entire nation observed a minute of silence—the train traveled north to Hyde Park. There, on April 15, 1945, before a gathering of dignitaries, friends, and family—including his beloved Fala—the body of the thirty-second president of the United States was laid to rest in the rose garden of the place he loved most of all.

Franklin Delano Roosevelt had passed into the pages of history.

The Cover-Up Continues

CHAPTER 14

From the moment Franklin Roosevelt died, much of the White House press corps—and not just veteran FDR critics, like Walter Trohan—began to lift the tight censorship they had imposed on themselves. The same newspaper editions that reported FDR's death finally contained candid accounts of what those reporters who covered the president had all seen and heard. For the first time the American people were told, in stark terms, of the precarious condition of their president's health during the last year and a half of his life.

An editorial in the *Washington Post* noted that "to be sure, many knew that the President had been in ill health. But rumors about this condition had so often been proven false that most of us had put aside the fear that he might not live to see the peace established."[1] The Associated Press reported FDR's illness deep in its news account of his death but made it seem like a new revelation, even for the journalists who'd covered him regularly: "Mr. Roosevelt had not been in the best of health for some time, it was disclosed last night," the wire service wrote in an unsigned piece. At a recent dinner, according to the article, Senate Majority Leader Alben Barkley had told the First Lady that FDR "looked thin and haggard and Mrs. Roosevelt said she also felt he was too thin," adding that "*for several days previous* the president had been taking only gruel because he had no taste for other foods" (emphasis added).[2]

Merriman Smith of United Press, who later wrote that he'd spent the better part of 1944 chasing down and discrediting rumors about FDR's health—even as he acknowledged privately that the president looked increasingly "ghastly"[3]—filed a lengthy report in which he asked: "Did President Roosevelt know that he was an ill man and that the time had come for him to husband his strength? Many of us who saw him often and traveled with him believe he did." But, like McIntire and those around him, Smith insisted that "there was nothing wrong with him organically," save for a noticeable loss of hearing and his increasingly inaudible voice, and that he'd simply been overwhelmed by "the tremendous pressure of the toughest job on earth."[4] A front-page story in the *New York Times* the morning after the president's death (unsigned, but probably written by Washington bureau chief Arthur Krock) stated flatly what nearly every journalist covering the president, including Krock, had long refused to report: "The condition of the health of President Roosevelt raised doubts in the minds of those in the capital who have had regular contact with him over the last two years, largely because official statements regarding it appeared to be in conflict with visible evidence of his physical condition." In fact, the article stated flatly, FDR "appear[ed] to decline more in the last year than might be attributable to his advancing age." And it noted pointedly that "factual accounts of his health . . . could only be based on the official statements of Vice Admiral Ross T. McIntire, the President's official physician, and White House secretaries." The *Times* account added that the February 1944 wen operation had "given rise to rumors" that "a large tumor," possibly malignant, actually had been involved—although the article did not specifically refute or deny those rumors.[5]

Walter Lippman, arguably the nation's most distinguished political columnist, wrote that "Harry S. Truman was nominated at Chicago last July by a convention which was fully aware that it was almost certainly choosing a President of the United States. There was no secret about this during the campaign." That column provoked a sharply critical jab from the *Saturday Evening Post*, the hugely popular weekly magazine, whose chief editorial writer, Garet Garrett, was a longtime critic of FDR's domestic and foreign policies. In an editorial headlined "Everybody Knew But the People: Roosevelt's Health," Garrett called it "extraordinary that Mr. Lippman could make such a statement and pass no judgment on its implications." Added Garrett:

> Actually, the state of Mr. Roosevelt's health was a secret from millions of Americans who voted for the President on the theory that he could reasonably be expected to live out his term of office. . . . To be sure, some voters thought they detected signs of unfamiliar weakness in Mr. Roosevelt's radio voice. Others thought the pictures of the President revealed signs of serious illness, but doubters were continually assured by Admiral Ross McIntire, the President's medical advisor, that the patient was "in better physical condition than the average man of his age," that his health was "good, very good" and that he was "in splendid shape." . . .
>
> Journalists or politicians who hinted that Mr. Roosevelt was not a well man were rebuked as little better than fifth columnists by the President's associates, who saw their one chance of continued power in the ability of the President to get through one more election. . . .
>
> Why do we bring up this disagreeable subject now? For the only reason that can be given for mentioning it—namely, that it must not happen again. . . . It is impossible to plan a precise course which will prevent a courageous President from daring fate once more. . . . But at least we can make it plain that those who ask questions shall receive answers, and not be brushed off as malicious obstructionists by the very same people who come up after the fatal event with the news that they knew it all along.[6]

Yet save for some isolated criticism of McIntire on the floor of the House of Representatives, there was no follow-up, no calls for investigations or explanations. Perhaps the American people were overwhelmed by the sudden tragedy, or preoccupied with the ongoing turmoil of the rapidly approaching end of the war in Europe,* but there was little concern

*In the three weeks following Roosevelt's death, Benito Mussolini was executed, Adolf Hitler committed suicide, Berlin fell to the Red Army, and Germany surrendered.

over whether the White House had engaged in massive deception over the perilous state of Roosevelt's health. Most Americans seemed to accept the insistence by both McIntire and Bruenn that, however ill FDR might have been, the cerebral hemorrhage that killed him was both unforeseen and unpredictable.

Not everyone accepted that explanation, though. Joseph Pulitzer II, publisher of the *St. Louis Post-Dispatch*, "thought that we should have known that Roosevelt was going to die," according to his longtime Washington bureau chief, Raymond "Pete" Brandt, who was ordered to pursue the story.[7] Pursue it he did: In the days following the president's death, Brandt approached both Ross McIntire and Frank Lahey (whose role in examining Roosevelt was not widely known, even among the White House press corps), demanding not only an interview about their examinations of FDR but also their complete medical records and files.*

To say that the White House physician was alarmed by this inquiry, and where it might possibly lead, is putting it mildly. On May 8, a little more than three weeks after the president's death, McIntire sent an urgent letter to Eleanor, even as she was busy coping with the burden of her unexpected relocation from the White House after a dozen years of residence. Warning her that Brandt, acting on "a direct order from his publisher," had tried "to secure my permission to publish all the physical and clinical records on the president," he said that "very naturally, I told him that my answer was 'no,' that no good could come of it. . . . Notwithstanding this, a few days later he called on Doctor Frank Lahey in Boston and asked him to comment on the president's condition throughout the past year of his life, knowing that Doctor Lahey had been a consultant. Doctor Lahey's reply was much more emphatic than mine."

---

*The previous fall, Pulitzer had personally dispatched another of his reporters, Charles Ross, to visit Lahey in Boston and sound him out on a rumor that Roosevelt would resign following Germany's collapse, which the doctor labeled "ridiculous." Ross also asked Lahey point-blank whether he had "seen the President professionally" and was told that "that was something that I felt he had no right to ask, and that the only answer I could make was what [McIntire] had told me, and it was my opinion, that [FDR] was now in excellent health." Lahey immediately fired off an account of the interview to McIntire in order "to protect myself against any mis-statement that may be made." (Frank Lahey to Ross McIntire, September 12, 1944, RTM papers, FDRL-HP)

McIntire said he was telling the grieving widow all this "for I know that the next move will be to request from you the release of the records on the President. You, of course, have the right to say whatever you will care to do about it. But I can see no good coming from such a thing, and moreover, as you have said, the story is closed."[8]

There is no record of Mrs. Roosevelt's response, and it does not appear that Brandt, or any other reporter, formally asked for the president's medical records to be released—a move that would have been without historical precedent.* Yet that is not the argument McIntire offered, either to Brandt or to Eleanor, for not opening up FDR's file. To both, he said the same thing: "No good can possibly come from this." The warning is clear: Trust me, you don't want to go there. Moreover, McIntire stressed to the now-former First Lady that "*you* have said the story is closed" (emphasis added). Not, he argued, that he and his colleagues had authoritatively pronounced the cause of the president's death, which certainly would have been reasonable grounds for a refusal, but that Eleanor, as he very pointedly reminded her, had declared the medical issue "closed" and, thus, there was no reason to reopen it.

It was a curious suggestion, especially since there is no evidence that Eleanor ever made any such assertion, even privately. Indeed, Mrs. Roosevelt apparently continued to have doubts about the treatment her husband had received—doubts she would make public, and then investigate privately, a decade later.

But did fear that Mrs. Roosevelt might agree to such a request—or that Congress might subpoena the medical records—lead McIntire to take a drastic step to ensure that they would remain closed? Later inquiries would disclose that Roosevelt's complete medical file, kept under lock and key in the safe at Bethesda, at some point went missing; repeated efforts over the coming years to locate it would prove fruitless. Besides McIntire, the only people with access to the safe were Captain John Harper, commanding officer of the National Naval Medical Center,

---

*Brandt eventually wrote a piece that appeared on April 23. Though McIntire and Lahey were not sources for the article, Brandt did secure information from Howard Bruenn, and privately thanked him for his "kind cooperation." (Raymond P. Brandt to Howard Bruenn, April 23, 1945, Bruenn papers, FDRL-HP)

and Captain Robert Duncan, Bethesda's executive officer. It is not unreasonable to suspect that the surgeon general—who had the most to lose if the records ever were made public—destroyed the file, save for a few lab slips and other reports.

Meanwhile, Roosevelt's death presented Walter Trohan with an opportunity to publish some of the more sensational rumors he'd heard from his sources, who—he revealed in his 1975 memoir—included several of the Secret Service agents guarding Roosevelt (and who he claimed "didn't like" the president)[9] as well as William Calhoun Stirling.[10] Ten weeks after Roosevelt's death, the *Chicago Tribune* published a sensational story in which Trohan declared that the president "almost met death last Palm Sunday, March 25, just 19 days before he was fatally stricken" at Warm Springs. According to Trohan, FDR had "suffered a severe stroke in his family home at Hyde Park"—an attack that was "so severe . . . that it was feared the end was at hand."

Indeed, he claimed, this attack was one of "a long series of such seizures," dating back to "the late summer of 1938 at Rochester, Minn.," when FDR "was then visiting the Mayo Clinic."* That particular stroke, he wrote, "was light, the breaking of a small capillary in the brain. Other light attacks followed thru the years. The first serious stroke came in late 1943," during the Teheran conference.[11]

There was no response from the Roosevelt family to Trohan's story, which was not given a particularly prominent display by the *Chicago Tribune*. Nor was it picked up by any other major newspapers, which was not surprising for one of his stories. But Trohan continued to quietly disseminate his information to anyone who would listen and, though it took four years, eventually created a national sensation with it.

Just days after Trohan's story appeared, a monthly magazine called *News Story* published the first installment of a three-part investigative series titled "The Strange Death of President Roosevelt." The title was clearly meant to recall "The Strange Death of President Harding," a best-selling, but widely discredited, book written in 1930 by Gaston B. Means, a lawyer turned con man, which claimed that the twenty-ninth

---

*FDR's eldest son, Jimmy, then serving as his father's White House secretary, underwent surgery at the Mayo Clinic for a stomach ulcer in September.

News Story, a little-known magazine, trumpeted its investigation just weeks after FDR's death, based largely on information from the *Chicago Tribune*'s Walter Trohan, that concluded Franklin Roosevelt had died of cancer. But no one paid much attention. (Authors' collection)

president had been poisoned by his wife.* The series, which carried no byline except "The Editors,"** was written in a wildly over-the-top, melodramatic style as a "court of inquiry" into FDR's death. "Suppressed Medical Facts and Uncalled-For Secrecy Give Rise to Sinister Rumors," the magazine declared. Its conclusions mirrored exactly those put forward by Trohan in his *Tribune* postmortem, though his name never appeared in any of the three articles. "I have learned that Mr. Roosevelt

*Means died in prison after swindling $100,000 from Washington socialite Evalyn Walsh McLean in connection with a purported scheme to ransom the kidnapped baby of Charles Lindbergh.

**Despite its tabloid style, the magazine was produced by well-known, reputable journalists. Its executive editor, James W. Barrett, had been the final city editor of the legendary *New York World* until it folded in 1931; its managing editor, Rex Goad, would become the chief editor of NBC News during the '50s and early '60s; and its publisher, Herbert Moore, was a veteran newsman who'd founded Transradio Press Service, the first wire service for broadcast news.

died of cancer," intones "the first witness, a news reporter" identified in the article as Gene Davis, when "called to the witness stand." According to his account, an examination at Bethesda on October 13, 1944, had disclosed "malignant cancer somewhere in the uro-genital system" with an "unfavorable prognosis." An unnamed prominent New York City urologist was called in, it continued, who "confirmed the prognosis," pronouncing it "a case of inoperable cancer." The article added that Roosevelt—who had "faced his advisors and requested them to tell him the whole truth and to withhold nothing—was informed that he had no more than six months to live." In response, it said, he "lit a cigarette, inhaled deeply, blew out smoke and smiled."[12]

The third installment provided more detail about the March 25 incident first written about by Trohan. An unidentified reporter who was in Hyde Park at the time—almost certainly Trohan—"testifies" about having learned "on the very best authority that Mr. Roosevelt had suffered a stroke, a cerebral hemorrhage; that he was unconscious for some time, and physicians feared it might be fatal. But, miraculously, he soon recovered and in a few hours appeared quite normal."[13]

The March 25 incident, if indeed something actually occurred, was most likely just another of the president's many seizures, perhaps this one more alarming than the others. Had he been found on the floor after falling from his wheelchair during an attack, as he'd done several times at the White House, according to authoritative eyewitness accounts? Except for Trohan's account, there are no other reports that anything out of the ordinary occurred at Hyde Park that day. Certainly the symptoms of a major brain hemorrhage—of the kind suggested by Trohan and *News Story*—could not have been resolved in a matter of hours. (Roosevelt left for Warm Springs the following day.)

The Trohan-instigated magazine series also erred seriously in reporting that the October 13 examination at Bethesda by "recognized specialists" had determined that FDR's heart "was normal." That was Ross McIntire's public story—though none of the president's inner circle of doctors, including McIntire, could possibly have believed it to be true. In September, Roosevelt's blood pressure had been measured at 240/130; a few weeks after the examination, it was 210/112—both of which were indicative of severe hypertension. By then, he had long been under the daily care of a cardiologist.

The *News Story* series attracted no attention from the rest of the press. Nor, unsurprisingly, did another book with the same title—even though its author was the first person to correctly, in our view, diagnose Roosevelt's lesion as melanoma.

Dr. Emanuel Josephson was a fifty-year-old eye specialist, trained at Johns Hopkins and Columbia universities and a former assistant medical director of the American Red Cross in Europe. He also had a long record of political activism but was a conspiracy theorist of the most extreme variety. Over the years, he wrote dozens of books, self-published by his Chedney Press, accusing everyone from the Rockefellers to Dwight Eisenhower of being communists. FDR, he wrote in 1948, had been a conscious agent of the Rockefeller-Mellon interests, who replaced him after the Teheran conference with a lookalike body double, and claiming that this substitute Roosevelt actually lies buried in Hyde Park.

Such absurd allegations pretty much explain why no one outside the insular world of anti-Roosevelt conspiracy-mongers paid the slightest attention to it. But, in one respect, Josephson's speculation was entirely accurate:

> It takes no great medical skill to diagnose the character of the growth over President Roosevelt's left eyebrow. It had the characteristic appearance and behavior of a mole turned malignant and rapidly growing, a type of cancer, or sarcoma, known as melanosarcoma . . . one of the most malignant forms of cancer.[14]

Yet even if Josephson had more credibility and been taken seriously, it's unlikely his conclusion would have been accepted, given that it was based solely on photographic evidence, and that McIntire had repeatedly denied that Roosevelt ever had a malignancy.

In the months after FDR's death, McIntire was working on what he expected would be the definitive—and final—word on Roosevelt's health. Even while the president was still alive, he'd entered into an agreement with George Creel, a former journalist and longtime Democratic Party activist,* to write two articles for *Collier's* about FDR's health that would then be expanded into a book.[15] But the book project stretched on and on, much to Creel's dismay; at one point he pleaded with McIntire to "*please* get on the job at once."[16]

Yet even though McIntire clearly meant the book to be a defense of his treatment of the president, he was decidedly reluctant to give Creel specific facts and figures to bolster his case. "Regarding the use of medical reports," he wrote his coauthor, "I doubt very much that we would want to put in such things as the actual laboratory reports. They would not be of interest to the lay public, but there is no reason why each physical examination could not be outlined and statements made as to the condition of certain vital organs."[17]

Which is exactly how the book, *White House Physician*, appeared in late 1946—filled with personal anecdotes that stressed the closeness of the FDR-McIntire relationship and an unapologetic defense both of the president's medical care and McIntire's clearly disingenuous public statements touting the wellness of his health. Except for the results of one checkup in May 1944, the book contains no specific facts or figures—allowing McIntire, amazingly, to declare that while high blood pressure and arteriosclerosis would have predicted a cerebral hemorrhage, "President Roosevelt did not have either of these. His blood pressure was not alarming at any time; in fact, on the morning of the day he died, it was well within normal limits for a man of his age."[18] (The last readings of which a record survives, taken less than a week before his death, ranged from a high 170/88 to an alarming 240/130.)[19]

There is no other way to characterize McIntire's statement except as a bald-faced lie, as was his assertion as late as March 1945 that FDR's "stout" heart was "in good condition" and "never failed."[20] Yet without any specific data, and in the absence of Roosevelt's records, there was no way to refute him. Little reason, then, why McIntire could reiterate in the book his statement that Roosevelt had always been "in excellent condi-

*During Roosevelt's first term, Creel had written a number of articles for *Collier's* that, he later admitted, were practically dictated by the president himself; among them was a "prophecy" right after FDR's 1936 reelection suggesting that the Supreme Court be enlarged—which Roosevelt himself proposed only a few months later. (George Creel, *Rebel at Large: Memoirs of Fifty Crowded Years*. New York: G. P. Putnam's, 1947)

tion for a man of his age" and flatly declare: "*I stand by that judgment today without any amendment or apology*" (emphasis in original).[21]

Surprisingly, *White House Physician* received warm, even glowing reviews—even in the *Chicago Tribune*, much to McIntire's astonishment and obvious delight. The review by Cabel Phillips in the *New York Times* was typical: "This slender, reverent and unpretentious contribution . . . has much that is solid and informative to recommend it." The book, he added, "will remain as source material for the serious student and historian."[22] That proved sadly true; for years, historians cited it uncritically, despite its many inaccuracies and its fundamental purpose, which was to tell a story rather than establish the facts.

But McIntire would find himself on the defensive three years later—once more, thanks to Walter Trohan, who had found someone else to put forward his theory about FDR's multiple strokes. This time the agent was Dr. Karl C. Wold of Minneapolis, in an article for *Look* magazine, "The Truth About FDR's Health," based on a chapter in his book detailing the medical histories of past presidents. Like Trohan's original piece, it alleged that Roosevelt had suffered a series of four strokes: in 1938 at the Mayo Clinic; in December 1943, after which two physicians doubted he'd live six months; on March 25, 1944; and, finally, the fatal attack at Warm Springs. It also reported the "rumor" that a separate exam at the Mayo Clinic in 1944 had revealed inoperable cancer of the prostate.[23]

Unlike the earlier stories, this one attracted nationwide attention. McIntire immediately blasted the article as "not true," adding that "no such thing ever occurred."[24] This time, however, he was not alone: For the first time, the Roosevelt family, which had maintained virtual silence on the medical front, went public to attack the skeptics. Anna Roosevelt Boettiger issued a statement calling the article "utterly and entirely misleading" and noting that "only a few days" after the supposed first stroke in 1938, her father "went on a long fishing trip to the Galapagos Islands," during which he "landed a 235-pound shark. Does that sound like a man who had a stroke?"[25]

Her brother Elliott wrote a lengthy rebuttal for *Liberty* magazine, titled "They're Lying About FDR's Health!" that slammed *Look* for its "smear" and "dirty journalism." Quoting not only McIntire, his own mother, and his siblings but also numerous members of the White House staff, he offered firm denials of each one of the alleged strokes. Finally, he phoned Wold directly and demanded to know the sources of his information.

The clearly embarrassed doctor first tried to disassociate himself from the magazine piece. "The article as it appeared in *Look* magazine has been highly sensationalized by the magazine and much of the material that appears in my book has been omitted, giving rise to a completely false impression as to the intent of my writing," he told Elliott. In fact, the information in the article was almost identical to what appeared in the book.

Finally Elliott, "after much insistence on my part," won from Wold the admission, based on "a hazy recollection," that "he had received much of the information in a letter from Walter Trohan," whom the president's son identified as the Washington correspondent for "the most anti-Roosevelt newspaper in the United States," meaning he could "hardly be regarded as a reliable source."[26] As far as the national press was concerned, the revelation of Trohan's involvement automatically refuted Wold's credibility: *Time,* in its account of the controversy, described Trohan as the "topflight hatchetman of the *Chicago Tribune*" (and reported that the *Look* issue had sold an extra 10,000 copies on the newsstand).[27]*

Though Elliott Roosevelt successfully put to rest the issue of prior strokes, the question of just how ill FDR had been flared up again in 1951, prompted by a letter to the editor in the *New York Times* from James A. Farley discussing the newly adopted Twenty-Second Amendment to the Constitution, which limits a president to two terms. The former postmaster general recalled that he'd opposed a third term for Roosevelt in 1940—it was the issue that permanently destroyed their relationship—and insisted that history had borne out his judgment.

"We saw tragically in the case of President Roosevelt an utter breakdown of his great strength in his third term," Farley wrote. "Worse, we saw his nomination in 1944 when it was widely known among political leaders that he was a dying man."[28]

---

*Trohan himself made no public comment about his role in the controversy. Interestingly, his 1975 autobiography makes no mention of FDR's having suffered any strokes before the fatal attack.

Those last five words set McIntire off even more than had Wold's article—notwithstanding that many of the articles in the days following FDR's death had said pretty much the same thing. But Farley was the first onetime member of Roosevelt's inner circle to publicly make such a claim. So McIntire sent a letter of his own to the *Washington Star*, which had published an editorial agreeing with Farley's assessment*—though it hardly constituted a denial. Farley's letter, he charged, was an attack on the "excellent doctors who worked with me and whose reputations cannot be challenged." Besides, he added, Farley hadn't seen the president "for a period of several years," so "it could not have been his personal observation that the President was a dying man." And finally, said McIntire, *FDR well knew his own physical condition at all times*—which, while undoubtedly true, does not answer the question of what his condition was.[29]

At the same time, McIntire gave a lengthy interview to *U.S. News & World Report*, which published an edited transcript under the headline "Did the U.S. Elect a Dying President?" In it, McIntire conceded that Roosevelt had had "moderate arteriosclerosis"—though he insisted "it was nothing" for "a man who had lived as he did, under great stress and strain"—but continued to maintain that "he never had what I would consider alarming blood pressure." Instead, McIntire insisted that Roosevelt had what he called "a peculiar blood pressure. It bounced. He could vary 20 to 30 points easily in two or three hours" when "he got annoyed by little things." However, McIntire quickly added, "when he got into the big stuff, no, it came down and stayed."[30] Once again McIntire loyally burnished the myth that whenever there were great issues to be faced—"the big stuff"—Roosevelt was fully competent and able. It just wasn't true.

Most of the press let McIntire's interview speak for itself. One exception was the Hearst-owned *Boston Herald*, which ran an editorial saying it was "not the least bit surprised" that McIntire had "denied what Dr. Wold reported," because "not to have denied it would have made [McIntire] a liar." After all, the paper wrote:

*Coincidentally, there was a Trohan connection here, too. Though his name did not come up in connection with this episode, Trohan had ghost-written Farley's 1948 memoir, which acknowledges the reporter for his "editorial help."

> Many leading specialists throughout the country who never had the opportunity of examining the late President found ample basis for dire diagnosis from his declining physical appearance. These external symptoms were particularly noticeable to the correspondents, even though they lacked the medical competence to judge their meaning. They long suspected something on the order of what Dr. Wold reports.[31]

During all these controversies, Eleanor Roosevelt remained silent, except for giving a brief statement for use by her daughter. And she continued to hold her tongue until the summer of 1956, when—for the first time—she opened up about her husband's health in an interview with Clayton Knowles of the *New York Times*. It was an auspicious moment for such a discussion: President Dwight Eisenhower had recently been hospitalized with ileitis just after being cleared by his doctors to seek reelection, having suffered a heart attack the previous year. Now Mrs. Roosevelt disclosed that FDR's physicians similarly had told him in the summer of 1944 that he "could quite easily go on with the activities of the presidency." At the same time, however, she insisted that health played no role in his decision to run: "He never gave his health much thought," she said, "and neither did any of us."[32]

Her statements fly in the face of every available piece of evidence. The Lahey memorandum says quite plainly that Roosevelt was warned not to seek reelection; Daisy Suckley's diary confirms that FDR gave his health much thought and was concerned about it; and the mother-daughter correspondence between Eleanor and Anna demonstrates that the Roosevelt women likewise were disturbed over the president's ill health. But none of this was publicly known, so the interview reinforced the official line, propagated by Ross McIntire, of the martyr president who persevered with complete disregard for his physical well-being—not that there was really anything noticeably wrong with him, anyway.

But did Eleanor Roosevelt really believe this—or did she retain some doubts? About a year after the story ran on the *Times*'s front page, the former First Lady—unbeknownst to her family—wrote to the surgeon general of the Navy, Bartholomew W. Hogan, requesting a copy of her husband's medical records. Because no records could be found at Bethesda, Hogan contacted McIntire, who replied that he only had copies of some lab reports and nothing else; these were forwarded to Mrs. Roosevelt, who eventually sent them to the FDR Library at Hyde Park and apparently dropped the matter.[33]

Ten years passed before Anna Roosevelt learned of her mother's inquiry—and then, only when she herself called the surgeon general's office asking about FDR's medical records. She was told that "no actual records had been kept because Father had never spent a night at the Bethesda Medical Center and that all lab test reports would not have Father's name on them as, in the case of VIPs, no names were ever used for lab test orders and reports or x-rays." Anna pronounced herself thoroughly mystified as to "why Mother never requested the medical records until 1957; and I wonder what prompted her [to do so] at that time."[34]

The answers to these questions went to the grave with Eleanor Roosevelt, who died on Election Day 1962* after a six-week battle with what was only correctly diagnosed postmortem as a rare form of tuberculosis. Her death might have closed the books on the debate over FDR's final illness. Instead, it opened a whole new chapter—one that would make medical history.

*Her obituary shared the front page of the next day's newspapers with accounts of Richard Nixon's bitter "you won't have Nixon to kick around anymore" press conference after losing the California gubernatorial election.

A Certain Narrative

CHAPTER 15

For Howard Bruenn, the turn of 1963 must have seemed like an opportune time to break his nearly two-decades-long silence. Not only had Eleanor Roosevelt just died, but all the rest of the inner circle of doctors who'd been publicly identified as having had a major role in the president's care now also were gone.

James Paullin was the first to pass away, from a heart attack in 1951 at age sixty-nine while examining a patient at his Atlanta office.[1] Frank Lahey succumbed two years later at seventy-three, widely hailed as the "outstanding general surgeon in the world today" and for having pioneered the concept of group care, in which specialists cooperate to provide comprehensive medical treatment.[2] Most important, Ross McIntire also was dead. After retiring from the Navy in 1947, he'd been appointed to organize the Red Cross's blood program, a position he held for four years. In 1954, he made an unsuccessful run for Congress from a district in California, then was named executive director of the International College of Surgeons. He suffered a fatal heart attack in 1959 and was buried in Arlington National Cemetery.

Besides Bruenn, William Calhoun Stirling was the only other one of the major doctors still alive. But he had long ago stopped talking about his critical link with the FDR mystery, and it would be decades before his name became publicly known in connection with Roosevelt. (He died in 1969.)

Moreover, there had recently been renewed interest in Roosevelt's health within the medical community. Though the issue of serial strokes seemingly had been laid to rest with Elliot Roosevelt's convincing rebuttal of Karl Wold back in 1949, a new book and an article in a respected medical journal had repeated the allegation. Dr. Rudolph Marx's *The Health of the Presidents*, published in 1960, and a paper by Dr. Ben H. McConnell in the February 1961 issue of the *Journal of the American Geriatric Society*, both stated that Roosevelt had suffered a series of "little strokes." Surprisingly, there was no reaction from the Roosevelt family until an article by J. D. Ratcliff in *Today's Health*, a magazine sponsored by the American Medical Association for a general audience, also claimed that "Franklin D. Roosevelt had five minor strokes before the final catastrophe which killed him."[3]

The magazine agreed to publish a rebuttal by Dr. James A. Halsted, a Harvard-educated internist who in 1952 had married Anna Roosevelt and who now assumed the role of principal family spokesman on medical issues regarding the late president. He gave a flat denial that FDR had suffered any minor strokes, and explained why he believed the issue was critical—the "sick man of Yalta" accusation had become a rallying cry for conservatives convinced that a mentally disabled Roosevelt had sold out Eastern Europe to Stalin:

> It is important to get at the truth in order to set the record straight. Otherwise this myth would lend credence to the assumption by some people that Roosevelt's judgment was seriously impaired by his supposed ill-health. Going on unchallenged, it might become a part of documented "history" which is actually mythical in the years to come.[4]

Besides citing both his wife and mother-in-law, Halsted quoted another source to support his contention—a rather startling one, given the lack of confidence his course of treatment is supposed to have engendered in the Roosevelt family: "Presumably, [Ratcliff] did not read Doctor McIntire's book, *White House Physician*, published in 1946. Otherwise, he must have been willing to assume that Doctor McIntire, a vice-admiral in the United States Navy, who was in nearly daily attendance upon the President from 1933 to 1945, did not tell the truth."[5] There was no response from Ratcliff, but—as Halsted surely must have known—he would not have been the first to believe that Ross McIntire had been less than truthful, both before and after FDR's death.

Yet another medical journal article about Roosevelt did not prompt a reaction from Halsted or anyone else in the Roosevelt circle, either—perhaps because they were unaware it had been published. A surgeon named Francis Massie wrote a paper in 1961 for *Modern Medicine* in which he commented on FDR's pigmented lesion and its eventual disappearance, concluding that it was a malignant melanoma.[6] He based this assessment not just on photos of the lesion but on a slide that had been featured a dozen years earlier in a medical paper by Dr. William S. McCune of Georgetown University and Walter Reed Army Hospital.[7] The slide, which was taken from Walter Reed, showed a section of brain demonstrating a fatal hemorrhage from a metastatic melanoma in the right cerebral hemisphere; although the patient was not otherwise identified, the slide contained the label "A-14-45"—which Massie concluded meant April 14, 1945, the day FDR's body arrived back in Washington from Warm Springs. The fact that a slide from the capital's main Army hospital showing a brain hemorrhage from a metastatic melanoma, and which carried that date made the connection unmistakable, as far as Massie was concerned, notwithstanding the denials from all those involved that FDR's body had undergone an autopsy.

But though he was on the right track—and his was the first paper in a medical journal to connect Roosevelt with melanoma—the "smoking gun" for Massie's diagnosis was based on faulty evidence. Dr. Robert Joy, a former pathologist at Walter Reed, told Dr. Robert Hudson, and also confirmed to the authors, that Massie had misinterpreted the slide's label: A-14 indicates only that it came from the fourteenth autopsy performed at Walter Reed in 1945. A check of the records by Dr. Joy revealed that the subject was a twenty-seven-year-old soldier.[8]

Were Halsted aware that a reputable medical journal was reporting that his father-in-law had suffered from cancer, he undoubtedly would have sought to refute it. For that's exactly what did happen when the allegation was raised again, more visibly, a few years later.

This, then, was the background of Howard Bruenn's reaction when he was contacted—without the Roosevelt family's knowledge or authorization—by David Gurewitsch, Eleanor's confidant, doctor, housemate, and traveling companion during the last fifteen years of her life, about whether he would be willing to deposit his personal FDR file at Hyde Park.[9]

When Bruenn expressed interest, Anna and her husband told him they were convinced that whatever documents he had should remain closed to outsiders "for a considerable period yet to come"—suggesting twenty-five years as an appropriate time span. Indeed, they wrote, "the more thought we have given to this problem, the more strongly we have felt."[10] This despite a private warning from her brother Jimmy that the family should have no say in allowing access to Bruenn's records: "I would be afraid of something like this," he wrote his sister, "for fear that we would be accused of trying to hide some late information. After all, we are just about eighteen years after Father's death and there would not seem to be much excuse for putting any restrictions on medical records concerning him at this time."[11]

Fully four years later, Bruenn and the Halsteds still had not reached agreement on terms for depositing his records at Hyde Park, at which point the two doctors decided on a face-to-face meeting to discuss the matter. In his handwritten notes of their March 8, 1967, conference, Halsted wrote that he once again "explained the possibility of [Bruenn] depositing his records at the Library under conditions he could stipulate as to their availability," but repeated his earlier suggestion that they remain "closed for 25 years."[12] However, Bruenn now raised another possibility, saying he "had thought about publishing the record, but had wished to wait until enough time had passed."[13] Obviously trying to win Halsted over, Bruenn stressed that "it would be a purely factual account—not a 'Lord Moran' book," referring to Churchill's doctor, whose tell-all memoir after the prime minister's death was widely disapproved of in the medical community (and had also questioned whether FDR was still "fit for his job" at Yalta).[14] Still, Bruenn said, he was undecided about whether to publish his own account, adding that he "wished to avoid any political or international implications."[15]

One would think that Bruenn's offer to publish was exactly what the Halsteds wanted: an objective medical account, based on documented records, that could refute, once and for all, the notion that the United States had been badly represented by the "sick man of Yalta." But, again, James Halsted's response was far from enthusiastic—indeed, he raised objections to the very notion of going public, warning that "it might still have adverse effects."[16]* That initial reluctance would change before long—and quite dramatically. Halsted suggested that Bruenn discuss the matter with two respected, but decidedly friendly, Roosevelt biographers, Frank Freidel and Arthur Schlesinger Jr.[17] The two doctors then discussed the details of FDR's case—with Bruenn again saying that he "first saw the president in late 1943," the same time period both he and McIntire had cited back in 1946, and several months before the date he would later claim.

During this drawn-out negotiation, another development was taking place: Dr. George T. Pack, one of the world's leading experts in cancer surgery, had been presenting a series of lectures to medical students and professionals about the impact of illness on world history. Pack certainly knew whereof he spoke; among his many well-known patients had been Admiral William "Bull" Halsey and Argentina's first lady, Eva "Evita" Peron. In 1963, Pack gave his talk to a group of surgical residents at New York's Memorial Sloane-Kettering Hospital, where he'd been an attending surgeon for over three decades and head of the melanoma service. In the audience that day was a young doctor named Harry Goldsmith, who was impressed by Pack's disclosure that an old friend and colleague, Frank Lahey, had seen FDR in consultation in 1944, determined that the president had a metastatic tumor, and advised him not to run for a fourth term.[18] The memory of that lecture, and his subsequent discussions about it with Pack, would eventually lead Goldsmith on a three-decade investigation of Roosevelt's health and the 1979 publication of his paper in a highly regarded medical journal that raised the possibility that FDR had had cancer, which garnered national attention.

---

*Both Bruenn and the Halsteds might have felt differently had they known that George Fox was thinking about beating them to the punch. In late 1962, he wrote William Rigdon, FDR's naval aide, that he had "been urged by many to do a book on the medical aspects of my twenty years at the White House. While I realize this is a ticklish subject, it could be very interesting and difficult to do without opening the bedroom doors too wide." For whatever reasons, Fox never did write a memoir. (George A. Fox to William Rigdon, September 24, 1962, William Rigdon papers, Georgia Southern University)

But Goldsmith was not the only one who recalled hearing Pack make such claims. Dr. Samuel Day, former president of the Florida Medical Association, wrote that Pack told him years earlier that, according to Lahey, Roosevelt was examined in 1944 at the Lahey Clinic, where he was told that he had advanced, inoperable cancer of the stomach. According to Day, Lahey told Pack that this information could not be made public as long as any of the involved figures were still alive.[19] Day repeated this account in a letter to syndicated columnist Jack Anderson following publication of Goldsmith's paper. And he added that in 1965, he'd again asked Pack about the FDR incident and was told, "I spoke to Dick Cattell [Lahey's top assistant and eventual successor] about it and he seemed upset by my inquiry. Cattell was quite short with me, saying that was confidential information and would not be released."[20]

In preparing his paper, Goldsmith reached out to other doctors who had attended Pack's 1963 lecture. One, Andrew A. Kiely, who'd been chief surgical resident at Memorial Sloane-Kettering at the time, recalled not only that talk but a similar one Pack delivered at a private dinner of the Strollers Club, at which he'd said "that he was told by Dr. Frank Lahey that President Franklin D. Roosevelt went to see him as a patient in the summer prior to his nomination for his fourth term. Dr. Lahey told him that he had a metastatic carcinoma primary in the prostate, advising him not to run for re-election as he would never complete his term in office."[21]

At least one doctor recalled hearing a similar story directly from Lahey in the years following Roosevelt's death. Robert Bradley, attending a lecture at the College of Physicians in Philadelphia, disclosed that Lahey, while visiting friends at a club in New Hampshire, related that he'd examined the president at the White House and found what was later described as an appalling situation. As he prepared to inform FDR of his findings, telling him, "Mr. President, you may not care for what I have to say," Roosevelt curtly dismissed him, saying, "That will be all, Dr. Lahey."[22]

None of this ever got back to the Roosevelt family, but by mid-1967 Bruenn was beginning to write his paper, with the active help of Anna, who was constantly sending him suggestions, and her husband, who forwarded his notes and ideas based on the available medical records at Hyde Park.[23] On October 21, Bruenn informed Anna that he was "almost finished," needing about "2 weeks more work."[24] But it would be over a year before Bruenn completed his manuscript, at which point there began a series of back-and-forth revisions—with both Halsteds exerting a very heavy editorial influence.

"Jim and I have gone over your mss [manuscript] quite carefully," Anna wrote in the summer of 1969, "and think your changes are clarifying and excellent and we are pleased with the summary."[25] The same letter contained a proposed change designed to ward off "the possible reaction of gossip mongers" who, she feared, "*might* decide to contact you as to what you know about Mrs. [Lucy Mercer] Rutherfurd."[26] And it included a new final paragraph, written entirely by the Halsteds in Bruenn's voice, which stressed their principal concern in seeing the piece published:

> In conclusion, I should like to reiterate that this clinical record is written in the interest of accuracy and to answer some unfounded rumors. . . . As a result of this unforgettable experience, and as a practicing physician, I have often wondered what turn the subsequent course of history might have taken if the modern methods for the control of hypertension had been available.[27]*

During these negotiations, Anna had been contacted by historian James MacGregor Burns, who was preparing the second volume of his FDR biography and wanted her help in contacting Bruenn. Anna urged Bruenn to collaborate with Burns, assuring him that he would receive full credit in whatever Burns published, even suggesting that Burns would write a magazine article for the general public in advance of, and based on, Bruenn's paper.[28] After reading Bruenn's manuscript, Burns agreed that it would "be an indispensable contribution to . . . diminishing the rumors of the 'sick man of Yalta' and the like," though he cautioned that it "may raise more questions than it settles."[29]

Bruenn submitted his paper to the prestigious *Annals of Internal Medicine*, whose editors were decidedly interested but questioned whether Bruenn might be violating his late patient's confidentiality and whether the Roosevelt family—by which they meant all of the president's children—

*The paragraph appeared in Bruenn's paper exactly as written by the Halsteds.

had agreed to its publication. Anna agreed to get her brothers' consent (though noting that Elliot, from whom she was then estranged, might balk)[30] but raised serious concerns about how the journal would present that permission.

"We feel it will detract from the strength of the document itself if . . . mention of its 'approval' could be construed to mean that we had pressured Dr. Bruenn into writing his paper and, possibly, that our reason for doing so was to put the best possible light on Father's decisions during the last year or so of his life," she wrote editor R. Russell Elkinton—which, of course, is precisely what had happened. "If any mention is made of the family," she added disingenuously, "it should merely be made on the basis that Dr. Bruenn has notified the five of us that the paper he planned to write for some time is now being published. (Or something to that effect!)"[31] Bruenn, for his part, stressed to the *Annals*' associate editor, Edward Huth, that he'd written the paper only "at the urging of President Roosevelt's daughter, Anna."[32]

But something else had occurred—something that was giving Anna and her husband new concerns and considerably more reason to push hard for speedy publication of Bruenn's paper. Several weeks earlier, a *New York Times* article out of London had reported on the publication of *The Pathology of Leadership*, a new book by British medical historian Dr. Hugh L'Etang, which alleged that six of the last ten U.S. presidents, and eleven of the thirteen previous British prime ministers, had "suffered illness which incapacitated them to some degree while in office."[33] The article named Roosevelt as one of the six but did not elaborate. However, a British medical journal published a lengthy and detailed review of the book, which had been called to Bruenn's attention. Relaying what Bruenn told her, Anna informed her brothers that "the author's thesis is that these leaders were medically unfit to make important decisions, and he makes the unequivocal statement that Father was killed by a brain tumor."[34]

Actually, the book made no such "unequivocal statement." L'Etang had read Francis Massie's 1961 paper, based on the flawed autopsy slide identification, and devoted but a single paragraph of his chapter on FDR to the possibility that "Roosevelt's terminal illness was due to malignant deposits from a pigmented growth." Massie's since-discredited slide evidence, he added, "in default of information from the Roosevelt family, cannot be dismissed."[35] This, combined with L'Etang's stronger claim that FDR's cardiac and other ailments certainly had impaired his abilities at Yalta, clearly touched a nerve with both Bruenn and the Halsteds. Suddenly, publishing Bruenn's paper had become a race against time, as far as Anna was concerned. "It is Dr. Bruenn's present hope," she told her brothers, "that his article may appear in print either before or approximately at the same time as Dr. L'Etang's book." (Actually, the book already had been published in Britain.)

Bruenn's article was published on April 12, 1970—the twenty-fifth anniversary of FDR's death, which certainly helped maximize publicity. An advance copy was given to the *New York Times,* which ran an appraisal under a seven-column headline that read (doubtless to Anna's delight): "Roosevelt's Doctor Says Last Illness Did Not Prevent President From Performing Duties."[36]

Significantly, the issue of the *Annals* containing Bruenn's paper also featured an editorial, ostensibly written by the editors independent of any outside input. Though neither L'Etang's book nor the possibility of a metastatic melanoma were ever mentioned by Bruenn, the editorial pointedly noted that "the speculation in a recently published book (based on the showing of an unlabeled slide from Walter Reed Hospital) that the President was suffering from a metastatic melanoma in the brain, is laid to rest by Dr. Bruenn; there was no clinical evidence for such a lesion, and no autopsy was performed." And, it concluded—exactly as Anna Halsted would have wanted: "We are given by Dr. Bruenn the picture of a great and gallant man, fatigued by the burdens of his office and by his hypertension and reduced cardiac reserve, yet quite able to exercise his judgment and to use the fruits of his unique knowledge and experience in guiding the war effort."[37]

News articles hailed Bruenn's paper as a major revelation that, at long last, told the *real* story of Franklin Roosevelt's final illness and would become the standard reference for all time. Historians have accepted Bruenn's paper as the definitive account of FDR's health; Drs. Kenneth R. Crispell and Carlos F. Gomez, in their book, *Hidden Illness at the White House*, cite "the true medical facts as recorded so accurately by Bruenn."[38] And Matthew B. Wills, in his account of FDR's last year, lavishes praise on both Bruenn and Anna, "two people who insisted on [telling] the truth about Roosevelt's precarious state of health" and "to whom all those with a serious interest in the life of Franklin Delano Roosevelt should be extremely grateful."[39] Bruenn himself exhibited no false modesty about his paper's importance, saying that it "sort of blew the door down as far as the actual facts were concerned."[40]

But is this gospel according to Bruenn really as authoritative as he hoped future historians would believe? Only recently have questions been raised about the reliability of Bruenn's narrative. Dr. Barron H. Lerner, a medical historian and professor of medicine at Columbia University's College of Physicians and Surgeons (the same institution where Bruenn once practiced), published a paper in 2007 raising doubts about Bruenn's account. "Bruenn was no different from any other historical actor who later described events in which he had participated," Lerner wrote, noting that this "definitive" account "was colored by the political context of the 1940s and also that of 1970"—not to mention the unacknowledged collaboration of "several parties . . . all of whom had interests in what Bruenn would conclude."[41] Indeed, he quoted from a letter in which Dr. Howard B. Burchell, chief of cardiology at the University of Minnesota Medical School, asked point-blank whether the paper would either have been written or published "if there had been a less favorable review of the health problems of the president." Because, he suggested, Bruenn had a vested interest, too—having presumably given his medical clearance for FDR to attend the Yalta conference. "One could submit," wrote Burchell, "that Dr. Bruenn would have strong unconscious forces which would operate in his rendering a favorable report on the patient's health."[42]

In fact, those forces weren't so unconscious. Though a Republican, Bruenn, like so many others, had fallen under the spell of his closeness to the president of the United States and became a lifelong Roosevelt admirer. As he told Daisy Suckley just two weeks before the president's death, "Like all people who work with this man, I love him. If he told me to jump out of the window, I would do it, without hesitation."[43] Though he always insisted he'd never been asked whether Roosevelt was medically fit to run for another term, he admitted in a 1990 interview with Jan K. Herman, historian of the U.S. Navy's Bureau of Medicine and Surgery, that his political feelings probably would have swayed his judgment. Given that the war had been conducted through an intense personal relationship between FDR, Churchill, and Stalin, he said, "I thought that was damn important."[44]* But in an interview two years later with historian Robert H. Ferrell, Bruenn conceded that, had he been asked about a fourth term, he would have called it medically impossible.[45]

Lerner concluded that Bruenn's paper was flawed because it "conformed to a certain narrative"—namely, "a form that supported the decisions that Roosevelt, his family members, his political colleagues and his doctor, Howard Bruenn, had made"[46] And it's significant that the paper contains no direct criticism of Ross McIntire, particularly of his role as FDR's primary physician. True, the paper undermines McIntire's public pronouncements about Roosevelt's health, but even this is not done directly; though not widely noted, Bruenn's paper constitutes a rebuke to those who have derided McIntire as an incompetent physician. (As the years went on, Bruenn grew increasingly disparaging toward McIntire in his occasional interviews but never was openly critical.)

Lerner's analysis did not raise significant medical questions about what had been billed as a "clinical" history. Yet even if one discounts all of the medical information and suggestions about FDR this book raises, Bruenn's paper contains startling omissions and outright distortions, particularly the astonishing absence of any reference whatsoever to Roosevelt's seizures—those attacks of often frightening temporary impairment that had been witnessed, and later commented on, by more than a dozen eyewitnesses, many of them people close to the president. Given that some have attributed these attacks to encephalopathy brought about by FDR's alarmingly high blood pressure,[47] it should have been expected that a cardiologist—who certainly must have seen those attacks firsthand and also been told of them by other concerned witnesses—would take note of them. But Bruenn mentions not a word. Of Roosevelt's stumbling performance in the Yalta speech, Bruenn writes that the president "laughingly reported that while giving the speech he had

---

*For someone who initially had expressed his eagerness to "avoid any political or international implications," Bruenn included a surprising amount of unrelated political and historical analysis in his paper, which, after all, was written for a medical journal. And, in later interviews, he departed from his ostensible role as impartial medical observer to offer a passionate defense of Roosevelt's political decisions. (See Jan K. Herman interview for *Navy Medicine*, 1990)

spoken at intervals from memory and 'off the record' and that he had then had slight difficulty in finding the place when returning to read the printed words of his address."[48]

Nor did Bruenn comment in any way on the pigmented lesion above Roosevelt's eye and its eventual disappearance. Years later, after Harry Goldsmith's paper was published, he would give wildly varying accounts of the lesion's disappearance, suggesting at one point that it had been removed by Winchell Craig in 1944 at the same time as the wen, and at another that it never disappeared at all, calling pictures showing the area above FDR's eye free of any pigmentation "a photographic error or something."[49]

Bruenn does mention the president's "severe iron deficiency anemia" in 1941, which he attributes to "bleeding hemorrhoids," adding that it "responded quickly to ferrous sulfate [iron] therapy." Yet he makes no mention of any blood transfusions—though James Halsted had not only informed him of them in his analysis of the medical records at the FDR Library, but also mentioned that the president had experienced a "transfusion reaction." The fact that the president of the United States, having lost fully two-thirds of his blood, required multiple emergency blood transfusions, was, of course, never publicly acknowledged.

Finally, Bruenn made very selective use of the surviving medical records. Case in point: He cites numerous results from the Bethesda lab slip of a urinalysis conducted on March 29, 1944, including specific gravity, sugar, albumin, and blood cell counts, none of which indicated any serious problem. But he chose to omit two other results from the same slip, which showed white blood cell casts, meaning that Roosevelt literally was urinating pus, indicative of a serious urinary tract infection—which almost certainly required treatment with antibiotics.

Together with his advancement of other now-discredited myths about FDR's treatment—such as his insistence that Frank Lahey examined the president only once—it becomes clear that the "landmark" paper, while providing new and important medical facts, was little more than Howard Bruenn's final contribution to the cover-up of Franklin Roosevelt's health.

The Next Deadly Secret

CHAPTER 16

Franklin Delano Roosevelt was not the first president who, with the aid of his doctors, covered up life-threatening or debilitating illnesses; Grover Cleveland, Woodrow Wilson, and possibly Warren Harding had all done it before. Nor would he prove to be the last: Dwight Eisenhower's doctors suppressed, at least for a while, the serious extent of his cardiac and gastrointestinal problems; John F. Kennedy's physicians hid the fact that he had Addison's disease, a failure of the adrenal glands, and that it was treated with regular injections of corticosteroids laced with amphetamines. And Lyndon Johnson's secret operation to remove a skin cancer from his ankle was not disclosed until four years after his death.

Even in an era of greater White House transparency, top aides to Ronald Reagan carefully controlled the information that was given to the press following the 1981 assassination attempt in which he was critically wounded, again three years later when doctors removed a cancerous polyp from his colon, and once more in 1987, when he underwent a prostate operation. In the latter case, First Lady Nancy Reagan pointedly refused to make her husband's team of surgeons available to the news media for questioning, though the nature of the surgery was not hidden.[1]

The shock of FDR's death, the revelation that he'd been increasingly ill beforehand, and his succession by the still relatively unknown Truman, touched off concern in Congress that it was time to take a closer look at the process for filling a sudden vacancy in the White House. Over the next quarter-century, the procedure would undergo several substantive revisions. But, in the end, one key element remains unresolved: how to keep another president from successfully concealing, as Franklin Roosevelt did, such a deadly secret from the American people.

One month after FDR's death, Representative A. S. Mike Monroney (D-Oklahoma) introduced a bill proposing the first substantive change in the order of presidential succession in more than half a century. But his bill was a complicated affair, calling for a special commission to work out a long-term solution.[2] So, on June 19, 1945, President Truman sent a special message to Congress outlining a proposed solution to be codified in legislation without waiting for a commission to investigate.

As originally written, the U.S. Constitution specified only that the vice president ascends to the presidency in the case of a vacancy; the document left to Congress the task of selecting a new chief executive in the absence of a vice president. At no time—either then or for the next two centuries—was it suggested that the president nominate a new vice president should a vacancy occur. In 1792, Congress passed its first law on succession, specifying that the vice president be followed in the line of succession by the president pro tempore of the Senate (usually the body's senior member) and then the Speaker of the House. That was changed in 1886, five years after President James A. Garfield was assassinated and several months after Grover Cleveland's first vice president, Thomas A. Hendricks, died suddenly. This persuaded Congress that the vice president should be succeeded in line for the presidency by the members of the cabinet, in order of seniority, based on when their respective departments had been officially established; this placed the secretary of state first in line.

But Truman now objected to this method, noting that "each of these Cabinet members is appointed," which meant that "by reason of the tragic death of the late President, it now lies within my power to nominate the person who would be my immediate successor in the event of my own death or inability to act. I do not believe," he added, "that in a democracy this power should rest with the Chief Executive."[3]

Truman was not the first to argue, as he did that day, that "insofar as possible, the office of the President should be filled by an elective officer." But that was precisely what he proposed to Congress, though with a significant difference from the 1792 law: Truman insisted that the Speaker of the House be placed ahead of the Senate's president pro tempore in the line of succession.

His official reasoning was somewhat tortured: The Speaker, he said, is elected not only by voters in his own district but by the members of the House, who are "all the Representatives of all the people in the country." According to Truman, this made the Speaker that elected official who "can be most accurately said to stem from the people themselves."[4] This, he said, is because the entire House—unlike the Senate—is elected every two years; members of the Senate, Truman insisted, "are not as closely tied in by the electoral process to the people as are the members of the House."

Actually, Truman had a more personal, and blatantly political, concern: He wanted his good friend Sam Rayburn of Texas* to be first in line to succeed him, rather than Senator Kenneth McKellar of Tennessee, a onetime New Dealer who had grown more conservative over the years (and would soon be involved in a fierce political fight with Truman over the renomination of David A. Lilienthal to head the Tennessee Valley Authority). But the president also recognized that, as the senior member of the Senate, the president pro tempore tended to be an elderly Southerner. In fact, McKellar just five months earlier had succeeded Senator Carter Glass of Virginia, who'd held the post until his retirement at age eighty-seven. As for Secretary of State Edward Stettinius, who was then first in line, *New York Times* Washington bureau chief Arthur Krock noted that most Democratic officials did not believe the onetime General Motors executive and veteran New Deal bureaucrat "has had the public and political training essential to the Presidency."[5]

In his message, Truman noted that during the impeachment proceedings against President Andrew Johnson in 1868, some had "suggested the possibility of a hostile Congress in the future seeking to oust a

---

*Truman had been in Rayburn's office, having drinks with some of the members of the speaker's famous "board of education" on April 12, when the call came from Steve Early following FDR's death telling him to go immediately to the White House.

Vice President who had become President, in order to have the President Pro Tempore of the Senate become President," which was one of the motives behind the 1886 change in the law. So he proposed another clause: No matter who succeeded a vice president who had become president, that person "should not serve any longer than until the next Congressional election, or until a special election [is] called for the purpose of electing a new President and Vice President."[6]*

Initial reaction to Truman's proposal was extremely positive, especially in Democratic circles; the *New York Times* hailed it as "fundamentally sound."[7] Within days, however, opposition began to develop, mostly on constitutional grounds, with some arguing that an amendment to the Constitution, rather than congressional legislation, was needed. Others in Congress suggested changes to Truman's idea: One bill proposed reconvening the Electoral College from the previous election to choose a new president and vice president. And there was near-unanimous opposition to a limited term or special election; general agreement was that whoever succeeded to office should serve out the remainder of the current presidential term.[8]

Eventually, the objections—including fears that a hostile Congress might impeach the president and vice president in order to install the Speaker—were met and, on July 19, 1947, Truman signed into law a bill changing the order of succession; the legislation, Public Law 199, also specified that anyone succeeding the vice president to the Oval Office would serve until the next scheduled presidential election.

But there had been a significant change in the political landscape since his initial proposal: When Truman first suggested placing the Speaker directly in line behind the vice president, he noted that the House "usually . . . is in agreement politically with the Chief Executive"; on the other hand, the Senate—one-third of whose members are elected every two years—might "have a majority hostile to the policies of the President, and might conceivably fill the Presidential office with one not in sympathy with the will of the majority of the people."[9] In 1946, however, the GOP had taken control of both houses of Congress—meaning that the

---

*Krock also wrote that, in his opinion, neither Rayburn nor McKellar "has Presidential qualifications," either. (*New York Times*, June 20, 1945)

two people now in line to replace Democrat Truman were Republicans: Speaker Joseph W. Martin and Senator Arthur H. Vandenberg.

Similarly, had this system still been effect during the Watergate scandal of the 1970s, when Vice President Spiro Agnew's resignation in a bribery scandal was followed ten months later by that of President Richard Nixon, the two ousted Republicans would have been succeeded by a Democrat, House Speaker Carl Albert of Oklahoma. And right behind him was the archconservative and outspokenly racist president pro tempore of the Senate, James O. Eastland of Mississippi.

Further concerns about presidential health led to yet another change in the succession system. President Dwight Eisenhower suffered a massive heart attack in 1955, as did Senate Majority Leader and future President Lyndon B. Johnson.* In 1958, Eisenhower and Vice President Richard Nixon reached an informal agreement regarding what they would do if the president became unable to serve.[10] But theirs was a personal and unofficial understanding, not binding either on them or on their successors.

The assassination in 1963 of the youthful John F. Kennedy and his succession by Johnson, whose past cardiac problems** were well documented—and the fact that immediately following LBJ in line were the seventy-two-year-old Speaker of the House, John W. McCormack and eighty-six-year-old Senator Carl Hayden—spurred calls for another comprehensive look at the issue. Of particular concern this time was how to determine, as in Franklin Roosevelt's case, whether a president was physically and/or mentally able to serve.

Earlier in the '60s, Congress had considered a proposal in which the vice president would notify the chief justice of the Supreme Court of any suspected inability; the jurist would then appoint a civilian panel to evaluate the president. This was rejected on two grounds: Involving the Supreme Court violated the constitutionally mandated separation of powers, and the panel would lack public accountability. Similarly, Congress rejected

---

*Johnson's attack came just days after his annual physical examination, at which he was pronounced medically fit. (Michael J. Halberstam, *New York Times Magazine*, October 22, 1972)

**He died ten years later of a heart attack at the age of sixty-five.

assembling a panel of physicians to examine the president, saying that legally forcing a chief executive to undergo an exam would violate presidential dignity and that, if a medical emergency existed, it would delay immediate action.[11]

Finally, in 1966, Congress passed, and the states ratified, the Twenty-Fifth Amendment. This provided for the first time that in the case of a vacancy in the office, the president would name a new vice president, who would then be confirmed by majority vote in both houses of Congress. This provision has been utilized twice: when Gerald Ford succeeded Spiro Agnew in 1973, and when Ford then named Nelson A. Rockefeller to replace him following Nixon's resignation.

(Ironically, this led to precisely the situation Truman had warned against nearly three decades earlier: America was led by a president and a vice president, neither of whom had been elected to those posts by the voters.)

The amendment also provided that a president can declare himself unable to "discharge the powers and duties of his office" by so notifying congressional leaders; he may reassume the presidency upon transmitting "a written declaration" of his fitness. This has been used several times in recent decades, as presidents who undergo medical procedures involving anesthesia, for example, have declared themselves temporarily unable to discharge their duties and turned power over to the vice president—though, significantly, this was not invoked following Reagan's assassination attempt or during his colon surgery.

In case a president cannot recognize his inability to serve, the amendment specifies that the vice president, along with a majority of the cabinet or some other "body" specified by Congress, can declare him disabled and temporarily remove him from office. If the president disagrees with their judgment or later tries to reclaim the office without the backing of the vice president and a cabinet majority, the matter moves to Congress for a vote.

At first glance, the Twenty-Fifth Amendment seems sufficiently comprehensive to prevent the kind of situation under which Franklin Roosevelt and his doctors were able to hide his medical unfitness for the presidency. But, as Aaron Seth Kesselheim of Harvard University has written, there are a number of serious problems with the process. For one thing, no single event is needed to invoke its protection. And the power to put the disability procedure into motion remains with the executive branch—specifically, he noted, "under the control of the people most beholden to the President. . . . Those same people who must initiate the Twenty-Fifth Amendment procedure are those whose power it most likely affects."[12] Though the process is spelled out and authorized in the nation's guiding legal document, the notion that a vice president and cabinet actually might use it remains almost inconceivable: Doubtless there would be considerable fear, particularly in a case where the president's disability was not undeniably clear, of the public seeing any such effort as a veritable coup d'état. Certainly no one in Roosevelt's cabinet would ever have initiated, or even supported, such a process, despite their considerable and growing concern for his health.

Besides, as Kesselheim points out, the amendment has a fatal flaw: Nowhere does it require a medical evaluation of the president, meaning that any decision to forcibly remove him from power is an entirely political one. This was no oversight; Congress specifically rejected the idea of creating a panel of neutral physicians, deciding that the removal of a president involves ramifications beyond a simple medical diagnosis. Indeed, it does not even require the White House physician, let alone an independent doctor, to certify the president's disability. Relying on the White House physician would be a dubious step, at best; while the relationship between president and doctor in recent years has become less intimate than that of FDR and Ross McIntire, who was a member of the president's inner circle, those doctors invariably are drawn from the ranks of the military. They still have the dual problem of loyalty to their patient as well as to their commander in chief.[13]

How, then, to solve the problem? Some have proposed establishing an independent board of medical experts, serving specific terms, who could be called on when needed to examine the president and submit their findings to the vice president and the cabinet. But concerns have been raised about forcing the chief executive to undergo an examination by doctors not of his own choosing. Also, it is not clear how any disagreement within the panel would be resolved.

Others have proposed upgrading the office of White House physician to a formal position: This would still allow presidents to choose their own doctors, remove the conflict involving the commander in chief, and give the physician a stronger and more independent voice. But, notes Kesselheim, this might also drive a wedge between doctor and president, leading the latter not to confide fully in his physician and to withhold potentially dangerous symptoms.

It's ironic that top government agencies, like the Central Intelligence Agency, the Pentagon, and the State Department, have no problem requiring those appointed to senior positions to undergo advance medical screenings—and by an independent board, not their own physicians. Franklin Roosevelt required such an examination, at the Lahey Clinic, of Joseph E. Davies before naming him ambassador to the Soviet Union. Yet no such requirement—save for preelection public pressure—obtains on a presidential candidate. And once the president takes office, no independent doctor or board exists to monitor his health, or to confirm the publicly announced results of his annual medical examinations.

Franklin Delano Roosevelt and his doctors kept the full extent of his serious medical problems from the American people and—until now—from the pages of history, as well. But as things now stand more than sixty years later, another president of the United States with a similar deadly secret can still keep it hidden. And that is the real peril of FDR's deception: Franklin Roosevelt rolled the dice with history and—with the debatable exception of Yalta—won. The next similarly stricken president may not prove to be so lucky.

ACKNOWLEDGMENTS

Writing this book would have been impossible without the foundation provided by the work of the many historians and biographers who have scrutinized Franklin Delano Roosevelt's life over the past seven-plus decades. Fortunately for us, several of them took the time to generously share their insights, answer our many questions, and evaluate our analyses, including Frank Costigliola, along with his colleagues at the University of Connecticut, and Alonzo Hamby. This was particularly true of those who have researched FDR's health, such as Dr. Hugh Evans, Robert Ferrell, Richard Thayer Goldberg, Dr. Robert Hudson (who provided us with the only existing videotape of his widely reported 1986 lecture that first linked FDR's fatal brain hemorrhage to a malignant tumor), and John Sotos, aka "Doctor Zebra." Also immensely kind and helpful was the ageless Dr. James Toole, one of the world's great neurologists and a pioneer in the ongoing debate over presidential disability.

Special thanks are due to Geoffrey C. Ward, historian extraordinaire, who over more than three years patiently responded to our every question and suggestion, no matter how seemingly outrageous, and, though not convinced of our thesis, helped steer us away from several wrong paths; and Dr. Harry Goldsmith, whose dogged forty-year pursuit of the unanswered mysteries regarding FDR's fatal illness not only provided us with a wealth of valuable information that served as an adjunct to our own research, but, in fact, inspired the present work. Harry spent countless hours discussing, debating, and arguing with us; he deserves not only our gratitude but also recognition for having written the first notable paper in a peer-reviewed medical journal that challenged the traditional beliefs about Franklin Roosevelt's health.

We first approached the late Dr. A. Bernard Ackerman for advice on the recommendation of Dr. Joseph Eastern, who thought his mentor, the world's foremost dermatopathologist, could help conclusively answer the question of whether FDR's lesion was, in fact, melanoma. To our delight, Bernie quickly became caught up in our research and not only spent hours examining hundreds of photos of FDR, but also joined us at Hyde Park to examine the FDR Library's holdings. His advice, encouragement, and counsel were invaluable. Moreover, his conclusion that the lesion most probably was malignant, and the paper he co-wrote with Dr. Lomazow to that effect, has played a major role in the acceptance of our research in the medical community. (We thank the editors of the *Archives of Dermatology* for reviewing and publishing that paper.) Sadly, Bernie passed away in December 2008, before seeing the fruits of our joint effort.

We could not have asked for more genuinely helpful colleagues than Jan K. Herman, official historian of the U.S. Navy's Bureau of Medicine and editor in chief of *Navy Medicine*, and his deputy, Andre Sobocinski, who went out of their way to provide their own prodigious research skills and guide us through Navy medicine's bureaucracy. Jan, it should be noted, was one of the last to interview Dr. Howard Bruenn, eliciting from him important information that had eluded earlier questioners.

We are extremely grateful to those hospitals and medical schools—among them Harvard, Columbia, Mount Sinai, Bowman Gray, and Albany Medical College—that invited Dr. Lomazow to present our findings at various lecture series and grand rounds, allowing us to receive valuable feedback and input from the medical community, without which this project would never have come to fruition. Particular thanks go to Vice Admiral Adam M. Robinson Jr., surgeon general of the U.S. Navy, for featuring Dr. Lomazow as the opening speaker of the Surgeon General's Lecture Series at the National Naval Medical Center at Bethesda; and Dr. Robert Goldwyn of Harvard Medical School, one of the giants in the field of plastic surgery.

The number of those directly involved in the events described in this book has dwindled with the passage of time to a precious few (though we did get to interview John R. Shrader, one of the three men who embalmed FDR's remains), but many of their children and grandchildren were able to provide both information and documentation. We especially want to thank

Margheritta "Mickey" Allardice, daughter of Dr. William Calhoun Stirling, and Dr. Hal Raper Jr., son of the longtime director of internal medicine at Warm Springs, who also provided us with an unpublished memoir of FDR's last visit there by the wife of that facility's chief surgeon.

Cynthia Koch, director of the Franklin D. Roosevelt Library at Hyde Park, and her staff, including head archivist Robert Clark, were extraordinarily helpful on each of our many visits, guiding us through the library's magnificent holdings. Our research assistant, Tim Frank, located material in several archives in the Washington, D.C., and Virginia area.

All of these people contributed greatly to our efforts. Any mistakes or faults, however, lie solely with the authors.

Our agent, Larry Kirshbaum, believed in this project from the outset. To him and the entire staff at LJK Literary Management, our deepest gratitude.

We were extremely lucky to have found a supportive and dedicated publisher in PublicAffairs, whose enthusiasm for this book from the very beginning was as great as our own. To the entire staff go our deepest thanks, but particularly to Peter Osnos, founder and editor-at-large, and publisher Susan Weinberg. We were especially fortunate that this book was edited by Clive Priddle, whose expert guidance is evident on every page. Thanks also to managing editor Melissa Raymond, project editor Meredith Smith, and copy editor Antoinette Smith.

Steven Lomazow and Eric Fettmann

Taking a medical history created in the 1930s and 1940s and applying it to the ever-increasing mountain of present-day medical understanding has been both daunting and challenging. At one time or another, I've probably cornered or cold-called every neurologist, oncologist, surgeon, urologist, radiologist, nuclear medicine specialist, cardiologist, pulmonologist, gastroenterologist, nephrologist, and dermatologist I know, especially the crew at Clara Maass Memorial Hospital in Belleville, New Jersey. The hospital librarian, Arlene Mangino, has been incredibly helpful and generous with her time in ferreting out some very obscure but highly important references in the medical literature.

Dermatologist Dr. Joseph Eastern has supported and validated this project from its very earliest stages. Dr. Eric Whitman, director of the

Atlantic Health Melanoma Center, provided me with guidance and much of the initial verification that we were indeed on the right track. Neurologist Dr. David Knopman, my fellow resident at the University of Minnesota and now of the Mayo Clinic (a facility that FDR so respected), provided his expertise and guidance. The enthusiasm and medical acumen of one of New Jersey's finest clinicians, Dr. Robert Lahita, and the brilliant Dr. Barry Weiner of Jersey City Medical Center have provided many stimulating and rewarding discussions. Oncologist Dr. Alan Lippman and the many other members of the New Jersey Medical History Society have provided insightful evaluation.

My friends, most notably Senator Raymond Lesniak, George Imperial, the consummate "occdoc" Peter Blumenthal, orthopedist Charles Granatir, fellow collecting fanatics Joseph Rainone and David Leishman, and all of my colleagues at the New Jersey State Board of Medical Examiners, have all been greatly supportive of this project, as has my office staff, anchored by the indispensable Kathleen Moran and Carol Greenwood, who have shared over a quarter-century of the vicissitudes of medical practice.

My father, Jacob M. Lomazow, who fought with General George Patton and later commanded a United Nations Relief and Rehabilitation camp in Austria for displaced Jewish refugees, has been a lifelong example of honesty, quiet compassion, intellect, and support. My late mother, Wanda, very much like FDR's mother, provided strong, consistent, and unqualified nurturing of her only child. Her sisters, Dr. Helen Neumark Fagin, a Holocaust educator of worldwide renown, and Theresa Neumark Dolgov, are superlative role models and living proof of the American dream that Franklin Roosevelt strived to guarantee.

My children, Tyson and Whitney, both now on the brink of rewarding careers in law and medicine, respectively, have been, as usual, tolerant of their father's latest obsession. And my partner in life and romance, Katherine Mitchell, is to be credited with not only having a focusing and modulating influence on my personal life, but also in sharing her invaluable computer expertise. While my previous marriage did not survive this journey, I'd like to thank my now friend, Marilynn, for her valuable help, as well.

S.L.

Over the past thirty-five years, I've had the real privilege of working with some of the finest journalists around and, better still, to call many of them not just colleagues, but also good friends. Thanks for years of friendship to George Arzt, Ken Auletta, Jami Bernard, Thom Bird, Hannah Brown, Jerry Capeci, Charles Carillo, Rita Delfiner, Steve Dunleavy, Roberta Brandes Gratz (my valued collaborator in our series of articles on the Statue of Liberty and Ellis Island), Clyde Haberman, Pete Hamill, Laura Harris, Michael Hechtman, Barbara Hoffman, Mike Kandel, Paul Kern, Ruth Kern, Ray Kerrison, Tony Mancini, David Margolick, the late Jerry Nachman, Mike Pearl, John Podhoretz, Michael Riedel, Joe Rabinovich, Jeff Roth, Michael Shain, Marvin Smilon, Leo Standora, and Tom Teicholz. And, from my too-brief sojourn in Israel, to Surie Ackerman, Sara Averick, Faye Bittker, Ilan Chaim, Aryeh Dean Cohen, Herb Keinon, Alisa Odenheimer, Abraham (Bumie) Rabinovich, Joel Rebibo, and Tom Sawicki.

I would need an entire book to describe the debt, both personal and professional, that I owe to Al Ellenberg. Apart from everything else, he is the best newspaper editor I've ever seen and likely ever will—a feeling that I know is shared by a lot of people in the list above.

Charles Lachman, former *New York Post* colleague and now executive producer of *Inside Edition*, introduced me to our agent, Larry Kirshbaum, for which I'll always be grateful. Bob McManus, editorial page editor of the *New York Post* and a fellow history buff, was both supportive of this project and exceedingly generous in giving me the time needed to pursue it.

"A true friend," the saying goes, "is one who knows us, but loves us anyway." So thanks to some very special friends: Bob and Lill Lansey (and their entire extended family), Toby and Hyman Schaffer, Irv and Lily Cantor, Joe and Joanne Lessem, Hinda Katz, Michael and Zahava Jeff, Rhonda Barad, Peter Zheutlin, Ron Radosh, Michael Rennert, Varda Uri, and Oron Uri. And to the memory of two very dear friends, Uri Dan and Zvika Malchin.

And, finally, to Kim Ginsberg, who keeps me sane.

E.F.

NOTES

Chapter 1

1. William Hassett, diary entry for March 29, 1945. The entry indicates he had expressed similar sentiments the previous December.

2. Newsreel excerpts, Franklin D. Roosevelt Library, Hyde Park, New York (FDRL-HP).

3. Diary entry for March 31, 1945; Geoffrey C. Ward, ed., *Closest Companion*, p. 403

4. Howard G. Bruenn, "Clinical Notes on the Illness and Death of President Franklin D. Roosevelt," p. 587.

5. "Tonic," *Time*, March 12, 1945.

6. Samuel I. Rosenman, *Working with Roosevelt*, p. 527.

7. Jim Bishop, *FDR's Last Year*, p. 481.

8. Ross T. McIntire, *White House Physician*, p. 236.

9. Bruenn, "Clinical Notes on the Illness and Death of President Franklin D. Roosevelt."

10. Ted Morgan, *FDR: A Biography*, p. 758.

11. *New York Times*, March 2, 1945.

12. Ibid.

13. Jonathan Daniels, *White House Witness*, p. 255.

14. Allen Drury, *A Senate Journal*, p. 373.

15. Ibid.

16. *Chicago Tribune*, March 2, 1945.

17. Ward, *Closest Companion*, p. 381.

18. Rosenman, *Working with Roosevelt*, p. 527.

19. Franklin D. Roosevelt death certificate, Hugh E. Evans, M.D., *The Hidden Campaign*, p. 135.

20. Dr. Wayne C. Levy to authors, May 27, 2009.

Chapter 2

1. *New York Times*, April 13, 1945.

2. Noah Fabricant, "Franklin D. Roosevelt's Nose and Throat Ailments," *Eye, Ear, Nose and Throat Monthly*, February 1957.

3. Geoffrey C. Ward, *Before the Trumpet,* pp. 122–123.

4. Sara Roosevelt, *My Boy Franklin,* quoted in Noah Fabricant, "Franklin D. Roosevelt, The Common Cold, and American History."

5. Noah Fabricant, "Franklin D. Roosevelt, the Common Cold, and American History," *Eye, Ear, Nose and Throat Monthly,* March 1958.

6. Ward, *Before the Trumpet*, p. 199.

7. Ibid., pp. 200–201.

8. *Harvard Alumni Bulletin,* April 28, 1945, quoted in Frank Freidel, *Franklin D. Roosevelt,* p. 15

9. *Time,* April 27, 1936.

10. The most complete account of the 1912 campaign appears in Jean Edward Smith, *FDR,* pp. 92–95.

11. Freidel, *Franklin D. Roosevelt,* p. 22.

12. Conrad Black, *Franklin Delano Roosevelt,* p.73.

13. Smith, *FDR,* p. 160.

14. *New York Times,* February 15, 1938.

15. Kenneth Crispell and Carlos Gomez, *Hidden Illness in the White House,* p. 68.

16. Freidel, *Franklin D. Roosevelt,* p. 39.

17. Blanche Wiesen Cook, *Eleanor Roosevelt,* p. 228.

Chapter 3

1. Hugh Evans, *The Hidden Campaign,* p. 18.

2. Hugh Gregory Gallagher, *FDR's Splendid Deception,* p. 11.

3. Elliot Roosevelt and James Brough, *An Untold Story,* p. 146.

4. Samuel A. Levine, "Some Notes Concerning the Early Days of Franklin D. Roosevelt's Attack of Poliomyelitis and Experience with Other Presidents' Illnesses," unpublished manuscript, quoted in Richard Thayer Goldberg, *The Making of Franklin D. Roosevelt,* p. 30.

5. Robert Lovett papers, Harvard, quoted in Jean Edward Smith, *FDR,* p. 191.

6. Ibid., p. 192.

7. *Daily Kennebec Journal,* August 27, 1921.

8. Davis W. Houck, *Rhetoric as Currency,* p. 99.

9. *New York Times,* September 16, 1921.

10. FDR to Adolph S. Ochs, FDRL-HP, quoted in Smith, pp. 192–193.

11. Hugh G. Gallagher, *FDR's Splendid Deception,* p. 20

12. Smith, *FDR,* pp. 196–197.

13. FDR to H. W. Chadeayne, October 5, 1921, FDRL-HP, quoted in Goldberg, *The Making of Franklin D. Roosevelt*, p. 39.

14. FDR to George Draper, September 30, 1925, quoted in Goldberg, ibid., pp. 89–90.

15. Roosevelt and Brough, *An Untold Story*, p. 170.

16. Frances Perkins, *The Roosevelt I Knew*, pp. 29–30.

17. Robert E. Gilbert, *The Mortal Presidency*, p. 46.

18. Geoffrey Ward, *Before the Trumpet*, p. 147.

19. "A History of the Case in Franklin D. Roosevelt's Own Words," *Journal of the South Carolina Medical Association*, January 1946. The letter was retained by Egleston's widow and not made public until several months after FDR's death.

20. Ibid.

21. FDR to Albert Maisel, March 19, 1926, Heritage Auction catalog.

22. Smith, *FDR*, p. 217.

23. Ibid.

24. Smith, *FDR*, p. 208.

25. *Syracuse Herald*, June 27, 1924.

26. Frank Freidel, *Franklin D. Roosevelt*, p. 52

27. *New York Times*, June 28, 1928.

28. *Chicago Tribune*, June 28, 1928, quoted in Conrad Black, *Franklin Delano Roosevelt*, p. 179.

29. Frank Freidel, *Franklin D. Roosevelt*, p. 255.

30. Unidentified clipping in Paul Hasbrouck file, FDRL-HP, quoted in Davis W. Houck and Amos Kiewe, *FDR's Body Politics*, p. 39.

31. Gilbert, *The Mortal Presidency*, p. 47.

32. Sam Rosenman, *Working with Roosevelt*, p. 31.

33. Conrad Black, *Franklin Delano Roosevelt*, p. 182

34. Betty Houchin Winfield, *FDR and the News Media*, p. 16.

35. Ibid., quoting William Leuchtenburg, *FDR and the New Deal*.

36. *New York Times*, November 10, 1928.

37. *New York Times*, November 11, 1928.

38. Smith, *FDR*, p. 242.

39. *New York Times*, April 28, 1930.

40. Goldberg, *The Making of Franklin D. Roosevelt*, p. 138.

41. "Newspaper Interview on Governor Roosevelt Accepting Delivery of $500,000 Life Insurance Policy, Albany, N.Y., October 18th, 1930," FDRL-HP; *New York Times*, October 19, 1930.

42. Smith, *FDR*, p. 245.

Chapter 4

1. *New York Times*, November 7, 1930.

2. Frank Freidel, *Franklin D. Roosevelt*, p. 66.

3. *New York Herald Tribune*, January 8, 1932, quoted in Freidel, *Franklin D. Roosevelt*, p. 68.

4. Jean Edward Smith, *FDR*, pp. 249–277.

5. *Time*, April 27, 1931.

6. *New York Times*, May 16, 1932.

7. *Time*, October 3, 1932.

8. *New York Times*, September 15, 1932.

9. *New York Times*, October 23, 1932.

10. Cross to *Newark Call*, February 19, 1930, FDRL-HP, quoted in David W. Houck and Amos Kiewe, *FDR's Body Politics*, p. 58.

11. Cross to *New Orleans Item*, February 1931, FDRL-HP, ibid.

12. FDR to *Danville Register*, December 18, 1930, FDRL-HP, ibid.

13. *New York Times*, July 31, 1932.

14. The fullest account of Earle Looker's involvement with FDR appears in Houck and Kiewe, *FDR's Body Politics*, pp. 66–76.

15. *Liberty*, July 25, 1931.

16. Houck and Kiewe, *FDR's Body Politics*, p. 67.

17. John Gunther, *Roosevelt in Retrospect*, p. 267.

18. *Springfield Republican*, July 18, 1931.

19. Looker to FDR, July 20, 1931, FDRL-HP, quoted in Houck and Kiewe, *FDR's Body Politics*, p. 70.

20. Looker to FDR, Aug. 26, 1931, ibid.

21. Looker, *This Man Roosevelt*, p. 147, quoted in Houck and Kiewe, *FDR's Body Politics*, p. 74.

22. Looker to FDR, November 13, 1933, FDRL-HP, ibid., p. 77.

23. FDR to Looker, November 21, 1933, FDRL-HP, ibid.

24. *New York Times*, February 17, 1933.

25. Freidel, *Franklin D. Roosevelt*, p. 88.

Chapter 5

1. Ross T. McIntire, *White House Physician*, pp. 58–61.

2. Christopher Hamlin, review of *The White House Physician*, by Ludwig M. Deppisch, *Journal of the American Medical Association* 299, no. 18 (May 14, 2008): 2214–2216.

3. Robert H. Ferrell, *The Dying President*, pp. 9–10.

4. *New York Times*, December 9, 1959; McIntire, *White House Physician*, pp. 55–56.

5. McIntire, *White House Physician*, pp. 55–56.

6. Ibid.

7. Ibid., p. 57.

8. Ibid., p. 68.

9. Ibid., p. 58.

10. Bert Edward Park, *The Impact of Illness on World Leaders*, p. 230.

11. Hamlin, review of *The White House Physician.*

12. Aaron Seth Kesselheim, "Privacy Versus the Public's Right to Know," p. 532.

13. McIntire, *White House Physician*, p. 64.

14. Conrad Black, *Franklin Delano Roosevelt*, p. 401.

15. Noah D. Fabricant, *13 Famous Patients*, p. 27, quoted in Robert E. Gilbert, *The Mortal Presidency*, p. 50.

16. John B. Moses and Wilbur Cross, *Presidential Courage*, p. 200; Grace Tully, *Franklin Delano Roosevelt—My Boss*, p. 273.

17. Associated Press, November 28, 1938.

18. *New York Times*, March 18, 1937.

19. Harold Ickes, *The Secret Diary of Harold Ickes*, vol. 2, p. 118, quoted in Kenneth Crispell and Carlos Gomez, *Hidden Illness in the White House*, p. 97.

20. *New York Times*, November 19, 1937.

21. James A. Farley, *Jim Farley's Story*, p. 108.

22. Ibid.

23. Anna Roosevelt Halstead papers, FDRL-HP.

24. Press conference of December 5, 1937, FDRL-HP.

25. Robert E. Gilbert, "Disability, Illness and the Presidency," p. 38.

26. Memo, February 18, 1936, Stephen T. Early papers, FDRL-HP.

27. Hugh Gregory Gallagher, *FDR's Splendid Deception*, p. 94.

28. Ibid.

29. J. B. West, *Upstairs at the White House*, p. 17.

30. John Gunther, *Roosevelt in Retrospect*, p. 239.

31. *New York Times*, February 4, 1936.

32. William McKinley Moore, *FDR's Image*, p. 465.

33. Ibid., p. 467.

34. Ibid., p. 468.

35. Ibid., p. 492.

36. Ibid., p. 306.

37. William R. Laue, *New York Times*, to William McKinley Moore, March 20, 1946, quoted in Moore, *FDR's Image*, p. 493.

38. Associated Press, December 19, 1944; *New York Times*, December 20, 1944.

Chapter 6

1. *Time*, May 28, 1923. The photograph traced to an article about FDR's role as president of the American Construction Council and contained the pointed declaration—at best, grossly misleading; at worst, flatly untrue—that "he is no longer an invalid."

2. Dr. Gary Williams and Dr. Murray Karcher, "Nomenclature of Skin Lesions," www.pediatrics.wisc.edu/education/derm/text.html.

3. S. Handley, "Progress of Simple Moles and Melanotic Sarcoma," *The Lancet*, June 15, 1935, p. 1401.

4. Hubert J. Farrell, "Cutaneous Melanomas with Special Reference to Prognosis," *Archives of Dermatology and Syphilology*, 1932.

5. Marc H. Friedberg, Eric T. Wong, and Julian K. Wu, "Management of Brain Metastases in Melanoma," www.uptodate.com/patients/content/topic.do?topicKey=~juew_O6HMOQ3am.

6. Ibid.

7. "State of the Union," *Time*, January 13, 1936.

8. William M. Pinkerton and Kirk Simpson, Associated Press, January 20, 1940.

9. See, for example, Cal Tinney, "Health of President Continues Good Despite Strain," *Nevada State Journal*, July 21, 1940.

10. *New York Times*, November 28, 1942.

11. *New York Times*, May 23, 1913.

12. Ross T. McIntire to Reuben Peterson, January 25, 1940, Ross McIntire papers, FDRL-HP.

13. Dr. Wolfgang Weyers, "A. Bernard Ackerman—'The Legend' Turns 70," *Journal of the American Academy of Dermatology*, November 2006.

14. Drs. A. Bernard Ackerman and Steven Lomazow, "An Inquiry Into the Nature of the Pigmented Lesion Above Franklin Delano Roosevelt's Left Eye," *Archives of Dermatology*, April 2008.

15. Ibid.

16. Interview with *Health Day Reporter*, April 25, 2008.

17. Ibid.

18. Ackerman and Lomazow, "An Inquiry Into the Nature of the Pigmented Lesion Above Franklin Delano Roosevelt's Left Eye."

19. Ibid.

20. Harold Ickes, *The Secret Diary of Harold Ickes*, quoted in Michael Barone, *Our Country*, p. 132.

21. Barone, ibid.

22. Henry Morgenthau diary, January 29, 1940, FDRL-HP, quoted in Jean Edward Smith, *FDR*, p. 442. Between the time of that entry and the Democratic convention, Hitler's blitzkrieg had overrun most of Western Europe.

23. Barone, *Our Country*, p. 133.

24. James T. Patterson, *The Dread Disease*, p. 111.

25. Harry S. Goldsmith, *A Conspiracy of Silence*, p. 2, n1. Goldsmith heard this from her doctor, George T. Pack—the same surgeon who said he'd been told by Dr. Frank Lahey that FDR had metastatic abdominal cancer.

26. Ibid., p. 112.

27. James A. Farley, *Jim Farley's Story*, p. 251.

28. Ibid., p. 254.

29. Ibid., p. 234.

30. Ibid., p. 206.

31. Robert Sherwood, *Roosevelt and Hopkins: An Intimate History*, pp. 148–149.

32. Handley, "Progress of Simple Moles and Melanotic Sarcoma."

33. Farrell, "Cutaneous Melanomas with Special Reference to Prognosis."

34. Margaret C. Tod, "Radiological Treatment of Malignant Melanoma," *British Journal of Radiology*, 1946, p. 224.

35. Ackerman and Lomazow, "An Inquiry into the Nature of the Pigmented Lesion Above Franklin Delano Roosevelt's Left Eyebrow," p. 530.

36. *Newsweek*, July 27, 1940.

37. White House usher's diary, FDRL-HP.

38. *New York Times*, February 15, 1940.

39. *New York Times*, February 16, 1940.

40. Ibid.

41. *New York Times*, March 3, 1940.

42. Geoffrey C. Ward, ed., *Closest Companion*, p. 134. Interestingly, this is the only record of the FDR–Daisy Suckley relationship from 1940 that survives. For unknown reasons, the diary that she began in 1933 is silent from June 1939, to be picked up again in late May 1941. Nor do any other of the many Roosevelt–Suckley letters from 1940 still exist; whether she chose not to write journal entries that year or later destroyed them is not known. But for the entire twelve years in which she faithfully recorded her diary, this is the only missing section.

43. *The Southern Cruise*, MP71–8:51, FDRL-HP.

44. *New York Times*, February 25, 1940.

Chapter 7

1. Charles Peters, *Five Days in Philadelphia*, p. 150.

2. Jean Edward Smith, *FDR*, p. 472.

3. Message to Congress, July 10, 1940; *New York Times*, July 11, 1940.

4. *New York Times*, May 5, 1941.

5. *Time*, May 12, 1941.

6. Doris Kearns Goodwin, *No Ordinary Time*, p. 235.

7. Kenneth R. Crispell and Carlos Gomez, *Hidden Illness in the White House*, p. 254, n79.

8. Lab slip, May 5, 1941, FDRL-HP.

9. Presidential news conference index, May 6, 1941, FDRL-HP.

10. Pare Lorentz Chronology, May 5, 1941, FDRL-HP.

11. "Did the U.S. Elect a Dying President?" *U.S. News & World Report*, March 23, 1951.

12. Jan K. Herman, "The President's Cardiologist," *Navy Medicine*, March/April 1990.

13. Crispell and Gomez, *Hidden Illness in the White House*, p. 78.

14. Ickes diary, May 10, 1941, FDRL-HP.

15. Ibid., May 17, 1941; Robert E. Gilbert, *The Mortal Presidency*, p. 53.

16. Eleanor Roosevelt to Anna Boettiger, May 15, 1941, FDRL-HP, quoted in Bernard Asbell, *Mother and Daughter*, p. 131.

17. Laboratory exam reports, FDRL-HP.

18. Eleanor Roosevelt to Anna Boettiger, June 22, 1941, quoted in Bernard Asbell, *Mother and Daughter*, p. 131.

19. Ibid.

20. Lab slip, July 15, 1941, FDRL-HP.

21. Anna Roosevelt Halsted papers, FDRL-HP.

22. Veronica Lake with Donald Bain, *Veronica*, p. 132.

23. E. Tillman Stirling to Dr. Harry S. Goldsmith, January 5, 1981, quoted in Goldsmith, *A Conspiracy of Silence*, p. 97.

24. *Washington Post*, September 9, 1969.

25. Walter Trohan, *Political Animals*, p. 198.

26. Ibid.

27. Margheritta Stirling Allardice to Harry Goldsmith, January 24, 1982, quoted in Goldsmith, *A Conspiracy of Silence*, p. 97. Allardice told us that she and her father became estranged shortly before her wedding in October 1943 and that she had been aware, before the estrangement, that her father had seen Roosevelt.

28. Ladislas Farago, *The Game of the Foxes*, pp. 330–331. The *Abwehr* files, discovered by Allied forces, are housed in the National Archives.

29. Farago, *The Game of the Foxes*, pp. 330–331.

30. "The Accidental Nurse: An Oral History," *Potomac Currents*, 2005.

31. "History of the White House Press Briefing Room," White House Press Office, U.S. Newswire, February 11, 2000.

32. Geoffrey C. Ward, *Closest Companion*, p. xix.

33. Daisy Suckley diary, entries for April 8, 1944, May 5, 1944, and December 15, 1944. Given the late dates of these entries, it is not clear whether she ever realized her mistake and that Roosevelt did not have leukemia.

34. Ross McIntire, *White House Physician*, p. 139.

35. Ibid.

36. Daisy Suckley diary entry, January 20, 1942.

37. McIntire, *White House Physician*, p.151.

38. James MacGregor Burns, *Roosevelt: Soldier of Freedom*, p. 332.

39. Daisy Suckley diary, February 27, 1943.

40. Ted Morgan, *FDR: A Biography*, p. 658.

41. Daisy Suckley diary, March 9, 1943.

42. Ibid.

43. Ibid., October 2, 1943, and October 29, 1943.

44. Ibid., October 18, 1943.

45. Ibid., November 5, 1943.

46. Ibid., September 30, 1943.

47. Charles Bohlen, *Witness to History*, pp. 143–144.

48. Lord Moran, *Churchill: Taken From the Diaries of Lord Moran*, p. 150, quoted in MacGregor Burns, *Roosevelt: Soldier of Freedom*, p. 409.

Chapter 8

1. Drew Pearson, "Washington Merry-Go-Round," January 7, 1944.

2. Matthew B. Wills, *FDR in 1944: A Diminished President*, p. 20.

3. Ross McIntire, *White House Physician*, p. 182; *U.S. News & World Report*, March 23, 1951.

4. Daisy Suckley diary, January 22, 1944.

5. Ibid., February 2, 1944.

6. Dr. George Webster to Dr. Harry Goldsmith, December 4, 1979, quoted in Goldsmith, *A Conspiracy of Silence*, p. 51.

7. Ibid.

8. Ibid.

9. Suckley diary, February 2, 1944.

10. Webster to Goldsmith, *A Conspiracy of Silence*, p. 52.

11. *New York Times*, February 5, 1944.

12. *Washington Post*, February 5, 1944.

13. Suckley diary, March 23, 1944.

14. Bert Edward Park, *The Impact of Illness on World Leaders*, p. 226. Park cites Howard Bruenn's 1970 paper on FDR as his source, but nowhere in Bruenn's paper is this mentioned.

15. William Hassett, *Off the Record with FDR*, p. 239 (diary entry for March 24, 1944) .

16. Ibid., p. 240 (diary entry for March 26, 1944).

17. Grace Tully, *Franklin Delano Roosevelt—My Boss*, p. 274.

18. Ibid.

19. Bernard Asbell, *Mother and Daughter*, p. 177.

20. Daisy Suckley diary, March 26, 1944.

21. Jan K. Herman, "The President's Cardiologist," *Navy Medicine*, March–April 1990, p. 7.

22. Ibid.

23. Ibid.

24. Walter Trohan, *Political Animals*, p. 200.

25. Kenneth R. Crispell and Carlos F. Gomez, *Hidden Illness in the White House*, p. 76.

26. Robert Sherwood, *Roosevelt and Hopkins*, p. 671.

27. Dr. Jon Wahrenberger, "High Altitude and Heart Disease," www.uptodate.com.

28. "High-altitude sickness," www.americanheart.org.

29. Sherwood, *Roosevelt and Hopkins*, p. 672.

30. Ibid., pp. 673–674.

31. Elliott Roosevelt, *As He Saw It*, pp. 146–147.

32. Crispell and Gomez, *Hidden Illness in the White House*, p. 100.

33. Lab slips, Eleanor Roosevelt, May 11, 1943, Anna Roosevelt Halsted papers, FDRL-HP.

34. Ibid.

35. Ross T. McIntire to Howard G. Bruenn, February 18, 1946, McIntire papers, FDRL-HP.

36. Howard G. Bruenn to Ross T. McIntire, August 1, 1946, McIntire papers, FDRL-HP.

37. "Did the U.S. Elect a Dying President?" *U.S. News & World Report*, March 23, 1951.

38. Dr. James Halsted handwritten notes, March 8, 1967, Anna Roosevelt Halsted papers, FDRL-HP.

39. Doris Kearns Goodwin, *No Ordinary Time*, p. 494.

40. Howard Bruenn typewritten notes, undated, Bruenn papers, FDRL-HP.

41. Howard G. Bruenn, "Clinical Notes on the Illness and Death of President Franklin D. Roosevelt," *Journal of Internal Medicine*, pp. 571–579.

42. Ibid.

43. Memorandum to Captain Harper, undated, unsigned, Ross McIntire papers, FDRL-HP.

44. Bruenn notes, Bruenn papers, FDRL-HP.

45. Ibid.

46. Bruenn, "Clinical Notes."

47. "Did the U.S. Elect a Dying President?" *U.S. News & World Report*.

48. Bruenn notes, Bruenn papers, FDRL-HP.

49. Bruenn, "Clinical Notes."

50. Ibid.

51. Bruenn notes, Bruenn papers, FDRL-HP.

52. Herman, "The President's Cardiologist," p. 8.

53. Bruenn, "Clinical Notes."

54. Daisy Suckley diary, March 28, 1944.

55. Ibid., April 4, 1944.

56. *New York Times*, April 5, 1944.

57. "The President's Week," *Time*, April 10, 1944.

58. Herman, "The President's Cardiologist."

59. Bruenn notes, Bruenn papers, FDRL-HP.

60. Bruenn, "Clinical Notes."

61. Herman, "The President's Cardiologist."

62. Bruenn, "Clinical Notes."

63. Warren Kimball, *Churchill and Roosevelt*, vol. 3, p. 60.

64. FDR press conference, May 6, 1944, quoted in Jim Bishop, *FDR's Last Year*, p. 35.

65. Daisy Suckley diary, April 4, 1944.

66. Ibid., April 6, 1944.

67. Merriman Smith, *Thank You, Mr. President*, p. 135.

68. Robert Ferrell, *The Dying President*, p. 68.

69. Goldsmith, *A Conspiracy of Silence*, p. 36.

70. Ward, *Closest Companion*, p. 295.

71. John Boettiger to Anna Roosevelt Boettiger, April 10, 1944, Anna Roosevelt Halstead papers, FDRL-HP.

72. Telegram, Steve Early to Ross McIntire, April 15, 1944. Memo in Steve Early correspondence file, FDRL-HP.

73. FDR press conference, May 6, 1944.

74. Smith, *Thank You, Mr. President*, p. 139.

75. *New York Times*, June 9, 1944.

76. Smith, *Thank You, Mr. President*, p. 143.

77. Howard Bruenn diary entries for April 17, 1944; April 19, 1944; April 20, 1944; and April 21, 1944.

78. Ibid., April 19, 1944.

79. Ibid., April 23, 1944.

80. Bruenn diary, March 28, 1944.

81. Daisy Suckley diary, May 4, 1944.

82. Bruenn diary, May 26, 1944.

83. Goldsmith, *A Conspiracy of Silence*, p. 37.

84. Harold Ickes diary, May 20, 1944, p. 8910.

85. Ward, *Closest Companion*, p. 295.

86. Daisy Suckley diary, May 5, 1944.

87. Smith, *Thank You, Mr. President*, p. 144.

88. Ibid., p. 141.

89. Wills, *FDR in 1944*, p. 26.

90. Ickes diary, May 13, 1944, p. 8886.

91. Bishop, *FDR's Last Year*, p. 73.

92. *Time*, May 22, 1944.
93. Smith, *Thank You, Mr. President*, p. 144.
94. Ibid.
95. Press conference, June 8, 1944, quoted in Wills, *FDR in 1944*, p. 27.

Chapter 9

1. *New York Times*, May 8, 1944.
2. Frances Perkins, *The Roosevelt I Knew*, p. 388.
3. Harold Ickes diary, June 4, 1944.
4. Daisy Suckley diary, April 6, 1945.
5. Robert Hannegan to Robert Sherwood, quoted in Hugh E. Evans, *The Hidden Campaign*, p. 84.
6. *New York Times*, March 26, 1944.
7. Suckley diary, May 22, 1944.
8. Jim Bishop, *FDR's Last Year*, p. 72.
9. Hugh Gallagher, *FDR's Splendid Deception*, p. 193.
10. Jonathan Daniels, *White House Witness*, p. 220.
11. Joseph P. Lash, *Eleanor and Franklin*, p. 708.
12. Merriman Smith, *Thank You, Mr. President*, p. 25.
13. Lash, *Eleanor and Franklin*, p. 709.
14. Bishop, *FDR's Last Year*, pp. 22–23.
15. Ibid.
16. Suckley diary, June 20, 1944.
17. Evans, *The Hidden Campaign*, p. 61.
18. Frank Freidel, *Franklin D. Roosevelt*, p. 513.
19. "The President's Doctor," *Life*, July 28, 1944.
20. Ross T. McIntire, *White House Physician*, p. 193.
21. Ibid.
22. *New York Times Book Review*, October 13, 1974.
23. James Roosevelt and Sidney Shalett, *Affectionately, FDR*, p. 350.
24. Harry Goldsmith, *A Conspiracy of Silence*, p. 123.
25. Ibid.
26. Lash, *Eleanor and Franklin*, p. 708.
27. Edwin Pauley memorandum to Jonathan Daniels, 1950(?), Harry S. Truman Library, quoted in Evans, *The Hidden Campaign*, p. 66.
28. David McCullough, *Truman*, p. 295; quoted in Evans, *The Hidden Campaign*, p. 66.
29. Pauley memorandum, Harry S. Truman Library.
30. *Time*, July 24, 1944.
31. Samuel Rosenman, *Working with Roosevelt*, p. 439.

32. Bishop, *FDR's Last Year*, p. 100.
33. John Morton Blum, *The Price of Vision*, p. 313.
34. *Washington Post*, November 20, 1972.
35. Ibid.
36. Bishop, *FDR's Last Year*, p. 99.
37. Ibid., p. 100.
38. Jonathan Daniels, *The Man of Independence*, p. 239.
39. Ibid., p. 255.
40. *Washington Post*, November 20, 1972.

Chapter 10

1. *New York Times*, July 21, 1944.
2. Ibid.
3. Jim Bishop, *FDR's Last Year*, p. 111.
4. James Roosevelt, *Affectionately, FDR*, p. 352.
5. James Roosevelt, *My Parents: A Differing View*, p. 278.
6. Harold Ickes diary, August 6, 1944, p. 9145.
7. Douglas MacArthur, *Reminiscences*, p. 199.
8. Grace Tully, *Franklin Delano Roosevelt—My Boss*, pp. 198–199.
9. Harold Ickes diary, August 12, 1944, p. 9183.
10. Ibid.
11. Samuel Rosenman, *Working with Roosevelt*, p. 462.
12. Ibid.
13. Daisy Suckley diary, August 12, 1944.
14. Ibid., August 23, 1944.
15. Jan K. Herman, "The President's Cardiologist," *Navy Medicine*, March–April 1990.
16. Ross McIntire, *White House Physician*, p. 202.
17. Rosenman, *Working with Roosevelt*, p. 462.
18. Harold Ickes diary, August 6, 1944, p. 9145.
19. Robert G. Nixon oral history interview, Harry S. Truman Presidential Library.
20. Steve Early to Grace Tully, July 28, 1944, Early papers, FDRL-HP, quoted in Robert H. Ferrell, *The Dying President*, p. 79.
21. George Skadding to Steve Early, August 2, 1944, Early papers, FDRL-HP.
22. Ibid.
23. Walter Trohan, *Political Animals*, p. 200.
24. Breckinridge Long to Steve Early, October 29, 1944, Federal Bureau of Investigation.
25. *Nashville Tennessean*, March 6, 1940.

26. Ross McIntire to Fiorello H. LaGuardia, May 28, 1940, Early papers, FDRL-HP.
27. Stephen T. Early to J. Edgar Hoover, May 29, 1940, Early papers, FDRL-HP.
28. Kenneth Crispell and Carlos Gomez, *Hidden Illness in the White House*, p. 111.
29. Ibid.
30. "Memorandum Re: Circulation of story alleging the President has a serious heart affliction," October 29, 1944, FBI.
31. J. Edgar Hoover to Stephen Early, November 1, 1944, FBI.
32. J. Edgar Hoover to Stephen Early, December 14, 1944, Early papers, FDRL-HP.
33. FBI Memorandum, courtesy of Margheritta Stirling Allardice.
34. Phone interview by the authors, March 22, 2006.
35. *Time*, June 15, 1953.
36. Goldsmith, *A Conspiracy of Silence*, p. 170.
37. Stanley P. Lovell, *Of Spies & Stratagems*, p. 70.
38. Rosenman, *Working with Roosevelt*, p. 478.
39. Frances Perkins, *The Roosevelt I Knew*, p. 114.
40. *New York Times*, September 24, 1944.
41. Rosenman, *Working with Roosevelt*, p. 477.
42. Ibid.
43. Suckley diary, September 25, 1944.
44. Ferrell, *The Dying President*, pp. 84–85.
45. Ibid.
46. Ferrell, *The Dying President*, p. 85.
47. Suckley diary, September 27, 1944, and September 25, 1944.
48. White House press conference, October 17, 1944.
49. "The President's Health," *Chicago Tribune*, October 17, 1944.
50. "A Vote for FDR May Be a Vote for Truman," *Chicago Tribune*, October 28, 1944.
51. *Syracuse Post-Standard*, undated, Stephen T. Early papers, FDRL-HP.
52. *Time*, October 29, 1944.
53. Ibid.
54. *New York Times*, October 22, 1944.
55. Hugh Gallagher, *Splendid Deception*, p. 195.
56. Tully, *FDR—My Boss*, p. 281.
57. *Time*, October 29, 1944.

Chapter 11

1. Howard G. Bruenn, "Clinical Notes on the Illness and Death of President Franklin D. Roosevelt," *Journal of Internal Medicine*, pp. 579–591.
2. Daisy Suckley diary, November 11, 1944.
3. Thomas Fleming, *The New Dealers' War*, p. 327.
4. Turner Catledge, *My Life and The Times*, p. 146.

5. John T. Flynn, *The Roosevelt Myth*, p. 403.

6. Doris Kearns Goodwin, *No Ordinary Time*, p. 571. Goodwin identifies her source for the story as Eliot Janeway, the noted economist.

7. Interview with PBS, *The American Experience: FDR*, 1994.

8. Allen Drury, *A Senate Journal*, p. 388.

9. Ibid., p. 390.

10. Frances Perkins, Columbia University Oral History Project, Part 8, Session 12, pp. 283–284 and 1951–1955.

11. PBS, *The American Experience: FDR*.

12. Grace Tully, *Franklin Delano Roosevelt—My Boss*, p. 273.

13. Orville H. Bullitt, *For the President: Personal and Secret*, p. 398.

14. Suckley diary, May 6, 1944.

15. Robert H. Ferrell, *The Dying President*, p. 161.

16. Phone interview with authors, 2006.

17. Suckley diary, June 27, 1944.

18. Bruenn, "Clinical Notes."

19. *New York Times*, October 13, 1944.

20. Ross McIntire, *White House Physician*, p. 194.

21. Suckley diary, November 29, 1944.

22. Bruenn, "Clinical Notes."

23. Jim Bishop, *FDR's Last Year*, pp. 248–249.

24. Ibid., p. 248; Ward, *Closest Companion*, p. 383.

25. James Roosevelt, *Affectionately, FDR*, pp. 354–355.

26. Roosevelt, *My Parents*, pp. 283–284.

27. Bert Edward Park, *The Impact of Illness on World Leaders*, p. 258.

28. Ferrell, *The Dying President*, p. 103.

Chapter 12

1. *New York Times*, May 8, 2005.

2. David Dilks, *The Diaries of Sir Alexander Cadogan*, quoted in Hugh L'Etang, *Ailing Leaders in Power*, p. 36.

3. Charles Bohlen, *Witness to History*, p. 173.

4. Hugh G. Evans, *The Hidden Campaign*, p. 153.

5. Howard G. Bruenn, "Clinical Notes on the Illness and Death of President Franklin D. Roosevelt," *Journal of Internal Medicine*, pp. 579–591.

6. John Gunther, *Roosevelt in Retrospect*, p. 364.

7. Ibid., p. 365.

8. James F. Byrnes, *Speaking Frankly*, p. 23.

9. William Rigdon, *White House Sailor*, quoted in Hugh E. Evans, *The Hidden Campaign*, p. 87.

10. Bruenn, "Clinical Notes."

11. Anna Roosevelt Boettiger to John Boettiger, February 4, 1945, Anna Roosevelt Halsted papers, FDRL-HP.

12. Lord Moran, *Churchill: Taken from the Diaries of Lord Moran*, p. 242.

13. L. G. Stansbury and J. R. Hess, "Putting the Pieces Together: Roger I. Lee and Modern Transfusion Medicine," *Transfusion Medicine Reviews*, January 2005.

14. www.ama-assn.org/ama/pub/about-ama/our-history/full-list-annual-meetings-presidents.shtml.

15. Lord Moran, *Churchill*, p. 242.

16. Ibid., p. 234.

17. Ibid., p. 239.

18. Ibid., p. 243.

19. Ibid.

20. Winston Churchill, *The Second World War*, vol. 6, p. 416.

21. Dilks, *The Diaries of Sir Alexander Cadogan*.

22. Jan K. Herman, "The President's Cardiologist," *Navy Medicine*, March–April 1990; Bruenn interview with Patricia Heaster, quoted in Robert H. Ferrell, *The Dying President*, p. 107.

23. *New York Times*, February 3, 1954.

24. Ibid., February 16, 1954.

25. Bohlen, *Witness to History*, p. 211.

26. Robert Sherwood, *Roosevelt and Hopkins*, p. 870.

27. Ross McIntire to Howard Bruenn, August 12, 1946, McIntire papers, FDRL-HP.

28. Conrad Black, *Franklin Delano Roosevelt*, p. 1074.

29. Jacob Heilbrunn, "Once Again, the Big Yalta Lie," *Los Angeles Times*, May 10, 2005.

30. Jim Bishop, *FDR's Last Year*, p. 468.

31. W. Averell Harriman and Elie Abel, *Special Envoy to Churchill and Stalin*, p. 344, quoted in Beichman, "Roosevelt's Failure at Yalta," *Humanitas*, March 22, 2003.

Chapter 13

1. Daisy Suckley diary, February 15, 1945.

2. Ibid., February 19, 1945.

3. FDR to Daisy Suckley, February 12, 1945. Geoffrey Ward, *Closest Companion*, p. 395.

4. Suckley diary, February 20, 1945.

5. Ibid., March 5, 1945.

6. Ibid.

7. Ibid., March 25, 1945.

8. Marvin Jones oral history interview, Harry S. Truman Library, 1963.

9. Mackenzie King diary, quoted in Robert H. Ferrell, *The Dying President*, p. 112.

10. Jonathan Daniels oral interview, October 4, 1963, p. 74, Harry S. Truman Presidential Library.
11. Suckley diary, March 25, 1945.
12. Suckley diary, March 29, 1945.
13. Mabel Irwin, *Memories of FDR's Last Visit*, p. 2.
14. Ibid., p. 3.
15. Bernard Asbell, *When FDR Died*, p. 22.
16. William D. Hassett, *Off the Record with FDR*, pp. 327–328.
17. Ibid., p. 328.
18. Ibid.
19. Suckley diary, March 31, 1945.
20. Ibid., April 3, 1945.
21. Ibid., April 12, 1945.
22. Ibid., April 5, 1945.
23. Grace Tully, *Franklin Delano Roosevelt—My Boss*, p. 359.
24. Irwin, *Memories of FDR's Last Visit*, p. 6.
25. Hugh E. Evans, *The Hidden Campaign*, p. 99.
26. Suckley diary, April 12, 1945.
27. Howard G. Bruenn, "Clinical Notes on the Illness and Death of President Franklin D. Roosevelt," *Journal of Internal Medicine*, pp. 579–591.
28. Jan K. Herman, "The President's Cardiologist," *Navy Medicine,* March–April 1990.
29. Ross T. McIntire, *White House Physician*, pp. 241–242.
30. Hassett, *Off the Record with FDR*, April 12, 1945, diary entry.
31. Herman, "The President's Cardiologist."
32. Hal S. Raper Jr. to Steven Lomazow, July 31, 2008.
33. Jim Bishop, *FDR's Last Year*, p. 585.
34. Ibid., p. 586.
35. Suckley diary, April 12, 1945.
36. James Paullin to Ross McIntire, 1946, McIntire papers, FDRL-HP.
37. Ibid.
38. McIntire, *White House Physician*, p. 242.
39. Merriman Smith, *Thank You, Mr. President*, pp. 183–184.
40. Hassett, *Off the Record with FDR*, April 12, 1945, diary entry.
41. Undated memorandum, authors' collection, courtesy of Phyllis (Oliver) Abbott.

Chapter 14

1. "Looking Ahead," *Washington Post*, April 14, 1945.
2. Associated Press, April 13, 1945.
3. Merriman Smith, *Thank You, Mr. President*, pp. 133–145. Smith's chapter on Roosevelt's failing health is titled simply "He's Dying."

4. United Press, April 13, 1945.

5. "Roosevelt Health Long Under Doubt," *New York Times*, April 13, 1945.

6. *Saturday Evening Post*, May 19, 1945.

7. Raymond P. Brandt Oral History, Harry S. Truman Presidential Library, September 28, 1970.

8. Ross McIntire to Eleanor Roosevelt, May 8, 1945, McIntire papers, FDRL-HP.

9. Walter Trohan Oral Interview, Harry S. Truman Presidential Library, October 7, 1970.

10. Walter Trohan, *Political Animals*, pp. 192–198.

11. "Reveal Stroke Almost Killed FDR on Mar. 25," *Chicago Tribune*, June 24, 1945.

12. *News Story*, June–August 1945.

13. Ibid., September 1945.

14. Emanuel Josephson, *The Strange Death of Franklin D. Roosevelt*, pp. 236–237.

15. George Creel to Ross McIntire, January 16, 1945, McIntire papers, FDRL-HP.

16. Ibid.

17. Ross McIntire to George Creel, undated reply to letter of April 30, 1946, McIntire papers, FDRL-HP.

18. Ross McIntire, *White House Physician*, p. 239.

19. Howard G. Bruenn, "Clinical Notes on the Illness and Death of President Franklin D. Roosevelt," *Journal of Internal Medicine*, pp. 579–591.

20. Ibid.

21. McIntire, *White House Physician*, p. 17.

22. *New York Times*, November 24, 1946.

23. *Look*, February 15, 1949.

24. Associated Press, February 4, 1949.

25. Ibid.

26. *Liberty*, April 26, 1949.

27. "Counter-Fire," *Time*, May 2, 1949.

28. *New York Times*, March 5, 1951.

29. *Washington Star*, March 10, 1951.

30. *U.S. News & World Report*, March 22, 1951.

31. *Boston Herald*, September 30, 1951.

32. *New York Times*, August 9, 1956.

33. Anna Roosevelt Halsted to Howard G. Bruenn, July 14, 1967, Anna Roosevelt Halsted papers, FDRL-HP.

34. Ibid.

Chapter 15

1. *New York Times*, August 15, 1951.

2. *Boston Globe*, June 28, 1953; Lahey Clinic Web site, www.lahey.org/About/LaheyHistory.asp.

3. "How Science Is Saving Stroke Victims," *Today's Health*, March 1962.

4. James A. Halsted, "A Medical Myth," *Today's Health*, December 1962.

5. Ibid.

6. *Modern Medicine*, March 6, 1961, p. 211, quoted in Hugh L'Etang, *The Pathology of Leadership*, p. 95. Because a number of different publications with the same title existed at the time, efforts by numerous researchers, including the authors, to locate the original Massie article have been unsuccessful. Information is taken from a summary by L'Etang, who did read it.

7. William S. McCune, "Malignant Melanoma: Forty Cases Treated by Radical Resection," presented before the American Surgical Association, April 20, 1949.

8. Dr. Robert Joy to the authors.

9. Eleanor Roosevelt National Historic Site Web site, www.nps.gov/archive/elro/glossary/gurewitsch-david.htm.

10. Anna Roosevelt Halsted to Howard G. Bruenn, March 5, 1963, Anna Roosevelt Halsted papers, FDRL-HP.

11. James Roosevelt to Anna Roosevelt Halsted, February 25, 1963, Anna Roosevelt Halsted papers, FDRL-HP.

12. James A. Halsted notes, March 8, 1967, Anna Roosevelt Halsted papers, FDRL-HP.

13. Ibid.

14. Lord Moran, *Churchill: Taken From the Diaries of Lord Moran*, p. 103.

15. Halsted, "A Medical Myth."

16. Ibid.

17. Ibid.

18. Harry Goldsmith, "Unanswered Questions in the Death of Franklin D. Roosevelt," *Surgery, Gynecology & Obstetrics*, December 1979, p. 899; Harry Goldsmith, *A Conspiracy of Silence*, pp. 1–2.

19. Samuel M. Day to Hugh L'Etang, February 5, 1970, quoted in Hugh L'Etang, *Ailing Leaders in Power*, p. 37.

20. Jack Anderson column, July 2, 1987.

21. Andrew F. Kiely to Harry Goldsmith, January 25, 1977, quoted in Goldsmith, *A Conspiracy of Silence*, p. 9.

22. Robert H. Ferrell, *The Dying President*, pp. 18–19.

23. James A. Halsted to Howard G. Bruenn, August 6, 1967, Anna Roosevelt Halsted papers, FDRL-HP.

24. Anna Roosevelt Halsted handwritten note, October 21, 1967, Anna Roosevelt Halsted papers, FDRL-HP.

25. Anna Roosevelt Halsted to Howard G. Bruenn, July 15, 1969, Anna Roosevelt Halsted papers, FDRL-HP.

26. Ibid.

27. Ibid.

28. Anna Roosevelt Halsted to Howard G. Bruenn, July 20, 1969, Anna Roosevelt Halsted papers, FDRL-HP.

29. James MacGregor Burns to Anna Roosevelt Halsted, October 17, 1969, Anna Roosevelt Halsted papers, FDRL-HP.

30. Anna Roosevelt Halsted to R. Russell Elkinton, November 17, 1969, Anna Roosevelt Halsted papers, FDRL-HP.

31. Anna Roosevelt Halsted to R. Russell Elkinton, November 24, 1969, Anna Roosevelt Halsted papers, FDRL-HP.

32. Howard G. Bruenn to Edward J. Huth, October 16, 1969, Anna Roosevelt Halsted papers, FDRL-HP.

33. "Effect of Illness on Leaders Noted," *New York Times*, September 26, 1969.

34. Anna Roosevelt Halsted to James Roosevelt, et al., Anna Roosevelt Halsted papers, FDRL-HP.

35. L'Etang, *Ailing Leaders in Power*, p. 37.

36. *New York Times*, April 12, 1970.

37. "Medicine in History," editorial, *Annals of Internal Medicine*, April 1970.

38. Kenneth Crispell and Carlos Gomez, *Hidden Illness in the White House*, p. 158.

39. Matthew B. Wills, *FDR in 1944*, p. 155.

40. Bruenn interview with Jan K. Herman for *Navy Medicine*, 1990.

41. Barron H. Lerner, "Crafting Medical History: Revisiting the 'Definitive' Account of Franklin D. Roosevelt's Terminal Illness," *Bulletin of the History of Medicine*, pp. 387–388.

42. Ibid., p. 398.

43. Daisy Suckley diary, March 31, 1945. Geoffrey Ward, *Closest Companion*, p. 403.

44. Jan K. Herman, "The President's Cardiologist," *Navy Medicine*, March–April 1990, p. 12.

45. Ferrell, *The Dying President*, p. 76.

46. Lerner, "Crafting Medical History," p. 406.

47. See Bert Park, *The Impact of Illness on World Leaders*, p. 227.

48. Howard G. Bruenn, "Clinical Notes on the Illness and Death of President Franklin D. Roosevelt," *Journal of Internal Medicine*.

49. Howard Bruenn to Jan K. Herman, unpublished transcript of interview for *Navy Medicine*, 1990.

Chapter 16

1. For a comprehensive treatment and analysis of the issues surrounding presidential health, the role of the White House physician, and presidential succession, see

"Privacy Versus the Public's Right to Know: Presidential Health and the White House Physician," in the December 2002 issue of the *Journal of Legal Medicine*, by Aaron Seth Kesselheim, a health policy researcher at Harvard University's Brigham and Women's Hospital.

2. *New York Times*, June 20, 1945.

3. Harry S. Truman, Special Message to the Congress, June 19, 1945, American Presidency Project, www.presidency.ucsb.edu.

4. Ibid.

5. *New York Times*, June 20, 1945.

6. Truman, Special Message to the Congress.

7. *New York Times*, June 20, 1945.

8. Ibid., June 24, 1945.

9. Truman, Special Message to the Congress.

10. Kesselheim, "Privacy Versus the Public's Right to Know," p. 536.

11. Ibid., p. 537.

12. Ibid., p. 539.

13. Ibid.

BIBLIOGRAPHY

Personal, Phone, and E-Mail Interviews

Dr. A. Bernard Ackerman, Margheritta Stirling Allardice, Dr. Joseph Craig, Hugh E. Evans, Robert H. Ferrell, Richard Thayer Goldberg, Dr. Harry F. Goldsmith, John Gunnison, Jan K. Herman, Dr. Robert Hudson, Dr. Robert Joy, Dr. Barron H. Lerner, Dr. Wayne C. Levy, Dr. Elliot V. Miller, Dr. Hal Raper, John Shrader, Elaine Ober Skagestaad, Dr. Elizabeth Stirling, E. Tillman Stirling, Geoffrey C. Ward

Personal Papers

Franklin D. Roosevelt Presidential Library, Hyde Park, New York: Anna Roosevelt Halstead, Ross T. McIntire, Howard G. Bruenn, Franklin D. Roosevelt, Stephen T. Early, Harold Ickes diary, Margaret Suckley diary

Georgia Southern University, Statesboro, Georgia: William Rigdon

Library of Congress, Washington, D.C.: Harold L. Ickes

University of Virginia, Charlottesville: Edwin M. Watson

Oral Histories

Harry S. Truman Presidential Library, Independence, Missouri: Raymond P. Brandt, Jonathan W. Daniels, Oscar R. Ewing, Marvin Jones, Robert G. Nixon, Samuel I. Rosenman, Walter Trohan

Columbia University Oral History Project, New York: Frances Perkins

Wood Library–Museum Living History of Anesthesiology, Park Ridge, Illinois: Dr. John Pender

Books

Asbell, Bernard. *When FDR Died.* New York: Holt, Rinehart and Winston, 1961.

———. *The FDR Memoirs.* New York: Doubleday, 1973.

———, ed. *Mother and Daughter: The Letters of Eleanor and Anna Roosevelt.* New York: Coward, McCann and Geoghegan, 1982.

Barone, Michael. *Our Country: The Shaping of America From Roosevelt to Reagan.* New York: Free Press, 1990.

Bishop, Jim. *FDR's Last Year.* New York: William Morrow, 1974.

Black, Conrad. *Franklin Delano Roosevelt, Champion of Freedom.* New York, Public-Affairs, 2003.

Blum, John Morton, ed. *The Price of Vision: The Diary of Henry A. Wallace, 1942–1946.* Boston: Houghton Mifflin, 1973.

Bohlen, Charles E. *Witness to History, 1929–1969.* New York: W. W. Norton, 1971.

Bullitt, Orville H., ed. *For the President, Personal and Secret: Correspondence Between Franklin D. Roosevelt and William C. Bullitt.* Boston: Houghton Mifflin, 1972.

Bumgarner, John R., MD. *The Health of the Presidents: The 41 United States Presidents Through 1993 from a Physician's Point of View.* Jefferson, NC: McFarland & Company, 1994.

Burns, James MacGregor. *Roosevelt: Soldier of Freedom, 1940–1945.* New York: Harcourt, Brace, Jovanovich, 1970.

Byrnes, James F. *Speaking Frankly*. New York: Harper & Brothers, 1947.

Catledge, Turner. *My Life and the* Times. New York: Harper & Row, 1971.

Churchill, Winston. *The Second World War, Vol. 6: Triumph and Tragedy*. New York: Houghton Mifflin, 1948.

Cook, Blanche Wiesen. *Eleanor Roosevelt: Vol. I, 1884–1933.* New York: Viking, 1992.

Creel, George: *Rebel At Large: Memoirs of Fifty Crowded Years.* New York: G. P. Putnam's Sons, 1967.

Crispell, Kenneth R., and Gomez, Carlos F. *Hidden Illness in the White House.* Durham, NC: Duke University Press, 1988.

Daniels, Jonathan. *The Man From Independence*. Philadelphia: J. B. Lippincott, 1950.

———. *White House Witness.* Garden City, NY: Doubleday, 1975.

Davis, Kenneth S. *FDR: The Beckoning of Destiny, 1882–1928.* New York: Random House, 1972.

———. *FDR: The War President, 1940–1943.* New York: Random House, 2000.

Drury, Allen. *A Senate Journal, 1943–1945.* New York: McGraw-Hill, 1963.

Eubank, Keith. *Summit at Teheran.* New York: William Morrow, 1985.

Evans, Hugh E., MD. *The Hidden Campaign: FDR's Health and the 1944 Election.* Armonk, NY: M. E. Sharpe, 2002.

Fabricant, Noah D. *13 Famous Patients*. New York: Chilton, 1960.

Farago, Ladislas. *The Game of the Foxes: The Untold Story of German Espionage in the United States and Great Britain During World War II.* New York: David McKay Co., 1972.

Farley, James A. *Jim Farley's Story: The Roosevelt Years.* New York: Whittlesey House, 1948.

Ferrell, Robert H. *Ill-Advised: Presidential Health and Public Trust.* Columbia: University of Missouri Press, 1992.

———. *The Dying President: Franklin D. Roosevelt, 1944–1945*. Columbia: University of Missouri Press, 1998.

Fleming, Thomas. *The New Dealers' War: FDR and the War Within World War II*. Oxford: Perseus Press, 2001.

Flynn, John T. *The Roosevelt Myth: A Critical Account of the New Deal and Its Creator.* Garden City, NY: Garden City Publishing, 1948.

Freidel, Frank. *Franklin D. Roosevelt: A Rendezvous with Destiny.* Boston: Little, Brown, 1990.

Gallagher, Hugh Gregory. *FDR's Splendid Deception*. Arlington, VA: Vandamere Press, 1994.

Gilbert, Robert E. *The Mortal Presidency: Illness and Anguish in the White House.* New York: Basic Books, 1992.

Goldberg, Richard Thayer. *The Making of Franklin D. Roosevelt: Triumph Over Disability.* Cambridge, MA: Abt Books, 1981.

Goldsmith, Harry S. *A Conspiracy of Silence: The Health and Death of Franklin D. Roosevelt.* New York: iUniverse Inc., 2007.

Goodwin, Doris Kearns. *No Ordinary Time: Franklin & Eleanor Roosevelt: The Home Front in World War II.* New York: Touchstone, 1995.

Gould, Jean. *A Good Fight: The Story of FDR's Conquest of Polio.* New York: Dodd, Mead and Co., 1960.

Gunther, John. *Roosevelt in Retrospect: A Profile in History.* New York: Harper & Brothers, 1950.

Harriman, W. Averell, and Elie Abel. *Special Envoy to Churchill and Stalin, 1941–1946.* New York: Random House, 1975.

Hassett, William D. *Off the Record with FDR, 1942–1945.* New York: Allen and Unwin, 1949.

Houck, Davis W. *Rhetoric as Currency: Hoover, Roosevelt and the Great Depression.* College Station: Texas A&M University Press, 2001.

Houck, Davis W., and Amos Kiewe. *FDR's Body Politics: The Rhetoric of Disability.* College Station: Texas A&M University Press, 2003.

Ickes, Harold L. *The Secret Diary of Harold L. Ickes: The First Thousand Days.* New York: Simon & Schuster, 1953.

Jackson, Robert H. *That Man: An Insider's Portrait of Franklin D. Roosevelt.* Oxford: Oxford University Press, 2003.

Josephson, Emanuel M. *The Strange Death of Franklin D. Roosevelt.* New York: Chedney Press, 1948.

Kimball, Warren, ed. *Churchill and Roosevelt: The Complete Correspondence.* Princeton, NJ: Princeton University Press, 1987.

Krock, Arthur. *Sixty Years on the Firing Line*. New York: Funk & Wagnall's, 1968.

Lake, Veronica, and Donald Bain. *Veronica.* New York: Citadel Press, 1971.

Lash, Joseph P. *Eleanor and Franklin: The Story of their Relationship, Based on Eleanor Roosevelt's Private Papers.* New York: New American Library, 1973.

———. *A World of Love: Eleanor Roosevelt and Her Friends, 1943–62.* Garden City, NY: Doubleday, 1984.

Lerner, Barron H. *When Illness Goes Public: Celebrity Patients and How We Look at Medicine.* Baltimore: Johns Hopkins University Press, 2006.

L'Etang, Hugh. *The Pathology of Leadership: A History of the Effects of Disease on 20th Century Leaders.* London: Hawthorne Books, 1970.

———. *Ailing Leaders in Power, 1914–1994.* London: Royal Society of Medicine Press, 1995.

Levin, Linda Lottridge. *The Making of FDR: The Story of Stephen T. Early, America's First Modern Press Secretary.* New York: Prometheus Books, 2008.

Lovell, Stanley P. *Of Spies & Stratagems.* New York: Penguin, 1963.

MacArthur, Douglas. *Reminiscences.* New York: McGraw-Hill, 1964.

Maney, Patrick J. *The Roosevelt Presence: The Life and Legacy of FDR.* Berkeley: University of California Press, 1998.

Marx, Rudolph. *The Health of the Presidents.* New York: G. P. Putnam's Sons, 1960.

McIntire, Ross, and George Creel. *White House Physician.* New York: G. P. Putnam's Sons, 1946.

Moran, Lord. *Churchill: Taken from the Diaries of Lord Moran. The Struggle for Survival, 1940–1965.* Boston: Houghton Mifflin, 1966.

Morgan, Ted. *FDR: A Biography.* New York: Simon & Schuster, 1985.

Moses, John B., MD, and Wilbur Cross. *Presidential Courage: The Dramatic Stories of Presidents Confronted by the Combined Challenges of Health and Political Crisis.* New York: W. W. Norton, 1980.

Park, Bert Edward. *The Impact of Illness on World Leaders.* Philadelphia: University of Pennsylvania Press, 1986.

Patterson, James T. *The Dread Disease: Cancer and Modern American Culture.* Cambridge, MA: Harvard University Press, 1987.

Perkins, Frances. *The Roosevelt I Knew.* New York: Viking Press, 1946.

Persico, Joseph. *Franklin and Lucy: President Roosevelt, Mrs. Rutherford and the Other Remarkable Women in His Life.* New York: Random House, 2008.

Peters, Charles. *Five Days in Philadelphia: The Amazing "We Want Willkie!" Convention of 1940, and How It Freed FDR to Save the Western World.* New York: PublicAffairs, 2004.

Rigdon, William McKinley, and James Derieux. *White House Sailor.* Garden City, NY: Doubleday, 1962.

Roosevelt, Elliott. *As He Saw It: The Story of the World Conferences of FDR.* New York: Duell, Sloan and Pearce, 1946.

Roosevelt, Elliott, and James Brough. *An Untold Story: The Roosevelts of Hyde Park.* New York: G. P. Putnam's Sons, 1973.

Roosevelt, James. *My Parents: A Differing View*. Chicago: Playboy Press, 1976.

Roosevelt, James, and Sidney Shalett. *Affectionately, FDR*. New York: Harcourt, Brace Jovanovich, 1959.

Rosenman, Samuel I. *Working with Roosevelt*. New York: Harper & Bros., 1952.

Sherwood, Robert. *Roosevelt and Hopkins: An Intimate History*. New York: Bantam, 1950.

Smith, Jean Edward. *FDR*. New York: Random House, 2007.

Smith, Merriman. *Thank You, Mr. President: A White House Notebook*. New York: Harper & Bros., 1946.

Smith, Tim, ed. *Merriman Smith's Book of Presidents: A White House Memoir*. New York: W. W. Norton, 1972.

Trohan, Walter. *Political Animals: Memoirs of a Sentimental Cynic*. Garden City, N.Y.: Doubleday, 1975.

Tully, Grace. *FDR—My Boss*. New York: Charles Scribner's Sons, 1949.

Walker, Frank C. (Robert H. Ferrell, ed.) *FDR's Quiet Confidant: The Autobiography of Frank C. Walker*. Niwot: University Press of Colorado, 1997.

Ward, Geoffrey C. *Before the Trumpet: Young Franklin Roosevelt, 1882–1905*. New York: Harper & Row, 1985.

———, ed. *Closest Companion: The Unknown Story of the Intimate Friendship Between Franklin Roosevelt and Margaret Suckley*. New York: Houghton Mifflin, 1995.

West, J. B. *Upstairs at the White House: My Life with the First Ladies*. New York: Coward, McCann & Geoghegan, 1973.

White, Graham J. *FDR and the Press*. Chicago and London: University of Chicago Press, 1979.

Wills, Matthew B. *FDR in 1944: A Diminished President*. Raleigh, NC: Ivy House, 2003.

Winfield, Betty Houchin. *FDR and the News Media*. New York: Columbia University Press, 1994.

Wold, Karl C., MD. *Mr. President—How Is Your Health?* Minneapolis–St. Paul: Bruce Publishing Co., 1948.

Medical/Scholarly Journal Papers

Ackerman, A. Bernard, and Steven Lomazow. "An Inquiry into the Nature of the Pigmented Lesion Above Franklin Delano Roosevelt's Left Eyebrow." *Archives of Dermatology* 144, no. 4 (2008): 529–532.

Alen, J. "A Review of FDR's Mental Capacity During His Fourth Term and Its Impact on History." *Forensic Examiner*, March 22, 2005.

Au, Sheila, Jason K. Rivers, and Frederick M. Vincent Sr. "CNS Melanoma." http://emedicine.medscape.com/article/1158059-overview.

Behrens, Charles F. "Fluoroscopic Hazards Including Use of Unprotected Radiographic Screens." *United States Naval Medical Bulletin* 44 (1945): 333–340.

Beichman, Arnold. "Roosevelt's Failure at Yalta." *Humanitas*, March 22, 2003.

Bruenn, Howard G. "Clinical Notes on the Illness and Death of President Franklin D. Roosevelt." *Journal of Internal Medicine* 72 (1970): 579–591.

Buhite, Russell D. "Patrick J. Hurley and the Yalta Far Eastern Agreement." *Pacific Historical Review* 37, no. 3 (August 1968): 343–353.

Byrne, Thomas N., Terrence L. Cascino, and Jerome B. Posner. "Brain Metastasis from Melanoma." *Journal of Neuro-Oncology* 1, no. 4 (2004): 313–317.

Colmes, Selma Harrison, MD. "John William 'Bill' Pender, M.D., 1912–2000." *Bulletin of Anesthesia History* 19 (2001): 2–3.

Costigliola, Frank. "Broken Circle: The Isolation of Franklin D. Roosevelt in World War II." *Diplomatic History* 32, no. 5 (November 2008): 677–718.

Crabtree, E. G., and N. Chaset. "Vascular Nephritis and Hypertension: A Combined Clinical and Clinicopathologic Study of 150 Nephrectomized Patients." *Journal of the American Medical Association* 115 (1940): 1842–1848.

Crispell, Kenneth R., and Carlos Gomez. "What If? A Chronicle of F.D. Roosevelt's Failing Health." *Journal of Medical Biography* I (1993): 95–101.

Cutler, Sidney J., Max H. Myers, and Sylvan B. Green. "Trends in Survival Rates of Patients with Cancer." *New England Journal of Medicine*, July 17, 1975, pp. 122–124.

De la Monte, S. M., G. William Moore, and Grover M. Hutchins. "Patterned Distribution of Metastases from Malignant Melanoma in Humans." *Cancer Research* 43 (July 1983): 3427–3433.

Denmeade, Samuel R., and John T. Isaacs. "A History of Prostate Cancer Treatment." *Nature Reviews* 2, no. 5 (May 2002):389–396.

Egleston, Mrs. William. "A History of the Case in Franklin D. Roosevelt's Own Words." *Journal of the South Carolina Medical Association* 53 (January 1946): 1.

Evans, H. E., and R. H. Ferrell. "The Illness and Death of President Franklin D. Roosevelt." *Transactions and Studies of the College of Physicians of Philadelphia* 19 (December 1997): 53–64.

Fabricant, Noah D. "Franklin D. Roosevelt's Nose and Throat Ailments." *Eye, Ear, Nose and Throat Monthly* 36, no. 2 (February 1957): 103–106.

———. "Franklin D. Roosevelt's Tonsillectomy and Poliomyelitis." *Eye, Ear, Nose and Throat Monthly* 36, no. 6 (June 1957): 348–349.

———. "Franklin D. Roosevelt, the Common Cold and American History." *Eye, Ear, Nose and Throat Monthly* 37, no. 3 (March 1958): 179–185.

Farrell, Hubert J. "Cutaneous Melanomas with Special Reference to Prognosis." *Archives of Dermatology and Syphilology* 26 (1932): 110–124.

Friedberg, Marc H., Eric T. Wong, and Julian K. Wu. "Management of Brain Metastases in Melanoma." www.uptodate.com/patients/content/topic.do?topicKey=~juew_O6HMOQ3am.

Gilbert, Robert E. "Disability, Illness and the Presidency: The Case of Franklin D. Roosevelt." *Politics and the Life Sciences* 7, no. 1 (August 1988): 33–49.

Goldsmith, Harry S., MD. "Unanswered Mysteries in the Death of Franklin D. Roosevelt." *Surgery, Gynecology & Obstetrics*, (December 1979) 149: 899–908.

Halsted, James E. "Severe Malnutrition in a Public Servant of the World War II Era: The Medical History of Harry Hopkins." *Journal of American Clinical Climatological Association* 86 (1974): 23–32.

Handley, S. "Progress of Simple Moles and Melanotic Sarcoma." *The Lancet*, June 15, 1935, p. 1401.

Kesselheim, Aaron Seth. "Privacy Versus the Public's Right to Know: Presidential Health and the White House Physician." *Journal of Legal Medicine* 23, no. 4 (December 2002): 523–545.

Lain, Edward L., Ida F. Orengo, and Ted Rosen. "Metastatic Melanoma." *Radiologic Images in Dermatology*, 2005: 314–317.

Lerner, Barron H. "Crafting Medical History: Revisiting the 'Definitive' Account of Franklin D. Roosevelt's Terminal Illness." *Bulletin of the History of Medicine* 81 (2007): 386–406.

McConnell, Ben H.: "The Little Stroke. A Report on 89 Cases." *Journal of the American Geriatric Society* 9 (February 1961): 110–118.

McCune, William S. "Malignant Melanoma. Forty Cases Treated By Radical Resection." *Annals of Surgery*, September 1949, pp. 318–332.

Meland, Orville N., and Ludwig Lindberg. "Malignant Melanoma; Course and Treatment." *Southwestern Medicine* 20 (1936): 336–346.

Miller, Elliot V., MD. "Dr. John Pender: An Appreciation." *American Society of Anesthesiology Newsletter* 64, no. 5 (April 2001): 2.

"Otic Complications of Streptomycin Therapy: A Preliminary Report." Resident Program, U.S. Army Reserve Board, October 21, 1946, p. 942.

Owen, The Rt. Hon. Lord David. "Diseased, Demented, Depressed: Serious Illness in Heads of State." *QJ Med* 96 (2003): 325–336.

Pack, George T., I. Scharnagel, and M. Morfit. "The Principle of Excision and Dissection in Continuity for Primary and Metastatic Melanoma of the Skin." *Surgery* 17 (1945): 849–866.

Patlak, Margie. "From Viper's Venom to Drug Design: Treating Hypertension." *FASEB Journal* 18 (2004): 421E.

Rovitt, Richard L., and William T. Couldwell. "No Ordinary Time, No Ordinary Men: The Relationship Between Harvey Cushing and Franklin D. Roosevelt, 1928–1939." *Journal of Neurosurgery* 95 (August 2001): 354–368.

Rubin, H. H. "The Treatment of Hypertrophied Prostate by a Newer Method of Radiation." *Urology & Cutaneous Review*, 1924.

Schnargel, Isabel M. "Melanoma of the Skin." *Journal of the American Medical Women's Association*, June 1946, pp. 76–83.

Skibber, J. M., S. J. Soong, L. Austin, C. M. Balch, and R. E. Sawaya. "Cranial Irradiation After Surgical Excision of Brain Metastases in Melanoma Patients." *Annals of Surgical Oncology* 3, no. 2 (1996): 118–123.

Stansbury, L. G., and J. R. Hess. "Putting the Pieces Together: Roger I. Lee and Modern Transfusion Medicine." *Transfusion Medicine Reviews*, January 2005.

Stirling, W. Calhoun, and Oscar B. Hunter Jr. "Metastatic Melanoma to the Bladder with Possibility of Being Primary in the Thyroid Gland." *Medical Annals of the District of Columbia*, February 1952, pp. 84–87.

Tod, Margaret C. "Radiological Treatment of Malignant Melanoma." *British Journal of Radiology* 19 (1946): 223–229.

Webster, Jerome P., Thomas W. Stevenson, and Arthur Purdy Stout. "The Surgical Treatment of Malignant Melanomas of the Skin," *Surgical Clinics of North America* 24 (April 1944): 319–339.

Winfield, Betty Houchin. "FDR's Pictorial Image, Rules and Boundaries." *Journalism History* 5, no. 4 (Winter 1978–1979): 110–114, 136.

Wu, Y. H., G. H. Kim, J. D. Wagner, A. F. Hood, and T. Y. Chuang. "The Association Between Malignant Melanoma and Noncutaneous Malignancies." *International Journal of Dermatology* 45, no. 5 (May 2006): 529–534.

Other Works

Herman, Jan K. Unpublished portion of transcript of his interview with Dr. Howard G. Bruenn for article in *Navy Medicine*, 1990.

Irwin, Mabel. *Memories of FDR's Last Visit.* Unpublished memoir by the wife of Dr. Ed Irwin, chief surgeon and medical director of Warm Springs, 1950.

Linda M. Strand v. Herrick & Smith et al. Supreme Judicial Court of Massachusetts, Suffolk. Argued December 5, 1985. Decided February 18, 1986.

Moore, William McKinley. *FDR's Image: A Study in Pictorial Symbols.* PhD diss., University of Wisconsin, 1946.

Magazine and Web Site Articles

Burns, James MacGregor: "FDR: The Untold Story of His Last Year." *Saturday Review*, April 11, 1970.

Childs, Marquis W. "Mr. Roosevelt." *Survey Graphic*, May 1940.

Creel, George. "The President's Health." *Collier's*, March 3, 1945.

Davenport, Walter. "The President and the Press." *Collier's*, January 27, 1945.

"Did the U.S. Elect a Dying President? The Inside Facts of the Final Weeks of FDR." *U.S. News & World Report*, March 23, 1951.

Dunigan, Alice. "The Last Days of F.D.R." *Sepia*, April 1962.

Feldman, Ellen. "Polio Strikes Franklin Roosevelt." AmericanHeritage.com, August 2, 2007.

Halberstam, Michael. "Who's Medically Fit for the White House?" *New York Times Magazine*, October 22, 1972.

Halsted, James A. "A Medical Myth." *Today's Health*, December 1962.

Hamlin, Christopher. Review of *The White House Physician: A History from Washington to George W. Bush*, by Ludwig H. Deppisch. *Journal of the American Medical Association* 299, no. 18 (May 14, 2008): 2214–2216.

Herman, Jan K. "The President's Cardiologist." *Navy Medicine*, March–April 1990.

"How Science Is Saving Stroke Victims," *Today's Health*, March 1962.

Karig, Walter. "Is the President a Well Man Today?" *Liberty*, December 13, 1941.

Lerner, Barron H. "How Much Confidence Should We Have in the Doctor's Account of FDR's Death?" *History News Network*, July 9, 2007.

Levy, Daniel, and Susan Brink. "A Change of Heart." *U.S. News & World Report*, February 14, 2005.

Looker, Earle. "Is Franklin D. Roosevelt Physically Fit to Be President?" *Liberty*, July 25, 1931.

Novak, Robert. "My Brain Tumor." *Chicago Sun-Times*, September 7, 2008.

Roosevelt, Elliott. "They're Lying About FDR's Health." *Liberty*, May 1949.

Smith, Richard Norton. "'The President Is Fine' and Other Historical Lies." *Columbia Journalism Review*, September–October 2001.

"The Accidental Nurse: An Oral History." *Potomac Currents*, 2005.

Weyers, Wolfgang, MD. "A. Bernard Ackerman—the 'Legend' Turns 70." *Journal of the American Academy of Dermatology*, November 2006.

Wold, Karl C. "The Truth About FDR's Health." *Look*, February 15, 1949.

INDEX

Marilynn Hawkridge

Steven Lomazow, MD, is a board-certified neurologist in practice for over twenty-five years. He is Assistant Professor of Neurology at the Mount Sinai School of Medicine, a member of the New Jersey State Board of Medical Examiners, and president of the Neurological Association of New Jersey. He has lectured extensively in the fields of pain management, headache, and medical politics and has represented the American Academy of Neurology before the Federal Trade Commission. A prominent collector of American magazines and a frequent lecturer on U.S. periodical history, he is a consultant to the Freedom Forum Newseum.

New York Post

Eric Fettmann is associate editorial-page editor of the *New York Post*, where he has spent most of his thirty-five-year journalism career. He has been a political columnist and assistant metropolitan editor for the paper and is the former managing editor of *The Jerusalem Post*. He also has written for *New York*, *The Nation*, *National Review* and *USA Today*. He was coauthor of an investigative series that was runner-up for the Society of Professional Journalists' national award for magazine reporting. A journalism historian, he has contributed to numerous encyclopedias and has been a history consultant on documentary projects for the BBC and PBS.

PublicAffairs is a publishing house founded in 1997. It is a tribute to the standards, values, and flair of three persons who have served as mentors to countless reporters, writers, editors, and book people of all kinds, including me.

I.F. STONE, proprietor of *I. F. Stone's Weekly*, combined a commitment to the First Amendment with entrepreneurial zeal and reporting skill and became one of the great independent journalists in American history. At the age of eighty, Izzy published *The Trial of Socrates*, which was a national bestseller. He wrote the book after he taught himself ancient Greek.

BENJAMIN C. BRADLEE was for nearly thirty years the charismatic editorial leader of *The Washington Post*. It was Ben who gave the *Post* the range and courage to pursue such historic issues as Watergate. He supported his reporters with a tenacity that made them fearless and it is no accident that so many became authors of influential, best-selling books.

ROBERT L. BERNSTEIN, the chief executive of Random House for more than a quarter century, guided one of the nation's premier publishing houses. Bob was personally responsible for many books of political dissent and argument that challenged tyranny around the globe. He is also the founder and longtime chair of Human Rights Watch, one of the most respected human rights organizations in the world.

• • •

For fifty years, the banner of Public Affairs Press was carried by its owner Morris B. Schnapper, who published Gandhi, Nasser, Toynbee, Truman, and about 1,500 other authors. In 1983, Schnapper was described by *The Washington Post* as "a redoubtable gadfly." His legacy will endure in the books to come.

Peter Osnos, *Founder and Editor-at-Large*